THE LAW REFORM (MISCELLANEOUS PROVISIONS) (SCOTLAND) ACT 1990

THE LAW REFORM (MISCELLANEOUS PROVISIONS) (SCOTLAND) ACT 1990

By

J.M. THOMSON, LL.B., *Regius Professor of Law,*
University of Glasgow

R.A. BURGESS, LL.B., Ph.D., *Professor of Law,*
University of Strathclyde

SIR CRISPIN AGNEW OF LOCHNAW, Bt., *Advocate*

HEATHER M. BAILLIE, B.A., LL.B., *Solicitor*

FRASER P. DAVIDSON, LL.B., Ph.D.,
Senior Lecturer in Law, University of Dundee

and

KENNETH MILLER, LL.B., LL.M., Ph.D.,
Senior Lecturer in Law, University of Strathclyde

W. GREEN/Sweet & Maxwell
EDINBURGH
1991

First Published in 1991

ISBN 0 414 00974 6

Printed in Great Britain
by
The Eastern Press Ltd of Reading

LAW REFORM (MISCELLANEOUS PROVISIONS) (SCOTLAND) ACT 1990*

(1990 c. 40)

ARRANGEMENT OF SECTIONS

PART I

CHARITIES

Recognition of charities

---

*Annotations by Sir Crispin Agnew of Lochnaw Bt; Heather M. Baillie, Solicitor; Professor R.A. Burgess, University of Strathclyde; Fraser Davidson, Lecturer in Law, University of Dundee; Kenneth Miller, Senior Lecturer in Law, University of Strathclyde; Professor J.M. Thomson, Regius Professor of Law, University of Glasgow.

PART III

THE LICENSING (SCOTLAND) ACT 1976

75. Citation, commencement and extent.

An Act, as respects Scotland, to make new provision for the regulation of charities; to provide for the establishment of a board having functions in connection with the provision of conveyancing and executry services by persons other than solicitors, advocates and incorporated practices; to provide as to rights of audience in courts of law, legal services and judicial appointments, and for the establishment and functions of an ombudsman in relation to legal services; to amend the law relating to liquor licensing; to make special provisions in relation to the giving of evidence by children in criminal trials; to empower a sheriff court to try offences committed in the district of a different sheriff court in the same sheriffdom; to provide as to probation and community service orders and the supervision and care of persons on probation and on release from prison and for supervised attendance as an alternative to imprisonment on default in paying a fine; to amend Part I of the Criminal Justice (Scotland) Act 1987 with respect to the registration and enforcement of confiscation orders in relation to the proceeds of drug trafficking; to amend section 24 of the Housing (Scotland) Act 1987; to provide a system for the settlement by arbitration of international commercial disputes; to amend Part II of the Unfair Contract Terms Act 1977; and to make certain other miscellaneous reforms of the law.   [November 1, 1990]

PARLIAMENTARY DEBATES
   Hansard, H.L. Vol. 515, col. 166; Vol. 517, cols. 255, 293, 739, 758, 820, 841, 1043, 1104, 1146; Vol. 518, cols. 901, 926, 979; Vol. 519, cols. 159, 247, 269, 388, 1650; Vol. 522, cols. 1528, 1609; H.C. Vol. 174, col. 156; Vol. 177, cols. 1059, 1214.
   The Bill was considered in First Scottish Standing Committee from June 19 to July 25, 1990.

INTRODUCTION AND GENERAL NOTE
   Pt. I of the Act provides for the supervision of charities in Scotland. In their original form the provisions of Pt. I appeared to be to some extent, although not entirely, derivative in that they followed corresponding provisions in earlier English charities legislation, notably the Charities Acts of 1960 and 1985. Unlike the English measures, however, there has been no attempt to establish a comprehensive regulatory regime under a body such as the Charity Commissioners; instead, the Act directs its attention to specific detailed points and establishes a general supervisory rôle for the Lord Advocate.
   The Act creates its own terminology which has no real counterpart in English charity law and which is founded on the fact that in Scotland virtually the only significance of charitable status is in relation to the tax advantages it attracts. Accordingly, the primary distinction is drawn between "recognised bodies" and "non-recognised bodies" (ss.1 and 2), with the latter being prohibited from representing or holding themselves out as charities (s.2). Recognised bodies are subjected to obligations in relation to the keeping of accounts (s.4) and providing to

members of the public, on request, copies of their annual report and accounts, (s.5) although recognised bodies which are also "designated religious bodies" are exempted from these obligations (s.3). The "recognition" is that of the Commissioners of Inland Revenue that tax relief under s.505 of the Income and Corporation Taxes Act 1988 is available in respect of the income of that body which is applied to charitable purposes only.

Ss.6–8 seek to tackle abuse among charities. The Lord Advocate is given new powers to investigate the affairs of recognised charities and of non-recognised bodies which appear to him to be representing or holding themselves out to be charities (s.6); these powers include the power to suspend any person concerned in the management of a charity from the exercise of his functions. Where abuse has been discovered the Court of Session, on the application of the Lord Advocate, is empowered to take permanent or temporary action to remedy the situation (s.7). Persons who are bankrupt or who have been convicted of offences involving dishonesty are disqualified from involvement in the management or control of a charity (s.8).

Ss.9–11 are concerned with the administration of charities and in particular with the provision of mechanisms to enhance the effective use of funds held in trust. The criteria for the application of the *cy-près* doctrine are broadened so that the Court of Session may approve the application *cy-près* of funds from any public trust where social or economic changes have rendered the purposes of the trust obsolete or lacking in usefulness (s.9). The problems of small funds are addressed by enabling trustees of funds with an annual income of less than £5,000 to reform their objects or to transfer their assets to other trusts without recourse to the Court (s.10); where the annual income is less than £1,000, trustees are empowered to spend capital where such annual income is too small to enable the objects of the trust to be achieved (s.11).

S.12 deals with dormant charities, making provision for the utilisation of sums standing to their credit in bank accounts.

S.13 makes provision to permit the appointment of additional trustees so that the total number of trustees shall not be less than three.

S.14 empowers the Lord Advocate to petition the Court of Session for the winding-up of charitable companies, and prohibits such companies which have the power to alter their charitable objects from so doing without having first ensured that their revised objects will continue to be charitable for tax purposes.

S.15 is the definition section for Pt. I.

PART I

CHARITIES

Recognition of charities

Information as to recognised charities

1.—(1) No obligation as to secrecy or other restriction upon the disclosure of information imposed by statute or otherwise shall prevent the Commissioners of Inland Revenue (in this section referred to as "the Commissioners") from disclosing—

(a) to the Lord Advocate, information as regards any recognised body such as is mentioned in subsection (2) below,

(b) to any person who requests it, the name of any recognised body and the address last used by the Commissioners for any communication with the body and the year when such communication occurred.

(2) A recognised body referred to in subsection (1)(a) above is a body—

(a) which appears to the Commissioners to be or to have been carrying on activities which are not charitable or to be or to have been applying any of its funds for purposes which are not charitable;

(b) which is certified by the Lord Advocate as being a body in respect of which information has been provided to the Scottish charities nominee by a relevant institution in pursuance of section 12 of this Act.

(3) Where any information is made available to any person as mentioned in subsection (1)(b) above, the Commissioners shall include in such information any matter noted by them in respect of the body in pursuance of a requirement made by the Lord Advocate under this Part of this Act.

(4) A recognised body shall provide to any person who requests it, on payment of such reasonable charge in respect of copying and postage as the body may stipulate, a copy of its explanatory document.

(5) Where any recognised body, within one month of its being requested to do so by any person, fails to provide to that person a copy of its explanatory document as mentioned in subsection (4) above, the Lord Advocate, on a complaint being made to him by such person, may direct that the fact of such failure shall be noted for the purposes of subsection (3) above.

(6) Where there has been a failure such as is mentioned in subsection (5) above, the court may, on an application being made by the Lord Advocate, interdict the body and any person concerned in its management or control from engaging in any activity specified in the application until the Lord Advocate intimates to the court that he is satisfied that the explanatory document has been provided.

(7) In this Part of this Act "recognised body" means any body to which the Commissioners have given intimation, which has not subsequently been withdrawn, that relief will be due under section 505 of the Income and Corporation Taxes Act 1988 in respect of income of the body which is applicable and applied to charitable purposes only, being a body—
(a) which is established under the law of Scotland; or
(b) which is managed or controlled wholly or mainly in or from Scotland, and a recognised body shall be entitled to describe itself as "a Scottish charity."

(8) For the purposes of any proceedings under or by virtue of this Part of this Act, a certificate purporting to be signed by a person authorised to do so by the Commissioners and certifying that a body is a recognised body shall be sufficient evidence of that fact and of the authority of that person.

(9) In this section "explanatory document" means—
(a) the trust deed of a body or other document constituting the body; or
(b) such other document as the Lord Advocate may approve,
being a document which describes the nature of the body and of its charitable purposes.

GENERAL NOTE
This provision defines "recognised body" (s.1(7)) in terms of intimation of eligibility for tax relief under s.505 of the Income and Corporation Taxes Act 1988. "Body" is not defined as such but will include a trust and a company. Such body must either have been established under the law of Scotland or be managed or controlled wholly or mainly in or from Scotland. This last phrase enables companies registered in England but run from Scotland to be recognised bodies for the purposes of the Act; likewise it would appear that trusts created under English law but administered in Scotland by trustees resident here would also qualify. It would seem to be perfectly possible, therefore, for a trust to be both a registered charity governed by the (English) Charities Act 1960 and a recognised body for the purposes of Pt. I of this Act.

Certification by the Revenue that a trust or company is a recognised body is to be taken as conclusive evidence of that fact for the purpose of any proceedings under or by virtue of Pt. I (subs. (8)).

Recognised bodies are placed under a duty to supply copies of their documents of constitution to any person requesting them so that such person can ascertain the nature of the body and of its charitable purposes (subs. (4)); failure to comply with this duty within one month triggers an enforcement procedure operated via the Lord Advocate; on receiving a complaint by a person requesting such a copy the Court of Session, on an application being made by the Lord Advocate, may interdict the body and any person concerned in its management or control from engaging in any activity specified in the application until the Lord Advocate intimates to the Court that he is satisfied that the relevant documents have been provided (subs. (6)).

Details of the name of any recognised body may be supplied on request by the Revenue; such details will include the address last used by the Revenue for communication with the body and the year when such communication occurred (subs. (1)(b)). Where a complaint has been made concerning a failure by the recognised body to supply copies of its constitutional documents the Lord Advocate may direct that a note of the fact of such failure be made (subs. (5)); where information is disclosed under subs. (1)(b) such information is to include matters noted by the Revenue in pursuance of any direction or requirement made by the Lord Advocate (subs. (3)).

Subsection (1)(a) empowers the Revenue to disclose to the Lord Advocate information concerning two kinds of recognised body. The first is any recognised body which appears to it to be or to have been carrying on activities which are not charitable or to be or to have been applying any of its funds for purposes which are not charitable (subs. (2)(a)). "Charitable", in this context (see *Inland Revenue* v. *Glasgow Police Athletic Association* 1953 S.C. (H.L.) 13) has been given a definition by the House of Lords in *Income Tax Special Purposes Commissioners* v. *Pemsel* [1891] A.C. 531 (H.L.) as embracing (1) the relief of poverty; (2) the advancement of education; (3) the advancement of religion; and (4) other purposes beneficial to the community within the spirit and intendment of the preamble to the (English) Charitable Uses Act 1601.

The second kind of recognised body is a dormant charity (subs. (2)(b)), as to which see s.12 below.

The provision in subs. (1)(a) as to the disclosure of information to the Lord Advocate compares with provisions of s.9 of the Charities Act 1960 facilitating the exchange of information between the Revenue authorities and the Charity Commissioners.

Non-recognised bodies

2.—(1) A non-recognised body shall not be entitled to represent itself or hold itself out as a charity.

(2) For the purposes of this Part of this Act, any body which is not—
(a) a recognised body; or
(b) a body which is—
> (i) registered as a charity in England and Wales under section 4 of the Charities Act 1960; or
> (ii) a charity which is not required to register by virtue of subsection (4) of that section,

is a non-recognised body.

(3) Where a non-recognised body represents itself or holds itself out as a charity, the court may, on an application made by the Lord Advocate, interdict the body from so representing itself or holding itself out until it becomes a body such as is mentioned in paragraph (a) or (b) of subsection (2) above.

GENERAL NOTE

This section is directed towards the prevention of bodies which are not charitable from representing or holding themselves out as charitable (subs. (1)). Where such a "non-recognised body" does so represent or hold itself out as being a charity the Court of Session may, on an application made by the Lord Advocate, interdict the body (subs. (3)).

"Non-recognised body" is defined as a body which is neither recognised as charitable in Scotland under s.1 above, nor registered (or exempt from registration) in England under s.4 of the Charities Act 1960 (subs. (2)).

Designated religious bodies

3.—(1) The Secretary of State may from time to time, by order, designate for the purposes of this section such recognised bodies as appear to him—
(a) to have as their principal purpose the promotion of a religious objective;
(b) to have as their principal activity the regular holding of acts of public worship; and
(c) to be bodies which satisfy each of the conditions mentioned in subsection (2) below.

(2) The conditions referred to in subsection (1)(c) above are—
(a) subject to subsection (4) below, that the body has been established in Scotland for not less than 10 years;
(b) that the body can demonstrate to the satisfaction of the Secretary of State that it has a membership of not less than 3,000 persons resident in Scotland who are 16 years of age or more; and
(c) that the internal organisation of the body is such that one or more authorities in Scotland exercise supervisory and disciplinary functions in respect of the component elements of the body and, in particular that there are imposed on such component elements requirements as to the keeping of accounting records and the auditing of accounts which appear to the Secretary of State to correspond to those required by sections 4 and 5 of this Act.

(3) Where a body is, for the time being, designated under subsection (1) above the following provisions of this Part of this Act shall not apply to the body nor to any component or structural element of the body which is, itself, a recognised body—

section 1(6);

section 4;

section 5, other than subsections (6) to (8) and subsections (12);

section 6(2) and (6);

section 7; and

section 8.

(4) The Secretary of State may determine that the condition mentioned in subsection (2)(a) above shall not be required to be satisfied in the case of a body—

(a) which has been created by the amalgamation of two or more bodies each of which, immediately before the amalgamation, either was designated under this section or appears to the Secretary of State to have been eligible for such designation; or

(b) which has been constituted by persons who have removed themselves from membership of a body which, immediately before such removal, was so designated or appears to the Secretary of State to have been eligible for such designation.

GENERAL NOTE

The distinction established by ss.1 and 2 and the obligations that go with recognised body status were felt to be inappropriate to certain religious bodies. Accordingly, special provision is made by s.3 for the Secretary of State to "designate" particular bodies. Designation confers exemption from the obligations concerning the keeping of accounts (s.4) and the preparation of annual accounts and a report (s.5); further, the control powers of the Lord Advocate under ss.1(6), 6(2) and (6), 7 and 8 have no application to the officials of such bodies.

A body is eligible for designation (subs. (1)) if (a) it is a recognised body; (b) it has as its principal purpose the promotion of a religious objective; (c) it has as its principal activity the regular holding of acts of public worship; (d) it has been established in Scotland for not less than 10 years (except where the body has resulted from an amalgamation of other bodies, at least one of which was designated or appears to the Secretary of State to have been eligible for designation, or is a splinter group from a body which, immediately before the split, was designated); (e) it can demonstrate a membership of at least 3,000 people over 16 years of age; and (f) it has an internal organisation over which one or more authorities in Scotland exercise supervisory and disciplinary functions; in particular, this supervisory authority should require the keeping and auditing of accounts of the body.

Charities accounts

Duty to keep accounting records

4.—(1) The persons concerned in the management or control of every recognised body shall ensure that there are kept in respect of the body, accounting records which are sufficient to show and explain the body's transactions and which are such as to—

(a) disclose with reasonable accuracy, at any time, the financial position of the body at that time; and

(b) enable them to ensure that any statement of accounts prepared under section 5 of this Act complies with the requirements of that section.

(2) The accounting records shall in particular contain—

(a) entries showing from day to day all sums of money received and expended by the body, and the matters in respect of which the receipt and expenditure takes place; and

(b) a record of the assets and liabilities of the body.

(3) The accounting records which are required by this section to be kept in respect of a recognised body shall be preserved, without prejudice to any requirement of any other enactment or rule of law, for six years from the date on which they are made.

(4) The Secretary of State may, by regulations—

(a) prescribe requirements as to the places where and the persons by whom the accounting records of recognised bodies, including bodies which have been wound up or have ceased to be active, are to be kept; and

(b) provide that such class or classes of recognised body as may be prescribed shall be exempt from such requirements of this section and section 5 of this Act as may be prescribed.

GENERAL NOTE

This section imposes a duty on those concerned in the management or control of a recognised body to ensure that adequate accounting records are kept (subs. (1)). Such accounting records are to be preserved for a period of six years from the date on which they are made (subs. (3)).

The accounting records must be sufficient to (1) show and explain the body's transactions; (2) disclose, with reasonable accuracy, at any time, the financial position of the body at that time; and (3) comply with the formal requirements of s.5 (subs. (1)).

In particular, the accounting records must detail the body's income and expenditure and its assets and liabilities (subs. (2)).

Subs. (4) empowers the Secretary of State to make regulations concerning where such accounting records are to be kept and conferring exemptions from the accounting records requirements of ss.4 and 5.

The provisions of s.4 correspond to the provisions of s.8 of the Charities Act 1960.

Annual accounts and report

5.—(1) The persons concerned in the management or control of every recognised body shall ensure that, in respect of each financial year of the body, there is prepared a statement of accounts.

(2) Subject to subsection (3) below, the statement of accounts of every recognised body shall comprise—

(a) a balance sheet as at the last day of the year;

(b) an income and expenditure account; and

(c) a report as to the activities of the body, having regard to its charitable purposes.

(3) As regards such class or classes of recognised body as the Secretary of State may, by regulations, prescribe a recognised body may elect that in respect of any financial year its statement of accounts shall, instead of the requirements of subsection (2) above, comprise—

(a) a statement of balances as at the last day of the year;

(b) a receipts and payments account; and

(c) a report as to the activities of the body, having regard to its charitable purposes.

(4) The balance sheet shall give a true and fair view of the state of affairs of the body as at the end of the financial year; and the income and expenditure account shall give a true and fair view of the surplus or deficit of the body for the financial year.

(5) The Secretary of State may, by regulations, prescribe—

(a) the form and content of the statement of accounts;

(b) any additional information to be provided by way of notes to the accounts; and

(c) such requirements as to auditing of the balance sheet, statement of balances, income and expenditure account and receipts and payments account and any notes thereon and as to the consideration of the report as he considers appropriate,

and different provision may be prescribed for different bodies or classes of bodies.

(6) The Lord Advocate may require any recognised body to furnish him, without payment therefor, with a copy of its statement of accounts.

(7) Every such body shall—

(a) make available to any person who requests it, on payment of such reasonable charge in respect of copying and postage as the body may stipulate, a copy of its most recent statement of accounts;

(b) inform any person who requests it of its accounting reference date.

(8) Where any recognised body fails, within 10 months, or such longer period as the Lord Advocate may allow, after the end of a financial year, to have prepared a statement of accounts, the Lord Advocate may require that such fact shall be noted for the purposes of section 1(3) of this Act.

(9) Where a body has failed to have prepared a statement of accounts as mentioned in subsection (8) above, the Lord Advocate may require the persons concerned in the management or control of the body to have prepared a statement of accounts, by such date as he may require.

(10) In any case where the statement of accounts has not been prepared by the date specified under subsection (9) above, the Lord Advocate may appoint a suitably qualified person to prepare a balance sheet and income and expenditure account or, in the case of a body which belongs to a class to which subsection (3) above applies if it appears to such person more appropriate to do so, a statement of balances and receipts and payments account; and a person so appointed shall be entitled, for that purpose—

(a) on giving prior notice in writing, to enter, at all reasonable times, the premises of the body;

(b) to take possession of any document appearing to him to relate to the financial affairs of the body;

(c) to require any person concerned in the management or control of the body to give him such information as he may reasonably require relating to the activities of the body,

and the persons concerned in the management or control of the body shall be personally liable jointly and severally for the expenses incurred in the performance of his functions under this section by any person so appointed.

(11) A person appointed under subsection (10) above shall make a report to the Lord Advocate as to the affairs and accounting records of the body and shall send a copy of the report to any person appearing to him to be concerned in the management and control of the body.

(12) Where any such body, within one month of its being requested to do so by any person—

(a) fails to provide to that person a copy of its most recent statement of accounts as mentioned in subsection (7) above; or

(b) fails to inform that person of its accounting reference date,

the Lord Advocate, on a complaint being made to him by such person, may direct that the fact of such failure shall be noted for the purposes of section 1(3) of this Act.

(13) Where in the case of any recognised body, there has been a failure such as is mentioned in subsection (9) or (12) above the court may, on an application being made by the Lord Advocate, interdict the body and any person concerned in its management or control from engaging in any activity specified in the application until the Lord Advocate intimates to the court that he is satisfied that the failure has been rectified.

(14) Section 4 of this Act and subsections (1), (2), (3), (4), (5), (8), (9), (10) and (11) and, so far as it relates to a failure such as is mentioned in the said subsection (9), subsection (13) of this section shall not apply to any recognised body which is—

(a) a company within the meaning of section 735 of the Companies Act 1985; or

(b) an unregistered company to which Part VII of that Act (accounts and audit) applies by virtue of section 718 of that Act,

and, in the application of the remainder of this section to such a body, references to its income and expenditure account and its report shall be construed as references to its profit and loss account and its directors' report.

GENERAL NOTE

This section imposes a general duty on those concerned in the management or control of recognised bodies to prepare in respect of each financial year (a) a balance sheet as at the last day of the year; (b) an income and expenditure account; and (c) an annual report (subs. (1)).

The balance sheet and income and expenditure accounts are required to present a "true and fair view" of the matters to which they relate (subs. (2)).

This general duty is backed by the enforcement provisions of subss. (8)–(11); essentially, these involve a three stage process:

(1) Where, after 10 months (or such longer period as the Lord Advocate may allow) there has been failure to comply with the general duty, the Lord Advocate may require the fact of such failure to be noted under s.1(3) (subs. (8));

(2) the Lord Advocate may then set a date for compliance (subs. (9));

(3) failure to meet this date as regards the preparation of a balance sheet and income expenditure account (but not, it would seem, the annual report) may result in the Lord Advocate's appointing a suitably qualified person to do so, such person being granted access to premises, documents and management personnel for the purpose of obtaining the requisite information (subs. (10); the person so appointed will then make a report to the Lord Advocate as to the affairs and accounting records of the body, copies of which are to be sent to those concerned in the management or control of the body (subs. (11)).

The form and content of such balance sheet, income and expenditure account and annual report may be prescribed by regulations made by the Secretary of State; such regulations may also prescribe any additional information to be provided by way of notes to the accounts and any auditing requirements as may be considered appropriate (subs. (3)).

The Lord Advocate may require any recognised body to furnish him, without payment, with a copy of the balance sheet, income and expenditure account and report (subs. (6)).

Subs. (7) imposes on recognised bodies a duty to supply on request to any person (albeit subject to reasonable reimbursement) copies of their most recent balance sheet, income and expenditure account and annual report. This duty is in the same terms as the duty to supply copies of its constitutional documents and is backed up by corresponding enforcement powers (subss. (12) and (13)).

Subs. (14) applies where the recognised body is a charitable company; apart from the Lord Advocate's functions as to noting for the purposes of s.1(3) the accounting requirements of the Companies Act 1985 are substituted for those of ss.4 and 5.

The provisions of s.5 follow those of s.1 of the Charities Act 1985.

Supervision of charities

Powers of Lord Advocate to investigate charities and to suspend trustees

6.—(1) The Lord Advocate may at any time make inquiries, either generally or for particular purposes, with regard to—

(a) a recognised body;

(b) a registered, or non-registered, charity operating as such in Scotland; or

(c) a non-registered body which appears to him to represent itself or hold itself out as a charity and—

(i) is established under the law of Scotland;

(ii) is managed or controlled wholly or mainly in or from Scotland; or

(iii) has any moveable or immoveable property situated in Scotland,

or with regard to any class of any such bodies.

(2) Where it appears to the Lord Advocate—

(a) in the case of a body referred to in paragraph (a) or (b) of subsection (1) above—

(i) that there is or has been any misconduct or mismanagement in its administration; or

(ii) that it is necessary or desirable to act for the purpose of protecting its property or securing a proper application of such property for its purposes; or

(b) in any other case, that a body is a non-recognised body which appears to him to represent itself or hold itself out as a charity,

he may, if the body is managed or controlled wholly or mainly in or from Scotland, suspend any person concerned in its management or control from the exercise of his functions (but not for a period longer than 28 days), and may make provision as respects the period of the suspension for matters arising out of it.

(3) The Lord Advocate may from time to time nominate officers for the purpose of making inquiries such as are mentioned in subsection (1) above.

(4) A nominated officer may by notice in writing require any person who he has reason to believe has relevant information to answer questions or otherwise furnish information with respect to any matter relevant to inquiries being made under this section at a specified place and either at a specified time or forthwith.

(5) A nominated officer may, for the purpose of making inquiries under this section—

(a) require any person having in his possession or control any records relating to a body which is the subject of inquiries under this section to furnish him with copies of or extracts from any such records; or

(b) unless it forms part of the records of a court or of a public body or local authority, require such a person to transmit the record itself to him for inspection,

either by a specified time or forthwith.

(6) If any person fails or refuses to comply with a requirement made under subsection (4) or (5) above, the nominated officer may apply by summary application to the sheriff for an order requiring that person to—

(a) attend and to answer such questions or to furnish such information at a time and place specified in the order;

(b) furnish the nominated officer with copies or extracts of such records as are specified in the order and by such time as is specified in the order;

(c) transmit to the nominated officer such records as are specified in the order by such time as is specified in the order,

and the sheriff shall, if he considers it expedient to do so, make such an order.

(7) A person shall not be excused from answering such questions as he may be required to answer by virtue of subsection (6) above on the ground that the answer may incriminate or tend to incriminate him, but a statement made by him in answer to any such question shall not be admissible in evidence in any subsequent criminal proceedings against him, except in a prosecution for an offence under section 2 of the False Oaths (Scotland) Act 1933.

(8) A person who fails to comply with an order under subsection (6) above shall be guilty of an offence and liable on summary conviction to a fine not exceeding level 5 on the standard scale.

(9) Any person who wilfully alters, suppresses, conceals or destroys any record which he may be required to furnish or transmit under this section shall be guilty of an offence and liable on summary conviction to a fine not exceeding level 5 on the standard scale or to imprisonment for a term not exceeding 6 months or to both.

(10) Subject to subsections (11) and (12) below, there shall be paid to any person who complies with a requirement under subsection (4) or (5) above such expenses as he has reasonably incurred in so complying.

(11) A nominated officer shall, for the purpose of making inquiries under this section, be entitled without payment to inspect and take copies of or extracts from records in respect of which no requirement can be made under paragraph (b) of subsection (5) above.

(12) A nominated officer shall, for the purpose of making inquiries under this section, be entitled without payment to keep any copy or extract furnished to him under this section; and where a record transmitted to him for his inspection relates only to one or more recognised body and is not held by any person entitled as trustee or otherwise of such a body to the custody of it, the nominated officer may keep it or may deliver it to the trustees of such a body or to any other person who may be so entitled.

(13) In this section, "record" means a record held in any medium and includes books, documents, deeds or papers; and, in this Part of this Act—

"registered charity" means a body which is registered as a charity in England and Wales under section 4 of the Charities Act 1960; and "non-registered charity" means a charity which, by virtue of sub-section (4) of section 4 of that Act, is not required to register under that section.

GENERAL NOTE

S.6 contains provisions conferring powers on the Lord Advocate in connection with his supervisory rôle in relation to charities in Scotland. The Lord Advocate's jurisdiction covers

(a) recognised bodies;

(b) English-registered or non-registered charities (see subs. (12)) operating as such in Scotland; and

(c) non-recognised bodies which appear to represent themselves as being charities and

  (i) are established under the law of Scotland;

  (ii) are managed or controlled wholly or mainly in or from Scotland; or

  (iii) have any moveable or immoveable property situated in Scotland.

The first power is to make enquiries, either generally or for particular purposes, into the affairs of such bodies or class of such bodies (subs. (1)). These enquiries may be conducted by "nominated officers" (subs. (3)); no indication is given as to who these officers might be, although the appointment of accountants or lawyers would be appropriate. Subss. (4)–(6) detail the powers available to nominated officers; they include the making available of records (defined as records in any medium including books, documents, deeds or papers (presumably also records held on computer disk) (subs. (13)), or copies thereof (subs. (5)) and, after the service of a notice in writing, to answer questions relating to any matter relevant to the enquiry (subs. (4); compliance is enforced by order of a sheriff (subs. (6)), the failure to observe which is a criminal offence (subs. (8)), as also is suppression, destruction or alteration of any record (subs. (9)). Expenses reasonably incurred in complying may be reimbursed (subs. (10)).

With respect to bodies which have charitable status and in respect of which it appears that there has been maladministration or where it appears necessary for some action to be taken to protect a charity's property or to secure a proper application of such property for the purposes of the charity, in so far as the charity is run from Scotland the Lord Advocate may suspend persons concerned in management or control for up to 28 days. During the period of suspension the Lord Advocate is empowered to make provision for matters arising out of it (presumably for the management of the charity). Any suspension may be noted under s.1(3) (subs. (2)). Similar powers exist with regard to non-recognised bodies established, or managed from, or having property in Scotland, save that here it is not necessary for there to have been any appearance of maladministration or danger to or misapplication of property (subs. (2)).

Provisions corresponding to those contained in s.6 are to be found in ss.6 and 7 of the Charities Act 1960.

Powers of Court of Session to deal with management of charities

7.—(1) Where it appears to the court, in the case of a recognised body or a registered, or non-registered, charity which is managed or controlled wholly or mainly in or from Scotland, that—

(a) there is or has been any misconduct or mismanagement in its administration; or

(b) it is necessary or desirable to act for the purpose of protecting its property or securing a proper application of such property for its purposes,

it may, on the application of the Lord Advocate, exercise any of the powers specified in paragraphs (a) to (f) of subsection (4) below.

(2) Where the court is satisfied, in the case of such a body as is mentioned in subsection (1) above, that—

(a) there is or has been any misconduct or mismanagement in its administration; and

(b) it is necessary or desirable to act for the purpose of protecting its property or securing a proper application of such property for its purposes,

it may, on the application of the Lord Advocate, exercise any of the powers specified in paragraphs (f) to (j) of subsection (4) below.

(3) Where the court is satisfied that a non-recognised body—

(a) represents itself or holds itself out as a charity; and

(b) is established under the law of Scotland or is managed or controlled wholly or mainly in or from Scotland or has moveable or immoveable property situated in Scotland,

it may, on the application of the Lord Advocate, exercise any of the powers specified in subsection (4) below.

(4) The powers which may be exercised under this subsection by the court are—

(a) to interdict *ad interim* the body from representing itself or holding itself out as a charity or from such other action as the court, on the application of the Lord Advocate, thinks fit;

(b) to suspend any person concerned in the management or control of the body;

(c) to appoint *ad interim* a judicial factor to manage the affairs of the body;

(d) to make an order requiring any bank or other person holding money or securities on behalf of the body or of any person concerned in is control and management not to part with the money or securities without the court's approval;

(e) to make an order, notwithstanding anything in the trust deed or other document constituting the body, restricting the transactions which may be entered into, or the nature or amount of the payments which may be made, in the administration of the body without the approval of the court;

(f) to appoint a trustee, and section 22 of the Trusts (Scotland) Act 1921 shall apply to such a trustee as if he had been appointed under that section;

(g) to interdict the body from representing itself or holding itself out as a charity or from such other action as the court, on the application of the Lord Advocate, thinks fit;

(h) to remove any person concerned in the management or control of the body;

(j) to appoint a judicial factor to manage the affairs of the body.

(5) Where the court is satisfied, in the case of such a body as is mentioned in subsection (1) above, that—

(a) there has been in its administration any misconduct or mismanagement;

(b) it is necessary or desirable to act for the purpose of protecting its property or securing a proper application of such property for its purposes;

(c) it is not practicable nor in the best interests of the body to retain its existing administrative structure and, if appropriate, trustee body; and

(d) in its opinion, the body's purpose would be achieved better by transferring its assets to another such body,

or where the court is satisfied as mentioned in subsection (3) above in the case of a non-recognised body, it may approve a scheme, presented to it by the Lord Advocate and prepared by him in accordance with regulations made by the Secretary of State, for the transfer of any assets of the body to such body as the Lord Advocate specifies in the scheme, being a recognised body or a registered, or non-registered, charity which is managed or controlled wholly or mainly in or from Scotland.

(6) In the case of a registered, or non-registered, charity which is managed or controlled wholly or mainly outside Scotland but on behalf of which a bank or other person in Scotland holds moveable property, the court may, on the application of the Lord Advocate acting on information received from the Charity Commissioners for England and Wales, make an order requiring the bank or person not to part with that property without the court's approval and such an order shall be subject to such conditions as the court thinks fit.

(7) Where the court has made an order under subsection (6) above and is satisfied, in the case of such a charity, that—

(a) there has been in its administration any misconduct or mismanagement; and

(b) it is necessary or desirable to act for the purpose of protecting its property or securing a proper application of such property for its purposes,

it may, on the further application of the Lord Advocate, make an order confirming the order made under subsection (6) above and such an order shall be subject to such conditions as the court thinks fit.

(8) Where the court has made an order under subsection (6) above and it is satisfied as to the matters specified in subsection (7) above in respect of such a charity, if in its opinion the moveable property would not be applied for the purposes of the charity, it may, on the further application of the Lord Advocate, transfer that property to such body as the Lord Advocate specifies in the application, being a body—

(a) which is a recognised body or registered, or non-registered, charity the purposes of which closely resemble the purpose of the charity whose moveable property is transferred; and

(b) which has intimated that it will receive that property.

(9) The court shall have power—

(a) to vary or recall an order made under paragraph (d) or (e) of subsection (4) above or under subsection (6) or (7) above;

(b) to recall the suspension of a person under paragraph (b) of subsection (4) above;

(c) to approve a scheme under subsection (5) above subject to such modifications as it thinks fit;

(d) subject to subsection (10) below, to award expenses as it thinks fit in any proceedings before it under this section.

(10) In a case where, but for the provisions of this subsection, the court would have awarded expenses against the body which is the subject of the proceedings, the court—

(a) shall have regard to the desirability of applying the property of the body for the charitable purposes of that body, or the charitable purposes which are purported to be the purposes of that body, and

(b) may award expenses against a person concerned in the control or management of the body, or against any such persons jointly and severally.

(11) Where the court exercises in respect of a recognised body any power specified in subsection (4) or (5) above, the Lord Advocate may require that exercise to be noted for the purposes of section 1(3) of this Act.

(12) In this section "the court" means the Court of Session.

GENERAL NOTE

S.7 is supplemental to s.6 in that it provides for the next stages in the supervision process. Essentially, the scheme of s.7 is to confer on the Court of Session (not the Sheriff, who is the appropriate body for dealing with applications under s.6) powers to safeguard the funds of charitable bodies and to put a stop to the activities of those non-charitable bodies who represent or hold themselves out as having charitable status.

The primary powers available to the court are set out in subs. (4); they are (a) power to interdict *ad interim* the body from representing itself as a charity; also, power to interdict the body from such other action as the Court, on the application of the Lord Advocate, thinks fit; (b) power to suspend any person concerned in the management or control of the body; (c) power to appoint *ad interim* a judicial factor to manage the affairs of the body; (d) power to make an order freezing a body's bank or securities account; (e) power to place restrictions on the type of transactions that might be effected and on the nature or amount of payments that might be made without the approval of the court; (f) power to appoint a trustee; (g) power to interdict the body from holding itself out as a charity or such action as the court, on the application of the Lord Advocate, thinks fit; (h) power to remove any person concerned in the management or control of the body; (i) power to appoint a judicial factor to manage the affairs of the body.

With respect to bodies that have charitable status powers (a)–(f) are available to the court where it appears that maladministration has occurred or that the charities' property is in danger (subs. (1)); where the court is satisfied that such is the case powers (f)–(g) are available (subs. (2)). Where the court is so satisfied *and* (1) it is impracticable and not in the best interests of the body to retain its existing administrative structure and, if appropriate, trustee body; *and* (2) in the court's opinion, the body's purpose would be achieved better by transferring its assets to another charitable body, the court may approve a scheme for such transfer under s.7; such scheme must be prepared and presented to the court by the Lord Advocate.

With respect to non-recognised bodies which are shown to be representing or holding themselves out to be charities both the s.6 and s.7 powers are available.

Where the court exercises a power conferred by ss.6 or 7, the Lord Advocate may require that exercise to be noted under s.1(3) (subs. (11)).

Subss. (6)–(9) apply to English charities controlled or managed from outside Scotland but possessing money and securities held by banks or other persons in Scotland. Subs. (6) provides for a three-stage procedure in such cases.

Stage one requires an initiative from the Charity Commissioners by sending information to the Lord Advocate; stage two requires an application by the Lord Advocate to the court for an order to freeze the assets in question; and stage three empowers the court to make such an order.

Where the court has made such an order and it is satisfied that maladministration has occurred and that the property of the charity is at risk it may, on the further application of the Lord Advocate, confirm the previous order and make such confirmation subject to such conditions as the court thinks fit (subs. (7)).

Where an order has been made under subs. (6) and the court is satisfied that the maladministration has occurred and that the property of the charity is at risk it may, if it is of the opinion that the money or securities would not be applied for the purposes of the charity, on further application of the Lord Advocate, transfer the money or securities to a body named by the Lord Advocate in the application, provided that the body in question is a charity whose purposes "closely resemble" those of the first charity and the second charity agrees to the transfer (subs. (8)).

Subs. (9) confers on the court powers to modify or recall certain orders made under this section; specifically these powers relate to (i) the variation or recall of orders made under subss. (4)(d) or (e) or (6) or (7); (ii) the recall of a suspension under subs. (4)(b); or (iii) the approval, subject to modifications of a scheme, under subs. (5); (iv) subject to subs. (10), the award of expenses as it thinks fit.

Subs. (10) provides for the award of costs, if appropriate, against those managing or controlling the body.

Disqualification of persons concerned in the management or control of recognised bodies

8.—(1) A person who—

(a) has been convicted of an offence involving dishonesty;

(b) is an undischarged bankrupt;

(c) has been removed, under section 7 of this Act, from being concerned in the management or control of any body; or

(d) is subject to a disqualification order under the Company Directors Disqualification Act 1986,

shall, subject to the provisions of this section, be disqualified from being concerned with the management or control of a recognised body.

(2) A person shall not be disqualified under subsection (1) above if—

(a) the conviction mentioned in that subsection is spent by virtue of the Rehabilitation of Offenders Act 1974; or

(b) the Lord Advocate has thought fit to grant in writing a waiver of that disqualification in respect of that person,

but the Lord Advocate shall not grant a waiver where to do so would prejudice the operation of the Company Directors Disqualification Act 1986.

(3) A person who is concerned with the management or control of a recognised body whilst disqualified by virtue of this section shall be guilty of an offence and liable—

(a) on summary conviction, to imprisonment for a term not exceeding 6 months or to a fine not exceeding the statutory maximum or to both; and

(b) on conviction on indictment, to imprisonment for a term not exceeding 2 years or to a fine or to both.

(4) The acts, in relation to the management or control of such a body, of such a person as is mentioned in subsection (1) above shall not be invalid only by reason of his disqualification under that subsection.

(5) Proceedings for an offence under subsection (3) above shall not be commenced after the end of the period of 3 years beginning with the day on which the offence was committed but, subject to that, may be commenced at any time within 6 months from the date on which evidence sufficient in the opinion of the procurator fiscal to warrant proceedings came to his knowledge; and a certificate of the procurator fiscal as to the date on which such evidence came to his knowledge shall be conclusive evidence of that fact.

(6) In this section, "undischarged bankrupt" means a person who has had his estate sequestrated, been adjudged bankrupt or has granted a trust deed for or entered into an arrangement with his creditors and has not been discharged under or by virtue of—

(a) section 54 or section 75(4) of the Bankruptcy (Scotland) Act 1985;
(b) an order under paragraph 11 of Schedule 4 to that Act of 1985;
(c) section 279 or section 280 of the Insolvency Act 1986; or
(d) any other enactment or rule of law subsisting at the time of his discharge.

DEFINITIONS
"undischarged bankrupt": subs. (6).

GENERAL NOTE
S.8 disqualifies certain persons from being concerned with the management or control of a recognised body; these persons are
(a) those convicted of an offence involving dishonesty, unless the conviction is spent by virtue of the Rehabilitation of Offenders Act 1974 (subs. (2)(a));
(b) undischarged bankrupts;
(c) those removed under s.7 from being concerned in the management or control of a recognised body; or
(d) those subject to a disqualification order under the Company Directors Disqualification Act 1986 (subs. (1)).
These categories are subject to the power of the Lord Advocate to grant in writing a waiver of that disqualification; however, such a waiver may not be granted where it would prejudice the operation of the Company Directors Disqualification Act 1986 (subs. (2)). Failure to comply with a disqualification is an offence (subs. (3)) proceedings in respect of which are subject to the time limits mentioned in subs. (5). The *ultra vires* principle does not operate to invalidate acts done by disqualified persons in relation to the management or control of the recognised body (subs. (4)).

Reorganisation of public trusts

Reorganisation of public trusts by the court

9.—(1) Where, in the case of any public trust, the court is satisfied—
(a) that the purposes of the trust, whether in whole or in part—
(i) have been fulfilled as far as it is possible to do so; or
(ii) can no longer be given effect to, whether in accordance with the directions or spirit of the trust deed or other document constituting the trust or otherwise;
(b) that the purposes of the trust provide a use for only part of the property available under the trust;
(c) that the purposes of the trust were expressed by reference to—
(i) an area which has, since the trust was constituted, ceased to have effect for the purpose described expressly or by implication in the trust deed or other document constituting the trust; or
(ii) a class of persons or area which has ceased to be suitable or appropriate, having regard to the spirit of the trust deed or other

document constituting the trust, or as regards which is has ceased to be practicable to administer the property available under the trust; or

(d) that the purposes of the trust, whether in whole or in part, have, since the trust was constituted—

(i) been adequately provided for by other means; or

(ii) ceased to be such as would enable the trust to become a recognised body; or

(iii) ceased in any other way to provide a suitable and effective method of using the property available under the trust, having regard to the spirit of the trust deed or other document constituting the trust,

the court, on the application of the trustees, may, subject to subsection (2) below, approve a scheme for the variation or reorganisation of the trust purposes.

(2) The court shall not approve a scheme as mentioned in subsection (1) above unless it is satisfied that the trust purposes proposed in the scheme will enable the resources of the trust to be applied to better effect consistently with the spirit of the trust deed or other document constituting the trust, having regard to changes in social and economic conditions since the time when the trust was constituted.

(3) Where any of paragraphs (a) to (d) of subsection (1) above applies to a public trust, an application may be made under this section for the approval of a scheme—

(a) for the transfer of the assets of the trust to another public trust, whether involving a change to the trust purposes of such other trust or not; or

(b) for the amalgamation of the trust with one or more public trusts, and the court, if it is satisfied that the conditions specified in subsection (2) above are met, may approve such a scheme.

(4) Subject to subsection (5) below, an application for approval of a scheme under this section shall be made to the Court of Session.

(5) From such day as the Lord Advocate may, by order, appoint, an application for approval of a scheme under this section may be made by a public trust having an annual income not exceeding such amount as the Secretary of State may, by order, prescribe—

(a) to the sheriff for the place with which the trust has its closest and most real connection;

(b) where there is no such place as is mentioned in paragraph (a) above, to the sheriff for the place where any of the trustees resides;

(c) where neither paragraph (a) nor (b) above applies, to the sheriff of Lothian and Borders at Edinburgh.

(6) Every application under this section shall be intimated to the Lord Advocate who shall be entitled to enter appearance as a party in any proceedings on such application, and he may lead such proof and enter such pleas as he thinks fit; and no expenses shall be claimable by or against the Lord Advocate in any proceedings in which he has entered appearance under this subsection.

(7) This section shall be without prejudice to the power of the Court of Session to approve a cy-près scheme in relation to any public trust.

GENERAL NOTE

S.9 extends the powers of the Court of Session in relation to the approval of petitions for the application of funds *cy-près*. Apart from the powers conferred by this section, the Court could only approve a *cy-près* application where it was no longer possible to carry out the trust's purposes in the manner prescribed. Now, additionally, the Court may approve a petition where, having regard to social and economic changes since the trust was constituted, the purposes of the trust are obsolete or lacking in usefulness.

This reform brings the position in Scots law into line with the position in England. The corresponding provision in England is s.14 of the Charities Act 1960.

Small trusts

10.—(1) Where a majority of the trustees of any public trust having an annual income not exceeding £5,000 are of the opinion—

(a) that the purposes of the trust, whether in whole or in part—

(i) have been fulfilled as far as it is possible to do so; or

(ii) can no longer be given effect to, whether in accordance with the directions or spirit of the trust deed or other document constituting the trust or otherwise;

(b) that the purposes of the trust provide a use for only part of the property available under the trust;

(c) that the purposes of the trust were expressed by reference to—

(i) an area which has, since the trust was constituted, ceased to have effect for the purpose described expressly or by implication in the trust deed or other document constituting the trust; or

(ii) a class of persons or area which has ceased to be suitable or appropriate, having regard to the spirit of the trust deed or other document constituting the trust, or as regards which it has ceased to be practicable to administer the property available under the trust; or

(d) that the purposes of the trust, whether in whole or in part, have, since the trust was constituted—

(i) been adequately provided for by other means; or

(ii) ceased to be such as would enable the trust to become a recognised body; or

(iii) ceased in any other way to provide a suitable and effective method of using the property available under the trust, having regard to the spirit of the trust deed or other document constituting the trust,

subsection (2) below shall apply in respect of the trust.

(2) Where this subsection applies in respect of a trust, the trustees may determine that, to enable the resources of the trust to be applied to better effect consistently with the spirit of the trust deed or other document constituting the trust—

(a) a modification of the trust's purposes should be made;

(b) the whole assets of the trust should be transferred to another public trust; or

(c) that the trust should be amalgamated with one or more public trusts.

(3) Where the trustees of a trust determine as mentioned in subsection (2)(a) above, they may, subject to subsections (4) to (6) below, pass a resolution that the trust deed be modified by replacing the trust purposes by other purposes specified in the resolution.

(4) The trustees shall ensure that, so far as is practicable in the circumstances, the purposes so specified are not so far dissimilar in character to those of the purposes set out in the original trust deed or other document constituting the trust that such modification of the trust deed would constitute an unreasonable departure from the spirit of such trust deed or other document.

(5) Before passing a resolution under subsection (3) above the trustees shall have regard—

(a) where the trust purposes relate to a particular locality, to the circumstances of the locality; and

(b) to the extent to which it may be desirable to achieve economy by amalgamating two or more trusts.

(6) As regards a trust which is a recognised body, the trustees shall ensure that the purposes specified as mentioned in subsection (3) above are such as will enable the trust to continue to be granted an exemption from tax by the Commissioners of Inland Revenue under section 505(1) of the Income and Corporation Taxes Act 1988 (exemption from tax for charities).

(7) Subject to subsection (14) below, a modification of trust purposes under this section shall not have effect before the expiry of a period of two months commencing with the date on which any advertisement in pursuance of regulations made under subsection (13) below is first published.

(8) Where the trustees determine as mentioned in subsection (2)(b) above they may pass a resolution that the trust be wound up and that the assets of the trust be transferred to another trust or trusts the purposes of which are not so dissimilar in character to those of the trust to be wound up as to constitute an unreasonable departure from the spirit of the trust deed or other document constituting the trust to be wound up.

(9) Before passing a resolution under subsection (8) above, the trustees shall—

(a) where the trust purposes relate to a particular locality, have regard to the circumstances of the locality;

(b) where the trust is a recognised body, ensure that the purposes of the trust to which it is proposed that the assets be transferred are such as will enable the trust to be granted an exemption from tax by the Commissioners of Inland Revenue under section 505(1) of the Income and Corporation Taxes Act 1988 (exemption from tax for charities); and

(c) ascertain that the trustees of the trust to which it is proposed to transfer the assets will consent to the transfer of the assets.

(10) Where the trustees determine as mentioned in subsection (2)(c) above, they may pass a resolution that the trust be amalgamated with one or more other trusts so that the purposes of the trust constituted by such amalgamation will not be so dissimilar in character to those of the trust to which the resolution relates as to constitute an unreasonable departure from the spirit of the trust deed or other document constituting the last mentioned trust.

(11) Before passing a resolution under subsection (10) above, the trustees shall—

(a) where the trust purposes relate to a particular locality, have regard to the circumstances of the locality;

(b) where any of the trusts to be amalgamated is a recognised body, ensure that the trust purposes of the trust to be constituted by such amalgamation will be such as to enable it to be granted an exemption from tax by the Commissioners of Inland Revenue under section 505(1) of the Income and Corporation Taxes Act 1988 (exemption from tax for charities); and

(c) ascertain that the trustees of any other trust with which it is proposed that the trust will be amalgamated will agree to such amalgamation.

(12) Subject to subsection (14) below, a transfer of trust assets or an amalgamation of two or more trusts under this section shall not be effected before the expiry of a period of two months commencing with the date on which any advertisement in pursuance of regulations made under subsection (13) below is first published.

(13) The Secretary of State may, by regulations, prescribe the procedure to be followed by trustees following upon a resolution passed under subsection (3), (8) or (10) above, and such regulations may, without prejudice to the generality, include provision as to advertisement of the proposed modification or winding up, the making of objections by persons with an interest in the purposes of the trust, notification to the Lord Advocate of the terms of the resolution and the time within which anything requires to be done.

(14) If it appears to the Lord Advocate, whether in consideration of any objections made in pursuance of regulations made under subsection (13) above or otherwise—

(a) that the trust deed should not be modified as mentioned in subsection

      (3) above;

  (b) that the trust should not be wound up as mentioned in subsection (8) above; or

  (c) that the trust should not be amalgamated as mentioned in subsection (10) above,

he may direct the trust not to proceed with the modification or, as the case may be winding up and transfer of funds or amalgamation.

(15) The Secretary of State may, by order, amend subsection (1) above by substituting a different figure for the figure, for the time being, mentioned in that subsection.

(16) This section shall apply to any trust to which section 223 of the Local Government (Scotland) Act 1973 (property held on trust by local authorities) applies.

GENERAL NOTE

S.10 applies to small charities and creates mechanisms for their reorganisation in appropriate circumstances. The provisions apply to "any public trust" (not merely to charities) with an income of £5,000 or less (subs. (1)), although this figure may be changed by the Secretary of State by order (subs. (15)).

To bring the reorganisation procedure into operation the majority of trustees must be of the opinion that the purposes of the trust are obsolete or lacking in usefulness, or that it is no longer practicable to give effect to the intentions of the creator of the trust (subs. (1)). The reorganisation may take the form of a modification of the trust's purposes, a transfer of the entire assets of the trust to another public trust, or an amalgamation with one or more other public trusts (subs. (2)).

Subss. (3)–(7) deal with the procedure for effecting a modification. This is achieved by the trustees passing a resolution that the trust deed be modified replacing the trust purposes with other charitable purposes (subs. (3)); where the trust is a recognised body these substituted purposes must be cleared with the Revenue first in order to ensure that they continue to attract tax relief (subs. (6)); so far as is practicable the substituted purposes must be similar to the original ones (subs. (4)). Before passing the resolution the trustees are to consider whether it may be desirable to amalgamate with another trust or trusts; and, where the trust purposes relate to a particular locality, to have regard to the circumstances of that locality (subs. (5)). Any modification must be advertised and the modification will not be effective until two months have elapsed from the date of such advertisement (subs. (7)).

Where the trustees decide on transfer they may resolve that the trust be wound up and its assets transferred to another trust whose purposes are similar (subs. (8)). Where the trust is a recognised body the trustees must obtain Revenue clearance about the continued availability of tax relief before passing the resolution; they must be certain that its trustees consent to the transfer; and where the trust purposes relate to a locality they must have regard to the circumstances of that locality (subs. (9)).

A corresponding set of conditions applies in respect of proposed amalgamations (subss. (10) and (11)).

The two month period applies to transfers amalgamations as it does to modifications (subs. (12)).

Subs. (13) makes provision for the Secretary of State to make regulations governing the advertisement of any resolutions to modify trust purposes or wind up a trust. The object is to allow time for objections to be made; such objections should be notified to the Lord Advocate who is empowered (subs. (14)) to direct that the modifications, winding-up or amalgamation are not to be proceeded with.

The provisions of s.10 apply to trusts where the local authority is the trustee (subs. (16)).

The provisions of s.10 correspond to those of ss.2 and 3 of the Charities Act 1985.

Expenditure of capital

11.—(1) This section applies to any public trust which has an annual income not exceeding £1,000 where the trust deed or other document constituting the trust prohibits the expenditure of any of the trust capital.

(2) In the case of any trust to which this section applies where the trustees—

  (a) have resolved unanimously that, having regard to the purposes of the trust, the income of the trust is too small to enable the purposes of the trust to be achieved; and

  (b) are satisfied that either there is no reasonable prospect of effecting a transfer of the trust's assets under section 10 of this Act or that the expenditure of capital is more likely to achieve the purposes of the trust,

they may, subject to subsection (3) below, proceed with the expenditure of capital.

(3) Not less than two months before proceeding to expend capital, the trustees shall advertise their intention to do so in accordance with regulations made by the Secretary of State and shall notify the Lord Advocate of such intention.

(4) If it appears to the Lord Advocate that there are insufficient grounds for the expenditure of capital he may apply to the court for an order prohibiting such expenditure, and if the court is satisfied that there are such insufficient grounds it may grant the order.

(5) The Secretary of State may, by order, amend subsection (1) above by substituting a different figure for the figure, for the time being mentioned in that subsection.

GENERAL NOTE

S.11 applies to even smaller trusts, namely those with an annual income of less than £1,000 (or such other figure as the Secretary of State may by order substitute (subs. (5))) where the trust deed contains a prohibition on the expenditure of any of the trust capital (subs. (1)). What it does is provide a mechanism whereby such capital can be expended.

Essentially the procedure comprises three steps—

(1) the trustees must be satisfied that there is no reasonable prospect of a transfer of the trust's assets under s.10 or that the expenditure of the capital is more likely to achieve the purposes of the trust (subs. (2)(b));

(2) they must unanimously resolve that the income of the trust is too small to enable the purposes of the trust to be achieved (subs. (2)(a));

(3) they must advertise their intention of expending the capital and notify the Lord Advocate (subs. (3)).

The statutory two months delay is applied to action under s.11 and the Lord Advocate may within this period prevent the desired expenditure (subs. (4)).

The provisions of s.11 follow those of s.4 of the Charities Act 1985.

Dormant charities

Dormant accounts of charities in banks, etc.

12.—(1) The Secretary of State may appoint a person to be the Scottish charities nominee (in this section referred to as "the nominee") who shall have the functions conferred by this section.

(2) Where the nominee receives from a relevant institution the following information—

(a) that every account held by the institution in the name of or on behalf of a named body is dormant; and

(b) the amount of the balance standing to the credit of the body in each such account,

and he is satisfied that the body is a recognised body, subsection (3) or, as the case may be, subsection (5) below shall apply as regards the body and such accounts.

(3) Where the aggregate amount standing to the credit of the body in such accounts as are mentioned in subsection (2) above does not exceed £5,000, unless it appears to the nominee—

(a) that a person is concerned in the management or control of the body; or

(b) that there are circumstances relating to the body which would make it inappropriate to do so,

he shall transfer the balance standing to the credit of the body in such accounts to such other recognised body as he may determine, having regard to the purposes of the body in whose name or on whose behalf the accounts are held and those of the body to which it is proposed to transfer the funds; and the body to which the funds are transferred under this subsection or subsection (4) below shall be entitled to apply such funds for its purposes as it thinks fit.

(4) Where, in the case of a body to which subsection (3) above applies, the nominee is unable to ascertain the purposes of the body in whose name or on whose behalf such accounts are held, he shall transfer the balance standing in the name of the body concerned to such other recognised body as appeared to him expedient.

(5) Where the aggregate amount standing to the credit of the body in such accounts as are mentioned in subsection (2) above exceeds £5,000 or in any case to which paragraphs (a) or (b) of subsection (3) above applies, the nominee shall advise the Lord Advocate of the information received by him in respect of the body and of any other matter which appears to him to be relevant in the circumstances.

(6) Where the Lord Advocate receives information in pursuance of subsection (5) above he shall inform the nominee—

(a) in the case of a body which is a trust, whether he intends to exercise his power under section 13(2) of this Act to appoint new trustees to the body; or

(b) in any case, if he intends to apply to the Court of Session for the appointment of an interim judicial factor under section 7(4)(c) of this Act,

but if the Lord Advocate informs the nominee that he does not intend to proceed under either paragraph (a) or (b) above, subsection (3) above shall apply as regards the body and such accounts as are mentioned in subsection (2) above as if the aggregate amount of the balance referred to in subsection (3) did not exceed £5,000 and neither paragraph (a) nor (b) of that subsection applied.

(7) Notwithstanding anything in any enactment or rule of law to the contrary, the nominee shall, by virtue of this subsection, have the right to effect any transaction (including a transaction closing the account) in relation to any account to which subsection (3) above applies; and the receipt of the nominee in respect of any funds withdrawn or transferred from an account by virtue of this subsection shall, as regards the interest of the nominee in respect of such funds, be a full and valid discharge to the relevant institution holding the account.

(8) No liability (other than liability for a criminal offence) shall attach to the nominee in consequence of any act or omission of his in the performance of his functions under this section.

(9) The power of the nominee to effect transactions in relation to the accounts of a body shall cease to have effect—

(a) when the Lord Advocate notifies him of his intention to proceed under subsection (6) above;

(b) if the relevant institution by which the accounts are held notifies the nominee that the accounts held by or on behalf of the body are no longer dormant; or

(c) where the nominee becomes aware of the identity of a person concerned in the management or control of the body, when he informs the institution of that fact,

and in any case to which paragraph (c) above applies, the nominee shall also inform the Lord Advocate of that fact.

(10) The Secretary of State may, by regulations made under this section—

(a) make provision as to the procedure to be followed by the nominee in exercising his powers under this section;

(b) require the nominee to make to the Secretary of State an annual report as regards the exercise of his functions and such regulations may specify the form and content of such report; and the Secretary of State shall lay a copy of such report before each House of Parliament;

(c) prescribe the circumstances in which and the extent to which the nominee may apply any interest accruing the any account as regards which subsection (3) above applies during any period for which he is entitled to effect transactions in respect of the account for the purpose of defraying his expenses in connection with the exercise of his functions under this section;

(d) require the nominee to keep accounts as regards his outlays and expenses in connection with the exercise of his functions under this section; and

(e) amend subsections (3) and (5) above by substituting a different figure for the figure for the time being mentioned in those subsections.

(11) Where every account held by or on behalf of a body which appears to a relevant institution to be a recognised body is a dormant account, no obligation of confidentiality or requirement of secrecy (whether imposed by any enactment or rule of law of otherwise) shall prevent the institution from supplying to the nominee information such as is mentioned in subsection (12) below.

(12) Information referred to in subsection (11) above is information relating to any account such as is mentioned in that subsection which consists of any of the following—

(a) the amount of the balance of the account as at the date the information is supplied;

(b) the last date on which a transaction (other than a transaction consisting only of the accrual of interest to the account) was effected in relation to the account;

(c) so far as is known to the institution, the terms of the trust deed or other document constituting the body or any information as to the nature of the purposes of the body.

(13) For the purpose of this section—

(a) a "relevant institution" is—

(i) an institution which is authorised by the Bank of England to operate a deposit-taking business under Part I of the Banking Act 1987;

(ii) a building society which is authorised by the Building Societies Commission under section 9 of the Building Societies Act 1986 to raise money from its members;

(iii) such other institution mentioned in Schedule 2 to the Banking Act 1987 as the Secretary of State may, by regulations made under this section, prescribe;

(b) an account is dormant if—

(i) in the period of ten years preceding the date on which the institution reviews the account, no transaction (other than a transaction consisting only of the accrual of interest to the account) has taken place in respect of the account; and

(ii) the institution has no knowledge of the identity of any person concerned in the management or control of the body in whose name or on whose behalf the account is held.

GENERAL NOTE

S.12 confers powers to secure the application of funds of dormant charities to other purposes.

The function of dealing with dormant charities is vested in the Scottish Charities Nominee, a person appointed by the Secretary of State (subs. (1)). The nominee must, unless there are circumstances which appear to him to render it inappropriate to do so (subs. (3)), act when he receives information from a bank or building society (subs. (13)(a)) that an account held by a recognised body is dormant (subs. (3)); an account is dormant if no transaction has taken place in respect of it during the preceding 10 years and the relevant institution has no knowledge of the identity of persons concerned in its management or control (subs. (13)(b)).

Where the balance on the account is less than £5,000 the nominee is required to transfer the balance to such other recognised body as he shall determine (subs. (3)); where the balance exceeds £5,000 the nominee must advise the Lord Advocate (subs. (5)) who may (1) if the body is a trust, appoint new trustees, or (2) in any case, apply to the Court of Session for the appointment of an interim judicial factor, or (3) refer the matter back to the nominee to be dealt with as if the amount involved were less than £5,000 (subs. (6)).

The nominee is empowered to effect any transaction with respect to the account (including closing it) and his receipt shall constitute a valid discharge to the institution holding the account (subs. (7)) and no civil liability shall attach in relation to acts or omissions of the nominee (subs. (8)).

The powers of the nominee cease in respect of an account if (1) the account ceases to be dormant; (2) the nominee learns of the identity of persons with management or control of the body; or (3) the Lord Advocate appoints new trustees or applies to the Court of Session for the appointment of an interim judicial factor (subs. (9)).

The powers of the nominee and the procedures he may adopt may be further defined by regulations made by the Secretary of State (subs. (10)).

Relevant institutions are excused from their normal duties of confidentiality in respect of information provided to the nominee concerning dormant accounts (subss. (11) and (12)).

Miscellaneous

Appointment of trustees

13.—(1) Where a recognised body is a trust, notwithstanding anything to the contrary in the trust deed or other document constituting the trust, the trustees shall have power to appoint such number of additional trustees as will secure that, at any time, the number of trustees shall be not less than three.

(2) Where in the case of any trust which is a recognised body—

(a) the number of trustees is less than three; and

(b) it appears to the Lord Advocate that the trustees will not, or are unable to, exercise their power under subsection (1) above,

if it appears to the Lord Advocate expedient to do so, he may exercise the power in place of the trustees.

GENERAL NOTE

S.13 provides that notwithstanding anything in the trust deed the trustees are empowered to appoint additional trustees to ensure that at no time does the number of trustees fall below three (subs. (1)); the Lord Advocate is endowed with a reserve power should the trustees be unable to act (subs. (2)).

Alteration of purposes and winding-up of charitable companies

14.—(1) This section applies to a recognised body which may be wound up by the Court of Session under or by virtue of Parts IV or V of the Insolvency Act 1986.

(2) Where a body to which this section applies has power to alter the instruments establishing or regulating it, it shall not alter any charitable purposes in those instruments except in such a way as will enable the body to continue to be granted an exemption from tax by the Commissioners of Inland Revenue under section 505(1) of the Income and Corporation Taxes Act 1988 (exemption from tax of charities).

(3) Notwithstanding section 124 of the Insolvency Act 1986, a petition for the winding-up under section 122 of that Act of a body to which this section applies may be presented by the Lord Advocate to any court in Scotland having jurisdiction.

GENERAL NOTE

S.14 provides a procedure for the winding up or alteration of the purposes of charitable companies. A petition for the winding up of such a company may be presented by the Lord Advocate to any court in Scotland having jurisdiction (subs. (3)). Where the purposes of the company are amended, Revenue clearance to the effect that the purposes as modified will still attract tax relief must be obtained (subs. (2)).

The provisions of s.12 correspond to those of s.30 of the Charities Act 1960.

Interpretation

Interpretation of Part I, regulations and orders

15.—(1) In this Part of this Act—

"annual income" in relation to a recognised body means the income of
the body for the financial year to which its most recent statement of
accounts relates;

"accounting reference period," "accounting reference date" and
"financial year" shall be construed in accordance with subsections
(2) to (7) below;

"body" includes the sole trustee of any trust and, as regards any
reference in this Part of this Act to the institution of proceedings in
any court or to any order of a court in relation to an unincorporated
body, shall be construed—

    (a) in the case of a trust, as a reference to the trustees acting in
their capacity as such;

    (b) in any other case, as a reference to the persons concerned
in the management or control of the body;

"court," for the purposes of establishing jurisdiction to hear or determine any matter other than under sections 7 and 9 of this Act,
means the Court of Session or the sheriff court;

"non-recognised body" shall be construed in accordance with section 2
of this Act;

"non-registered charity" has the meaning given by section 6 of this Act;

"recognised body" has the meaning given by section 1 of this Act; and

"registered charity" has the meaning given by section 6 of this Act.

(2) For the purposes of this Part of this Act, a recognised body's first
financial year begins with the first day of its first accounting reference period
and ends with the last day of that period or such other date, not more than 7
days before or after the end of that period, as the persons concerned with the
management or control of the body may determine.

(3) Subject to subsection (4) below, subsequent financial years begin with
the day immediately following the end of the body's previous financial year
and end with the last day of its next accounting reference period or such
other date, not more than 7 days before or after the end of that period as the
persons responsible for its management or control may determine.

(4) A recognised body's accounting reference periods are determined
according to its accounting reference date.

(5) A recognised body's accounting reference date is the date upon which
its accounting reference period ends in each calendar year and it shall be
ascertained as follows—

(a) in the case of a body which is recognised at the commencement of this
section and in respect of which accounts have been prepared up to a
date not more than 12 months before such commencement, its
accounting reference date shall be that date;

(b) in the case of a body which is recognised at the commencement of this
section and in respect of which no such accounts have been prepared,
its accounting reference date shall be March 31, or such other date as
the Secretary of State may, by order, prescribe;

(c) in the case of a body which is not recognised at the commencement of
this section and in respect of which accounts have been prepared up to
a date not more than 12 months before its recognition, its accounting
reference date shall be that date; and

(d) a body which is not recognised at the commencement of this section
and in respect of which no accounts have been prepared up to a date
not more than 12 months before such commencement, unless it
determines that its accounting reference date shall be March 31, or
such other date as the Secretary of State may, by order, prescribe,
shall by notice given to the Lord Advocate specify its accounting
reference date;

(6) A recognised body's first accounting reference period is—

(a) in the case of a body which is recognised at the commencement of this section and in respect of which any accounts have been prepared for a period up to a date not more than 12 months before such commencement, the period beginning with that date;

(b) in the case of a body which is recognised at such commencement and in respect of which on such accounts have been prepared, the period beginning with such commencement;

(c) in the case of any other body, the period of more than 6 months but not more than 18 months, beginning with the date from which its recognition takes effect and ending with its accounting reference date.

(7) Its subsequent accounting reference periods are successive periods of 12 months beginning immediately after the end of the previous accounting reference period and ending with its accounting reference date.

(8) A recognised body may, on giving not less than one month's notice of its intention to do so to the Lord Advocate, unless the Lord Advocate notifies the body that he objects to the proposal, specify a new accounting reference date having effect in relation to the body's current accounting reference period and subsequent periods.

(9) Nothing in this Part of this Act, except section 1, shall affect any educational endowment within the meaning of section 122(1) of the Education (Scotland) Act 1980.

(10) The War Charities Act 1940 shall cease to have effect as regards Scotland; but nothing in this subsection shall affect any prosecution for an offence under that Act which has been instituted before the commencement of this section.

(11) Any power in this Part of this Act of the Secretary of State to make regulations or orders shall be exercisable by statutory instrument subject to annulment in pursuance of a resolution of either House of Parliament.

GENERAL NOTE
    S.13 contains the interpretation provisions for Pt. I of the Act; it also defines the financial years of recognised bodies.

PART II

LEGAL SERVICES

INTRODUCTION AND GENERAL NOTE
    Pt. II of the Act is part of the Government's continuing efforts at the deregulation of the legal profession, where we have already seen relaxation of the advertising rules which apply to solicitors and the abolition of scale fees in conveyancing. It seeks to implement many of the proposals for reform which were contained in the White Paper *The Scottish Legal Profession: The Way Forward*, which was published by the Secretary of State for Scotland in October 1989. This policy statement was itself based upon the two earlier consultation papers published by the Secretary of State, *viz. The Practice of the Solicitor Profession in Scotland* (1987) and *The Legal Profession in Scotland* (March 1989) and the responses to them. As the introduction to the consultation paper on the *Legal Profession in Scotland* makes clear, the Government's purpose in this reform process has been to remove anti-competitive restrictions on the supply of legal services which, it considers, are not in the public interest. The avowed aim of the Act is to increase choice for the client of legal services, while at the same time preserving and, where possible improving, consumer protection requirements. However, as a number of commentators have remarked, such an increase in choice only applies to those clients with adequate means. The Act does very little to improve the availability of legal aid.
    The Act will increase the choice for clients through the provisions which abolish the solicitors' conveyancing and executry monopolies and the Faculty of Advocates' monopoly on rights of audience in the higher courts. As far as the abolition of the solicitors' conveyancing monopoly is concerned, *The Scottish Legal Profession: the Way Forward* envisaged that individual banks and building societies who could certify to their regulatory authorities that they could comply with the requirements for authorisation and with a statutory code of conduct could operate as conveyancing practitioners. This arrangement was confirmed by the original Bill, which authorised the Board to grant applications from banks, building societies and insurance companies to offer conveyancing services. However, as a result of "understandings and agreements" reached

with the Law Society of Scotland on July 4, 1990, the Secretary of State undertook to withdraw from the Bill the provisions which authorised banks, building societies and insurance companies to act as conveyancing practitioners. The reason for this change of heart was largely because the Government realised that its backbenchers were not prepared to support such a proposal in Committee and given the paucity of Scottish Tory backbench MPs there was little chance of it surviving this legislative stage. Indeed, there was a time when it looked as if the whole Bill might be lost. Thus in order to ensure the enactment of the rest of its proposals on legal services, the Government tabled amendments at Committee Stage in the House of Commons which deleted the provisions concerning banks, etc. conducting conveyancing transactions from the Bill and restricted the right to practise as a qualified conveyancer to a "natural person".

Pt. II also creates the Scottish Conveyancing and Executry Services Board which is authorised to maintain a register of qualified conveyancers and a register of executry practitioners. The Board is also required to maintain a list of recognised financial institutions which provide executry services and also has the power to discipline qualified conveyancers and executry practitioners who are guilty of misconduct or provide inadequate professional services. Thus unlike the Courts and Legal Services Act 1990 which permits financial institutions to offer conveyancing services in England and Wales the Scottish Act restricts recognised financial institutions solely to the provision of executry services to the public.

Pt. II also fulfils the proposals in the *Scottish Legal Profession: The Way Forward* providing for a major expansion in the range of persons who may represent clients in court. The Faculty of Advocates has consistently opposed these proposals as being contrary to the public interest. However the Act extends the rights of audience of solicitors by enabling the Council of the Law Society of Scotland to authorise solicitors who have the necessary knowledge, training and experience to obtain rights of audience in, on the one hand, the Court of Session, House of Lords or Judicial Committee of the Privy Council or, on the other hand, the High Court of Justiciary. The Act also fulfils another proposal which the Faculty has resisted just as fiercely. This is the provision which allows "bare-foot" pleaders to acquire rights to conduct litigation on behalf of members of the public and to obtain rights of audience. Under the Act a member of a professional or other body which has made application to the Lord President and the Secretary of State for rights of audience on behalf of its members, will have a right to appear in court and to conduct litigation in conformity with a scheme which has been drawn up by the relevant body and approved by the Lord President and Secretary of State.

The Act also abolishes the statutory ban on fee-sharing with unqualified persons which prevented solicitors going into partnership with non-solicitors and, therefore, opens the door to the creation of multi-disciplinary practices. However, the Council of the Law Society will remain free to prevent the creation of such partnerships so long as the relevant rule has been approved by the Secretary of State. Equally, any rule which prevents an advocate entering into partnership with another advocate or with any other person offering professional services will have no effect unless it has been approved by the Lord President and the Secretary of State.

The complaints procedures for legal services are also strengthened by Pt. II. "Professional organisations" (*i.e.* the Faculty of Advocates, Council of the Law Society, the Board and any professional or other body which has obtained rights of audience for its members) will have a statutory duty to investigate complaints and to produce written reports on such complaints. Moreover, the office of the lay observer for Scotland is abolished, to be replaced by the Scottish legal services ombudsman who will be appointed by the Secretary of State and who will be able to deal with grievances about the handling of complaints about the conduct and quality of service offered by members of any of the professional organisations noted earlier. Finally, given that the Act seeks to introduce an element of competition into the provision of legal services, Pt. II also increases the advisory and supervisory functions of the Director General of Fair Trading. In particular, he is given the power to consider whether rules made by the Council of the Law Society extending solicitors' rights of audience and which prohibit the creation of multi-disciplinary practices will have the effect of restricting, distorting or preventing competition to any significant extent.

Organisations like the Scottish Consumer Council and Citizens' Advice Scotland have broadly supported many of the provisions in the Bill, particularly those aimed at the removal of the conveyancing monopoly and the extension of rights of audience. However, it has been argued that the above provisions, which repeal what the Government believes are unnecessary restraints on competition and which, it is intended, will have the effect of widening consumer choice, sound the death knell for the independence of the Scottish legal system. (See, in particular, W.A. Wilson's article in *The Scotsman* on January 1, 1990 on "The Death Sentence for Scots Law"). Professor Wilson, like all the opposition parties in the House of Commons and a number of influential peers in the House of Lords, has formed the view that the changes to the legal profession in Scotland introduced by this Act are much too important to have been left to a miscellaneous provisions measure. However, it is clear that the decision to include them in a statute of this nature was a function of the limited amount of time which is allocated to purely Scottish Bills.

Second, concern has been expressed in the debates on the Bill and in Professor Wilson's article about the extent of the powers which are bestowed upon the Secretary of State, Lord President and Director General and the fact that in many places the Act is largely an enabling measure granting powers to the Secretary of State or to organisations like the Council of the Law Society to make regulations or rules. It is the Government's view, however, that the Act, whilst increasing consumer choice, does so within the Scottish legal tradition and with proper regard for the rôles and functions of the persons and agencies which administer the Scottish legal system. (See, for example, the defence of the then Bill made by Alan Rodger Q.C., Solicitor General for Scotland in *The Scotsman* on January 1, 1990.) Finally, on the issue of whether the Act will damage Scots law, there are a number of places where the Act does diverge from its English counterpart. For example, there is no equivalent in the Scottish Act to the Lord Chancellor's Advisory Committee on Legal Education and Conduct which is created by the Courts and Legal Services Act for England and Wales. It must be noted that this omission has been criticised strongly by consumer groups in Scotland who have argued that there is as much need for an advisory body in Scotland as there is for England and Wales.

Conveyancing and executry services

The Scottish Conveyancing and Executry Services Board

16.—(1) There shall be a Board, to be known as the Scottish Conveyancing and Executry Services Board, which shall have the principal functions of regulating—

(a) the provision of conveyancing services by persons other than—
　　　(i) solicitors; and
　　　(ii) persons mentioned in section 32(2) of the 1980 Act (unqualified persons who may draw and prepare documents relating to heritable estate and confirmations); and

(b) the provision of executry services by persons other than—
　　　(i) solicitors;
　　　(ii) persons referred to in paragraph (a)(ii) above; and
　　　(iii) recognised financial institutions.

(2) The Secretary of State may, with the consent of the Treasury, make grants to the Board towards expenses incurred, or to be incurred, by them in connection with—

(a) the initial establishment of the Board; and
(b) the discharge by the Board of their functions.

(3) Any grant made under subsection (2) above may be made subject to such terms and conditions (including conditions as to repayment) as the Secretary of State, with the consent of the Treasury, thinks fit and the Secretary of State may, with such consent, vary such terms and conditions after the grant is made.

(4) Part I of Schedule 1 to this Act (constitution, duties, powers and status of the Board) shall have effect in relation to the Board.

GENERAL NOTE

The Scottish Conveyancing and Executry Services Board has been created to regulate the provision of conveyancing services by qualified conveyancers and the provision of executry services offered by executry practitioners. It has no responsibility for solicitors who provide conveyancing or executry services or for recognised financial institutions who will be entitled to provide executry services. The Scottish Board has a much broader remit than the English Conveyancing Practitioners Board since it also regulates executry practitioners and has greater responsibilities over qualified conveyancers than the English Board has over its nearest equivalent: the licensed conveyancer created by the Administration of Justice Act 1985. On the other hand, attempts in both Houses of Parliament to extend the remit of the Board to give it greater responsibility for maintaining and developing standards in education and training and as regards the conduct of those who provide legal services were defeated on the advice of the Government. These changes would have made the Board much more akin to the Lord Chancellor's Advisory Committee.

Subs. (1)

This makes it clear that the Board's principal responsibilities will be in relation to qualified conveyancers and executry practitioners. However, certain categories of unqualified persons are excluded from regulation by the Board. These are listed in the Solicitors (Scotland) Act 1980 and include any unqualified person who has proved that he drew or prepared a writ relating to heritable or moveable estate or papers relating to the confirmation of executors without receiving or expecting to receive, either directly or indirectly, any fee, gain or reward *other than by remuneration paid under a contract of employment* (words added by the 1990 Act, Sched. 8, para. 29(6)(a)). On the other hand, there is nothing to prevent solicitors who provide conveyancing services or executry services registering with the Board as qualified conveyancers or executry practitioners so long as they practise exclusively as qualified conveyancers or executry practitioners and do not offer these services as practising solicitors.

Subs. (2)

It is the Government's stated intention that the Board eventually become self-financing by relying on the income it receives from qualified conveyancers and executry practitioners. However, this subsection enables the Board to receive grants from the Secretary of State, with the consent of the Treasury to get it operational and to support the discharge of its functions.

Subs. (3)

This provision gives the Secretary of State the power to attach conditions to the award of a grant. Such conditions may include the requirement that the grant be repaid.

Qualified conveyancers

17.—(1) The Board shall establish and maintain a register of qualified conveyancers, which shall be available for inspection by any person without charge.

(2) Where, on an application made to them by a natural person in such form as they may determine, and on the provision of such information in connection with the application as they consider necessary, the Board are satisfied that the applicant—

(a) is a fit and proper person to provide conveyancing services as a qualified conveyancer; and

(b) complies with the requirements of rules made under subsection (3) below,

the Board shall grant the application and shall enter the applicant's name in the register of qualified conveyancers.

(3) The Board shall, subject to subsection (15) below and after such consultation as they consider appropriate, make rules as to the requirements to be satisfied by any person applying for registration under subsection (2) above, and such rules shall, in particular, make provision as to—

(a) educational qualifications; and

(b) practical training.

(4) Where the Board refuse an application under subsection (2) above they shall give the applicant written reasons for their decision.

(5) Where the Board refuse an application under subsection (2) above the applicant may, within 21 days of the date on which the Board's decision is intimated to him, apply to the Board to review their decision.

(6) Where the Board have reviewed a decision mentioned in subsection (5) above the applicant may, within 21 days of the date on which the outcome of such review is intimated to him, apply to the Court of Session and the Court may make such order in the matter as it thinks fit.

(7) Where a qualified conveyancers informs the Board that he intends to provide conveyancing services to the public for a fee, gain or reward and—

(a) satisfies the Board that he has made adequate arrangements for the satisfaction of any successful claims against him arising out of such provision by him of such services; or

(b) participates in the arrangements made by the Board for that purpose under subsection (13)(b) below,

the Board shall make an annotation on the register against his name to the effect that he is an independent qualified conveyancer; and where he subsequently informs them that he intends to cease providing such services to the public for a fee, gain or reward, they shall remove that annotation.

(8) Any person or body other than—

(a) an independent qualified conveyancer; or

(b) a solicitor; or

(c) an incorporated practice within the meaning of section 65 of the 1980 Act (interpretation); or

(d) a multi-disciplinary practice within the meaning of that section,

who employs a qualified conveyancer under a contract of employment for the purpose of providing conveyancing services for persons other than himself or, as the case may be, themselves, shall be guilty of an offence and liable on summary conviction to a fine not exceeding level 4 on the standard scale.

(9) Where a qualified conveyancer applies to the Board to remove his name from the register the Board shall—

(a) where, in the case of an independent qualified conveyancer, they are satisfied that he has made adequate arrangements with respect to the business he then has in hand; and

(b) in any other case, without further enquiry,

grant the application and amend the register accordingly.

(10) The Board shall send to the Keeper of the Registers of Scotland—

(a) as soon as practicable after April 1, in each year, a list of all qualified conveyancers; and

(b) written notice of any subsequent change to the register of qualified conveyancers.

(11) The Secretary of State shall, subject to section 40 of this Act and after consultation with such persons as he considers appropriate, by regulations make such provision as he thinks fit with a view to maintaining appropriate standards of conduct and practice of independent qualified conveyancers, and such regulations shall, in particular, make provision with respect to—

(a) the manner in which such conveyancers conduct the provision of conveyancing services;

(b) conflicts of interest;

(c) the contractual obligations of such conveyancers;

(d) the holding of clients' money; and

(e) the disclosure of and accounting for commissions.

(12) Regulations under subsection (11) above shall be made by statutory instrument and no regulations shall be made under that subsection unless a draft of the regulations has been laid before, and approved by a resolution of, each House of Parliament.

(13) The Board shall, in relation to the provision of conveyancing services by independent qualified conveyancers, and subject to subsection (14) below—

(a) establish and maintain suitable procedures for dealing with any complaints made to them in connection with the provision of conveyancing services by such conveyancers; and

(b) make suitable arrangements (whether by means of insurance policies or otherwise) to secure that any successful claims made against such a conveyancer in connection with the provision of conveyancing services are satisfied.

(14) Before establishing procedures or making arrangements under subsection (13)(a) or, as the case may be, (b) above, the Board shall submit particulars of the proposed procedures or arrangements to the Secretary of State for his approval.

(15) Before making any rules under subsection (3) above, the Board shall submit the rules to the Secretary of State for his approval, and before approving any such rules the Secretary of State shall consult—

(a) the Director in accordance with section 40 of this Act; and

(b) such other persons as he considers appropriate.

(16) It shall be the duty of—

(a) an independent qualified conveyancer to comply with the require-
    ments of regulations made under subsection (11) above and any
    direction of the Board under section 20(2)(a) or (b) of this Act; and
(b) the Board to ensure such compliance.

(17) Where, under or by virtue of any enactment—

(a) a warrant of registration is required for recording any deed in the
    General Register of Sasines; or
(b) an application for registration is required for registering an interest in
    land in the Land Register of Scotland,

any reference in that or any other enactment or any subordinate instrument
to such a warrant or application being signed by a solicitor or agent shall be
construed as including a reference to the warrant or application being signed
by a qualified conveyancer, and any enactment or subordinate instrument
making provision as to the form of such a warrant or application shall, with
the necessary modifications, apply in relation to a qualified conveyancer.

(18) A qualified conveyancer who signs a warrant or application by virtue
of subsection (17) above shall, in addition to any matters required to be
specified after his signature by any enactment or subordinate instrument,
specify the independent qualified conveyancer, solicitor or incorporated
practice by whom he is employed or, where he is himself an independent
qualified conveyancer, his designation as such.

(19) Any person who—

(a) wilfully and falsely—
    (i) pretends to be a qualified conveyancer; or
    (ii) takes or uses any name, title, addition or description implying
         that he is a qualified conveyancer; or
(b) being a qualified conveyancer, providers conveyancing services at a
    time when his registration as such is suspended,

shall be guilty of an offence and liable on summary conviction to a fine not
exceeding level 4 on the standard scale.

(20) Any qualified conveyancer not registered as an independent qualified conveyancer under subsection (7) above who—

(a) wilfully and falsely—
    (i) pretends to be an independent qualified conveyancer; or
    (ii) takes or uses any name, title, addition or description implying
         that he is an independent qualified conveyancer; or
(b) provides conveyancing services to the public for a fee, gain or reward,

shall be guilty of an offence and liable on summary conviction to a fine not
exceeding level 4 on the standard scale.

(21) Where an offence under subsection (19)(a) above is committed by a
body corporate and is proved to have been committed with the consent or
connivance of or to be attributable to any neglect on the part of—

(a) any director, secretary or other similar officer of the body corporate;
    or
(b) any person who was purporting to act in any such capacity,

he (as well as the body corporate) shall be guilty of the offence and shall be
liable to be proceeded against and punished accordingly.

(22) Where an offence under subsection (19)(a) above is committed by a
partnership and is proved to have been committed with the consent or
connivance of a partner, he (as well as the partnership) shall be guilty of the
offence and shall be liable to be proceeded against and punished
accordingly.

(23) Any independent qualified conveyancer who provides conveyancing
services upon the account of, or for the profit of, any person other than—

(a) a solicitor;
(b) an incorporated practice within the meaning of section 65 of the 1980
    Act;
(c) a multi-disciplinary practice within the meaning of that section; or

(d) another independent qualified conveyancer,

knowing that person not to be a solicitor, incorporated practice, multi-disciplinary practice or independent qualified conveyancer, shall be guilty of an offence and liable on summary conviction to a fine not exceeding level 4 on the standard scale.

(24) Any rule imposed by any professional or other body which purports to prevent a solicitor or any person mentioned in section 32(2) of the 1980 Act (unqualified persons who may draw and prepare documents relating to heritable estate etc.) from—

(a) acting as an employee of an independent qualified conveyancer in connection with the provision of conveyancing services; or

(b) acting on behalf of an independent qualified conveyancer in connection with the provision of such services,

shall be of no effect.

GENERAL NOTE

The original provisions of the Bill granted rights to practise as conveyancers to financial institutions as well as to individuals. However, the right to practise conveyancing granted to financial institutions by the Bill was deleted at Committee Stage in the House of Commons, ostensibly because the Government recognised as genuine the Law Society's fears for the future survival of rural solicitors. This was based on the argument that since much of the income of rural solicitors is derived from conveyancing work any loss of this business to banks and building societies would affect the viability of rural firms. Thus s.17 creates a framework whereby only natural persons can apply to the Board to be registered as qualified conveyancers. Although there is nothing in Scots law to prevent unqualified persons drawing up missives for the sale of heritage, the Solicitors (Scotland) 1980, s.32(1)(a), makes it an offence for an unqualified person to draw or prepare a writ relating to heritage or moveables. It is clear that this provision will not apply to a person who has registered as a qualified conveyancer with the Board. S.17 ensures that any person who satisfies the Board as to his character and education and training will be entitled to practise as a qualified conveyancer. A person whose application is rejected by the Board not only has the right to receive written reasons but can also seek review by the Board of that decision and eventually apply to the Court of Session for an order.

Subs. (1)

This provision enables the Board to maintain a register of qualified conveyancers and to make it available to the public without charge.

Subs. (2)

The Board is required to grant applications from natural persons who satisfy it that they are fit and proper persons to provide conveyancing services and who also satisfy the rules about education and training which the Board is entitled to make under the powers vested in it by subs. (3). S.17(2) also permits the Board to determine the application form for registration as a qualified conveyancer and to specify the necessary information which applicants must provide.

Subs. (3)

This is an enabling provision which authorises the Board to make rules as to the requirements for registration as a qualified conveyancer, and, in particular, to specify the requirements about educational qualifications and practical training. Any such rules must be approved by the Secretary of State who must first consult the Director General and such other persons as he considers appropriate. It is intended that such an arrangement will ensure the widest possible debate on the rules before they are introduced.

Subs. (4)

An applicant who is refused registration must be given written reasons by the Board.

Subs. (5)

Any such rejected applicant also has the right to apply to the Board to review its decision.

Subs. (6)

As a final safeguard on this issue, an applicant who has sought review by the Board of a refusal to register also has the right to apply to the Court of Session for an order within 21 days of the date of intimation of the outcome of the review.

Subs. (7)

This provision creates a specific breed of qualified conveyancer, *viz.* an independent qualified conveyancer, who is a qualified conveyancer who informs the Board that he intends to provide conveyancing services to the public for a fee, gain or reward; who satisfies the Board that he has made adequate arrangements to meet claims by clients and who participates in arrangements made by the Board for professional indemnity purposes. Such a person may set up in business offering conveyancing services and may employ qualified conveyancers as employees. Moreover, an independent qualified conveyancer is subject to the Board's intervention powers under s.21 to protect the interests of clients.

Subs. (8)
This is a provision which was introduced by Sir Nicholas Fairbairn, with the support of the Government, at Committee Stage in the House of Commons, to make it an offence for persons other than independent qualified conveyancers, solicitors, incorporated practices and multi-disciplinary practices to employ a qualified conveyancer to provide conveyancing services to the public. It is intended to ensure that financial institutions are denied the opportunity of offering conveyancing services by the backdoor route of employing qualified conveyancers.

Subs. (9)
The important issue under this provision is for the Board to ensure that an independent qualified conveyancer who intends to cease practice has made adequate arrangements as regards his current business.

Subs. (10)
This provision imposes upon the Board a duty to provide a list of qualified conveyancers to the Keeper and to give written notice of any changes to that list.

Subss. (11) and (12)
These provisions were introduced at Report Stage in the House of Commons. They are intended to place responsibility for making rules governing the conduct and practice of independent qualified conveyancers upon the Secretary of State who will be required to make such rules in the form of regulations which will be subject to affirmative resolution in both Houses of Parliament.

Subs. (13)
Before the Report Stage in the House of Commons it was the Board which was granted rule-making powers. Now the Board's powers are restricted to establishing and maintaining suitable complaints procedures and making suitable arrangements for indemnity purposes in relation to conveyancing services offered by independent qualified conveyancers.

Subs. (14)
The above procedures and arrangements can only be established after the Secretary of State has given his approval.

Subs. (15)
This provision specifies the preliminary steps that must be taken before the Board can make rules about education and training for qualified conveyancers.

Subs. (16)
This provision places duties upon independent qualified conveyancers to ensure compliance with the Secretary of State's rules and any directions made by the Board in relation to professional misconduct or inadequate professional services. The Board is also obliged to ensure compliance.

Subs. (17)
This provision gives qualified conveyancers the same rights as solicitors as far as registration of deeds in the General Register of Sasines or interests in land in the Land Register of Scotland are concerned.

Subs. (18)
Qualified conveyancers who are seeking registration and who are employees must specify the person or practice by whom they are employed and an independent qualified conveyancer who makes a similar application must intimate his designation.

Subs. (19)
This provision is along similar lines to that contained in the Solicitors (Scotland) Act 1980, s.31(1), as regards unqualified persons pretending to be solicitors or notaries public, with the addition of an offence applying to qualified conveyancers who are no longer registered as such.

Subs. (20)

This provision makes it an offence for a qualified conveyancer to act as an independent qualified conveyancer or to charge fees on his own behalf.

Subs. (21)

This provision makes it clear that where an offence is committed by a body corporate in relation to qualified conveyancers, other officers or persons, or the directors or company secretary, may also be prosecuted. It is similar in terms to the equivalent provision for bodies corporate who consent or connive in the impersonation of solicitors, notaries public or incorporated practices to be found in the 1980 Act, s.31(3) (as enacted by the Law Reform (Miscellaneous Provisions) (Scotland) Act 1985, s.56, Sched. 1, para. 8(b)).

Subs. (22)

A partner can also be convicted of an offence under s.17(19)(a) where it was committed by the partnership and it can be proved that it was committed with his connivance or consent.

Subs. (23)

This provision makes it an offence for an independent qualified conveyancer to provide services for the profit of some other person other than a solicitor, an incorporated practice, a multi-disciplinary practice, or another independent qualified conveyancer, knowing that the person concerned is not a solicitor, etc.

Subs. (24)

This section permits solicitors and any of the persons mentioned in the Solicitors (Scotland) Act 1980, s.32(2), to be employed as employees of independent qualified conveyancers or to act on their behalf.

Executry practitioners

18.—(1) The Board shall establish and maintain a register of executry practitioners, which shall be available for inspection by any person without charge.

(2) Where, on an application made to them in such form as they may determine, the Board are satisfied that the applicant fulfils the conditions specified in subsection (3) below, the Board shall grant the application and shall enter the applicant's name in the register of executry practitioners.

(3) The conditions referred to in subsection (2) above are that the applicant—

(a) is a fit and proper person to provide executry services;

(b) complies with the requirements prescribed by regulations made under subsection (10) below; and

(c) maintains suitable arrangements (whether by means of insurance policies or otherwise) to satisfy any successful claims made against it in connection with the provision of executry services.

(4) The Board may require an applicant under subsection (2) above to provide such further information in connection with the application as they consider necessary.

(5) Where the Board—

(a) grant an application under subsection (2) above, they may attach such conditions as they may determine, and shall record any such conditions against the applicant's name in the register;

(b) refuse such an application, they shall give the applicant written reasons for their decision.

(6) Where the Board—

(a) grant an application under subsection (2) above subject to conditions; or

(b) refuse such an application,

the applicant may, within 21 days of the date on which the Board's decision is intimated to it, apply to the Board to review their decision.

(7) Where the Board have reviewed a decision mentioned in subsection (6) above the applicant may, within 21 days of the date on which the

outcome of such review is intimated to it, apply to the Court of Session and the Court may make such order in the matter as it thinks fit.

(8) Where an executry practitioner applies to the Board to remove its name from the register the Board shall, if they are satisfied that the practitioner has made adequate arrangements with respect to the business it then has in hand, grant the application and amend the register accordingly.

(9) The Board shall send to the Keeper of the Registers of Scotland and to each sheriff clerk—

(a) as soon as practicable after April 1 in each year, a list of all executry practitioners; and

(b) written notice of any subsequent change to the register of executry practitioners.

(10) The Secretary of State shall, subject to section 40 of this Act and after consultation with such persons as he considers appropriate, by regulations make such provision as he thinks fit with a view to maintaining appropriate standards of conduct and practice of executry practitioners and such regulations shall, in particular, make provision as to educational qualifications and practical training.

(11) Regulations under subsection (10) above shall be made by statutory instrument and no regulations shall be made under that subsection unless a draft of the regulations has been laid before, and approved by a resolution of, each House of Parliament.

(12) It shall be the duty of—

(a) an executry practitioner to comply with the requirements of regulations made under subsection (10) above and any direction of the Board under section 20(2)(a) or (b) of this Act; and

(b) the Board to ensure such compliance.

(13) Any person who—

(a) wilfully and falsely—

(i) pretends to be an executry practitioner; or

(ii) takes or uses any name, title, addition or description implying that he is an executry practitioner; or

(b) being an executry practitioner, provides executry services at a time when his registration as such is suspended,

shall be guilty of an offence and liable on summary conviction to a fine not exceeding level 4 on the standard scale.

(14) Where an offence under subsection (13) above is committed by a body corporate and is proved to have been committed with the consent or connivance of or to be attributable to any neglect on the part of—

(a) any director, secretary or other similar officer of the body corporate, or

(b) any person who was purporting to act in any such capacity,

he (as well as the body corporate) shall be guilty of the offence and shall be liable to be proceeded against and punished accordingly.

(15) Where an offence under subsection (13) above is committed by a partnership or by an unincorporated association (other than a partnership) and is proved to have been committed with the consent or connivance of a partner in the partnership or, as the case may be, a person concerned in the management or control of the association, he (as well as the partnership or association) shall be guilty of the offence and shall be liable to be proceeded against and punished accordingly.

GENERAL NOTE

In *The Scottish Legal Profession: The Way Forward* the Secretary of State made it clear that he did not consider that the exclusive reservation of executry work to solicitors was in the public interest. Accordingly, he proposed that other bodies such as banks and building societies should be permitted to charge a fee for preparation of applications as appointment as an executor. The policy statement also suggested that bodies other than financial institutions should also have the right to perform executry work. However, it was made clear by the Lord

Advocate at Second Reading in the House of Lords that the Bill would also create a mechanism by which individuals would be permitted to offer executry services.

This section ensures that bodies other than financial institutions can apply to be executry practitioners and gives effect to the decision to permit individuals to offer executry services by authorising the Board to establish and maintain a register of executry practitioners. Persons who fulfil certain requirements as regards fitness to practise, educational qualifications and training and indemnity arrangements are entitled to have their names entered in this register. Further, s.18 also introduces rules which are intended to ensure that appropriate standards are maintained among executry practitioners registered by the Board.

Subs. (1)

This provision places a responsibility on the Board to establish and maintain a register of executry practitioners.

Subs. (2)

This provision requires the Board to enter the name of an applicant on the register who has satisfied the Board as to the conditions set out in s.18(3). It is interesting that there is no requirement that applicants for entry on the register of executry practitioners be "natural persons" the way that there is under s.17(1) as far as qualified conveyancers are concerned.

Subs. (3)

The Board must be satisfied that the applicant is a fit and proper person to provide executry services and will maintain suitable arrangements to satisfy any successful claims made by clients by means of indemnity insurance or by some other means. The Board is also required to ensure that the applicant complies with the regulations which the Secretary of State is empowered to make under s.18(10) so far as appropriate standards of conduct and practice are concerned and as regards educational qualifications and practical training.

Subs. (4)

The Board has the power to require an applicant to provide such other information as it considers necessary.

Subs. (5)

An application for entry on the register which is granted by the Board can be made subject to conditions. This allows the Board, where it does not believe that an applicant should be entitled to exercise the full range of functions of an executry practitioner, to allow that person to practise on a limited basis. On the other hand, if the application is refused the Board must give written reasons for that refusal.

Subs. (6)

This creates similar rights of review by the Board for executry practitioners as are applied to qualified conveyancers by s.17(5), save for the requirement that an executry practitioner can seek review when the application has been granted subject to conditions.

Subs. (7)

This provision gives an executry practitioner the right to apply to the Court of Session for an order after intimation by the board of the outcome of the review.

Subs. (8)

An executry practitioner can apply to have his name removed from the register by the Board and the Board will grant this application so long as it is satisfied that adequate arrangements have been made for the completion of outstanding business.

Subs. (9)

When the Keeper of the Land Register is dealing with applications for registration of interests in land, he is required to examine links in title which may be created through confirmation of executors so it is important for him to know the identities of those persons who are entitled to practise as executry practitioners. This provision places a statutory duty on the Board to provide him with the necessary information.

Subs. (10)

This provision requires the Secretary of State to make regulations not only as regards the educational qualifications and training of executry practitioners but also so as to maintain appropriate standards of conduct and practice. The Secretary of State must send a copy of the proposed regulations to the Director General of Fair Trading so that he can consider whether or not the regulations will restrict, distort or prevent competition. However, the Secretary of State is also required to consult with such persons as he considers appropriate. It is hoped that these arrangements will ensure the widest possible debate on the regulations before they are finally introduced. It is interesting that whereas in the case of qualified conveyancers it is the Board who is entitled to specify education and training requirements through the rule-making powers granted to it by s.17(3), in the case of executry practitioners standards of education and training will be set, ultimately, by the Secretary of State.

Subs. (11)

This makes it clear that the Secretary of State's regulations are required to be approved by a resolution of both Houses of Parliament so as to ensure some level of scrutiny of their contents.

Subs. (12)

This provision creates reciprocal duties on an executry practitioner to comply with the regulations and any determination by the Board under s.20(2)(a) and (b) and for the Board to ensure compliance.

Subs. (13)

This is a similar provision to that found in the Solicitors (Scotland) Act 1980, s.31(1), as regards impersonation of solicitors or notaries public.

Subs. (14)

This is similar in terms to the 1980 Act, s.31(3).

Subs. (15)

This ensures that partners or persons concerned with the management or control of an unincorporated association will also be guilty of an offence when the partnership or association has committed an offence under s.18(13) and it can be shown that the partner or person in control consented or connived in the commission of that offence.

Executry services by recognised financial institutions

19.—(1) Subject to subsection (3) below, a recognised financial institution may provide executry services if it has notified the Board that—
    (a) it intends to do so;
    (b) it complies with such requirements as may be prescribed by reg-
        ulations made by the Secretary of State with respect to the educa-
        tional qualifications and practical training of those of its employees
        who are to be engaged in the provision of executry services; and
    (c) it is a member of, or otherwise subject to, a scheme which—
            (i) has been established (whether or not exclusively) for the
        purpose of dealing with complaints about the provision of executry
        services; and
            (ii) complies with such requirements as may be prescribed by
        regulations made by the Secretary of State with respect to matters
        relating to such complaints.
    (2) In this section "recognised financial institution" means any institution
which is—
    (a) an institution authorised by the Bank of England to operate a deposit-
        taking business under Part I of the Banking Act 1987;
    (b) a building society authorised to raise money from its members by the
        Building Societies Commission under section 9 of the Building Socie-
        ties Act 1986;
    (c) a body authorised to carry on insurance business under section 3 or 4
        of the Insurance Companies Act 1982; or
    (d) any subsidiary (as defined by section 736(1) of the Companies Act
        1985) of a body falling within paragraph (a), (b) or (c) above whose
        business, or any part of whose business, consists of the provision of
        executry services.
    (3) Where—

(a) a recognised financial institution ceases (for whatever reason) to comply with the requirements with respect to educational qualifications and practical training referred to in paragraph (b) of subsection (1) above;

(b) a recognised financial institution ceases (for whatever reason) to be a member of, or otherwise subject to, a scheme referred to in a notice given by it under that subsection; or

(c) such a scheme ceases to comply with the requirements mentioned in paragraph (c)(ii) of that subsection,

the recognised financial institution shall notify the Board of that fact and shall forthwith cease providing executry services.

(4) The Board shall maintain a list of recognised financial institutions which have given notice under subsection (1) above and shall make the list available to any person without charge.

(5) The Board shall, as soon as practicable after April 1 in each year, send a copy of the list maintained under subsection (4) above to the Keeper of the Registers of Scotland and to each sheriff clerk.

(6) This section, so far as it relates to a body or subsidiary mentioned in subsection (2)(c) or (d) above, is without prejudice to section 16 of the Insurance Companies Act 1982 (restriction of insurance companies to insurance business).

(7) Regulations under subsection (1) above shall be made by statutory instrument and no regulations shall be made under that subsection unless a draft of the regulations has been laid before, and approved by a resolution of, each House of Parliament.

GENERAL NOTE

This section gives effect to the desire expressed in *The Scottish Legal Profession: The Way Forward* that banks and building societies should be entitled to perform executry work. It ensures that recognised financial institutions, *viz.* banks, building societies, insurance companies and their subsidiaries, will be entitled to notify the Board that they intend to offer executry services and the Board will grant their applications so long as certain conditions are fulfilled. This section was the subject of a number of important Government amendments at Report Stage in the House of Commons to ensure greater regulation and control of financial institutions which offer executry services. Much of this control is to be achieved through the regulation-making powers granted to the Secretary of State.

Subs. (1)

S.19(1)(b) was added at Report Stage so as to require financial institutions to comply with regulations as regards the educational qualifications and practical training of those of their employees who provide executry services. This provision ensures that financial institutions employ adequately trained staff and creates a similar requirement for education and training of the employees of financial institutions as is applied to executry practitioners by s.18(3). Financial institutions are also required to establish complaints procedures and must comply with any requirements as to complaints which the Secretary of State will specify in regulations.

Subs. (3)

This provision was also added at Report Stage and deals with the possibility that an institution might, for whatever reason, fail to maintain a suitable complaints machinery or suitable standards of training for its staff despite the fact that it did meet the requisite standards when it notified the Board of its intention to offer executry services. In such circumstances the institution is required to cease providing executry services and to notify the Board of this fact.

Subs. (4)

The Board has a duty to maintain a list of financial institutions offering executry services and to make this available to any person without charge.

Subs. (5)

A copy of such a list must be sent as soon as practicable after April 1 to the Keeper of the Registers of Scotland and to each sheriff clerk.

Subs. (6)

This provision should make it clear that s.19 is not intended to extend the area of business of insurance companies for the purposes of s.16 of the 1982 Act.

Subs. (7)
Until Report Stage the necessary regulations were to be made by the negative resolution procedure. The amendment ensures that the regulations must be approved by both Houses of Parliament.

Professional misconduct, inadequate professional services, etc.

20.—(1) Where, after such inquiry as they consider appropriate (whether or not following a complaint to them) and after giving the practitioner concerned an opportunity to make representations, the Board are satisfied that a practitioner—

(a) is guilty of professional misconduct;

(b) has provided inadequate professional services;

(c) has failed to comply with regulations made under section 17(11) or 18(10) of this Act; or

(d) has been convicted of a criminal offence rendering him no longer a fit and proper person to provide conveyancing services as a qualified conveyancer or, as the case may be, executry services as an executry practitioner,

they may take such of the steps set out in subsection (2) below as they think fit and shall, without prejudice to subsection (6) below, intimate their decision to the practitioner by notice in writing.

(2) The steps referred to in subsection (1) above are—

(a) to determine that the amount of fees and outlays which the practitioner may charge in respect of such services as the Board may specify shall be—

    (i) nil; or

    (ii) such amount as the Board may specify in the determination,

and to direct the practitioner to comply, or secure compliance, with such of the requirements set out in subsection (5) below as appear to them to be necessary to give effect to the determination;

(b) to direct the practitioner to secure the rectification at his or its own expense of any such error, omission or other deficiency arising in connection with the services as the Board may specify;

(c) to attach conditions (or, as the case may be, further conditions) to the registration of the practitioner or to vary any condition so attached;

(d) to suspend or revoke that registration;

(e) subject to subsection (3) below, to impose on the practitioner a fine not exceeding £10,000;

(f) in a case where the practitioner has provided inadequate professional services, to direct the practitioner to pay to the client by way of compensation such sum, not exceeding £1,000, as the Board may specify;

(g) to censure the practitioner; and

(h) to make a report of the Board's findings to any other person exercising functions with respect to—

    (i) the practitioner; or

    (ii) any person employed by or acting on behalf of the practitioner in connection with the provision of the services.

(3) The Board shall not impose a fine under subsection (2)(e) above where, in relation to the subject matter of the Board's inquiry, the practitioner has been convicted by any court of an offence involving dishonesty and sentenced to a term of imprisonment of not less than two years.

(4) Any fine imposed under subsection (2)(e) above shall be treated for the purposes of section 203 of the Criminal Procedure (Scotland) Act 1975 (fines payable to HM Exchequer) as if it were a fine imposed in the High Court.

(5) The requirements referred to in subsection (2)(a) above are—

(a) to refund, whether in whole or to any specified extent, any amount already paid by or on behalf of the client in respect of the fees and outlays of the practitioner in connection with the services; and

(b) to waive, whether wholly or to any specified extent, the right to recover those fees and outlays.

(6) Where the Board make a direction under subsection (2)(a), (b) or (f) above they shall, by notice in writing, require the practitioner to which the direction relates to give, within such period being not less than 21 days as the notice may specify, an explanation of the steps which he or it has taken to comply with the direction.

(7) Where a practitioner—

(a) fails to comply with a notice under subsection (6) above; or

(b) complies with such a notice but the Board are not satisfied as to the steps taken by the practitioner to comply with the direction to which the notice relates,

the Board may apply to the Court of Session for an order requiring the practitioner to comply with the direction to which the notice relates within such time as the court may order.

(8) Where the Board take a step set out in subsection (2)(c) or (d) above and—

(a) the period specified in subsection (11)(a) or (b) below has expired without an application for review or, as the case may be, an application to the Court of Session having been made, or

(b) where such an application is made, the matter is finally determined in favour of the Board's decision or the application is withdrawn,

they shall amend the register of executry practitioners or, as the case may be, the register of qualified conveyancers accordingly.

(9) The Board shall—

(a) subject to subsection (10) below, publish every decision taken by them under subsection (1) above (including a decision that they are not satisfied as to the matters mentioned in subsection (1)(a) to (d)); and

(b) make available a copy of every decision published under paragraph (a) above for inspection by any person without charge.

(10) In carrying out their duty under subsection (9) above, the Board may refrain from publishing any names or other information which would, in their opinion, damage or be likely to damage the interest of persons other than—

(a) the practitioner to whom the decision relates; or

(b) where the practitioner is an individual, his partners; or

(c) his or their families,

but where they so refrain, they shall publish their reasons for so doing.

(11) Where the Board take a step set out in subsection (2)(a) to (g) above, the practitioner concerned may—

(a) within 21 days of the date on which the Board's decision is intimated to it or him, apply to the Board to review their decision; and

(b) within 21 days of the date on which the outcome of such review is intimated to it or him, apply to the Court of Session, which may make such order in the matter as it thinks fit.

(12) Part II of Schedule 1 to this Act (Board's powers of investigation for the purposes of this section and section 21) shall have effect.

(13) The Secretary of State, after consulting the Board, may by order made by statutory instrument subject to annulment in pursuance of a resolution of either House of Parliament, amend subsection (2)(f) above by substituting for the sum for the time being specified in that provision such other sum as he considers appropriate.

(14) The taking of any steps under subsection (2) above shall not be founded upon in any proceedings for the purpose of showing that the practitioner in respect of whom the steps were taken was negligent.

(15) A direction under subsection (2)(f) above to a practitioner to pay compensation to a client shall not prejudice any right of that client to take proceedings against that practitioner for damages in respect of any loss which he alleges he has suffered as a result of that practitioner's negligence, and any sum directed to be paid to that client under that provision may be taken into account in the computation of any award of damages made to him in any such proceedings.

(16) The Secretary of State may, by order made by statutory instrument subject to annulment in pursuance of a resolution of either House of Parliament, amend subsection (2)(e) above by substituting for the amount for the time being specified in that provision such other amount as appears to him to be justified by a change in the value of money.

(17) In this section "executry practitioner" and "qualified conveyancer" respectively include any executry practitioner or qualified conveyancer whether or not it or he was registered as such at the time when the subject matter of the Board's inquiry occurred and notwithstanding that subsequent to that time it or he has ceased to be so registered.

GENERAL NOTE

This section specifies the disciplinary powers of the Board where a qualified conveyancer or executry practitioner (but not a recognised financial institution offering executry services) is guilty of professional misconduct, has provided inadequate professional services, has failed to comply with regulations which seek to maintain appropriate standards of conduct or practice or has been convicted of a criminal offence which renders him no longer a fit and proper person to practise. The disciplinary powers of the Board are largely based upon those provided to the Council of the Law Society and to The Scottish Solicitors' Discipline Tribunal by the Solicitors (Scotland) Act 1980 (as amended).

Subs. (1)

The inquiry powers of the Board can be exercised whether or not there has been a complaint and it is for the Board to decide upon the appropriate level of inquiry. However, the practitioner concerned must be given the opportunity to make representations and if the Board decides to take disciplinary action it must intimate this decision to the practitioner in writing.

Subs. (2)

This provision grants extensive disciplinary powers to the Board. By and large, the powers given to the Board are similar to those granted to the Council of the Law Society, certainly as far as s.20(2)(a) and (b) is concerned (see Solicitors (Scotland) Act 1980, s.42A(2)(a) and (b) as inserted by the Solicitors (Scotland) Act 1988, s.1) and to the Scottish Solicitors' Discipline Tribunal by the Solicitors (Scotland) Act 1980, ss.53 and 53A (this latter provision inserted by the Solicitors (Scotland) Act 1988, s.3). The most significant provision is s.20(2)(f), which authorises the Board, in a case where a practitioner has provided inadequate professional services, to direct that the practitioner pay the client compensation of up to £1,000. This was a provision which the Scottish Consumer Council had been pressing for ever since the Bill was introduced in the House of Lords. The point was only conceded by the Government at Report Stage in the House of Commons. It should be noted that Sched. 8, para. 29 gives similar powers to the Council and to the Tribunal to award compensation where a solicitor has provided inadequate professional services.

Subs. (3)

This provision places similar restrictions on the fining powers of the Board as those applied to the Scottish Solicitors' Discipline Tribunal by the 1980 Act, s.53.

Subs. (5)

There is also a similar provision granting rights to waive or refund fees for inadequate professional services in the 1980 Act.

Subs. (6)

Where the Board has served notice on a practitioner making a direction under s.20(2)(a), (b) or (f), the practitioner must be given an opportunity to provide an explanation as to the steps which will be taken to comply with the direction.

Subs. (7)

Where the practitioner fails to comply with the notice, or the Board is not satisfied with the steps which he has taken, it can apply to the Court of Session for an order of compliance.

Subs. (8)

The Board has the power to implement its decision, to attach conditions to the registration of a practitioner or to suspend or revoke that registration only once the various periods for review, or for application to the Court of Session have expired without any action being taken, or once the matter is finally determined in the Board's favour.

Subs. (9)

The Board has a duty to publish all of its decisions and to make these available to the public without charge.

Subs. (10)

This provision seeks to protect innocent third parties by authorising the Board to refrain from publishing names or other information where, in the opinion of the Board, damage would be caused to the interests of persons other than the practitioner, the practitioner's partners or his or their families. If the Board does so refrain it must publish its reasons for so doing.

Subs. (11)

This provision specifies the periods within which a practitioner may apply to the Board to review its decision or make application to the Court of Session.

Subs. (13)

Regulations which amend the maximum amount of compensation that can be awarded to a client under s.20(2)(f) will be made by the Secretary of State by reference to the negative resolution procedure and after consulting the Board.

Subs. (14)

This section makes it clear that any disciplinary action imposed by the Board upon a practitioner under s.20(2) cannot be used to establish a civil negligence claim against that practitioner.

Subs. (15)

The fact that the Board has awarded compensation to a client for inadequate professional services by a practitioner does not prejudice that person's right to sue the practitioner in damages for loss, although any such sum may be taken into account when computing the amount of damages to be awarded.

Subs. (16)

The provision gives the Secretary of State the power, by order, to increase the value of the fine which the Board can impose so as to take account of inflation.

Subs. (17)

The above disciplinary powers are available to the Board regardless of whether or not the practitioner was at the time of the "offence" on the relevant register or had his name removed at some subsequent time.

Board's intervention powers

21.—(1) The powers conferred on the Board by this section may be exercised if, after such inquiry (if any) as the Board consider appropriate, it appears to them to be desirable to do so for the purpose of protecting the interests of the clients, or prospective clients, of an independent qualified conveyancer or an executry practitioner (each of whom is in this section referred to as a "relevant practitioner").

(2) The Board may, in particular, exercise any such power where it appears to them that a relevant practitioner—

    (a) is no longer a fit and proper person to provide conveyancing services or, as the case may be, executry services;

    (b) has ceased, for whatever reason, to provide such services; or

    (c) has failed, or is likely to fail, to comply with regulations made under section 17(11) or, as the case may be, section 18(10) of this Act.

(3) The Board may direct the relevant practitioner not to dispose of, or otherwise deal with, except in accordance with the terms of the direction—

(a) any assets belonging to any client of the practitioner and held by or under the control of the practitioner in connection with his business as an independent qualified conveyancer or, as the case may be, an executry practitioner; or

(b) any assets of the practitioner which are specified, or of a kind specified, in the direction.

(4) The Board may direct the relevant practitioner to transfer to the Board, or to such persons (in this section referred to as "the trustees") as may be specified in the direction—

(a) all assets belonging to any client of the practitioner and held by or under the control of the practitioner in connection with his business as an independent qualified conveyancer or, as the case may be, an executry practitioner; or

(b) any assets of the practitioner which are specified, or of a kind specified, in the direction.

(5) A relevant practitioner to whom a direction is given may, within 21 days of the date on which the direction is received by him, apply to the Court of Session, which may make such order in the matter as it thinks fit.

(6) A relevant practitioner to whom a direction is given shall comply with it as soon as it take effect (and whether or not he proposes to apply to the Court of Session under subsection (5) above).

(7) If, on an application to the Court of Session by the Board, the court is satisfied—

(a) that a relevant practitioner has failed, within a reasonable time, to comply with any direction given to him; or

(b) that there is a reasonable likelihood that a relevant practitioner will so fail,

the court may make an order requiring the practitioner, and any other person whom the court considers it appropriate to subject to its order, to take such steps as the court may direct with a view to securing compliance with the direction.

(8) Any assets which have been transferred as a result of a direction given under subsection (4) above shall be held by the Board, or by the trustees, on trust for the client or, as the case may be, the practitioner concerned.

(9) The trustees may deal with any assets which have been transferred to them only in accordance with directions given to them by the Board.

(10) If the Board have reasonable cause to believe that a relevant practitioner or an employee of a relevant practitioner has been guilty of dishonesty resulting in pecuniary loss to a client of the relevant practitioner, they may apply to the Court of Session for an order that no payment be made by any bank, building society or other body named in the order out of any bank, building society or other account or any sum deposited in the name of the relevant practitioner without the leave of the court and the court may make such an order.

(11) Any direction under this section—

(a) shall be given in writing;

(b) shall state the reason why it is being given;

(c) shall take effect on such date as may be specified in the direction (which may be the date on which it is served on the relevant practitioner); and

(d) may be varied or revoked by a further direction given by the Board.

(12) In this section—

"assets" includes any sum of money (in whatever form and whether or not in any bank, building society or other account) and any book, account, deed or other document held by the relevant practitioner on his own behalf in connection with his business as a relevant practitioner or on behalf of the client concerned; and

"independent qualified conveyancer" and "executry practitioner" respectively include any independent qualified conveyancer or executry practitioner whether or not he was registered as such at the time when the matter in relation to which the Board exercise or propose to exercise their powers under this section arose and notwithstanding that subsequent to that time he has ceased to be so registered.

GENERAL NOTE

This section was only included in the Bill at Report Stage when Lord James Douglas-Hamilton introduced the clause for the first time. It is intended to enhance the regulatory structure of the Board and corresponds closely to an amendment brought forward at Report Stage of the Courts and Legal Services Bill as regards the powers of the Authorised Conveyancing Practitioners Board. The section in this Act gives the Board the power to intervene in the business of an independent qualified conveyancer or executry practitioner where it appears to the Board that it is desirable to do so in order to protect the interests of a practitioners' clients or prospective clients. It also gives the Board powers over the assets of a practitioner or any client's assets which are held by the practitioner and, in particular, authorises the Board to direct that the assets be transferred to it or to such trustees as may be specified in the direction. These powers are backed up by an enforcement mechanism that allows it to apply to the Court of Session for an order to secure compliance and which authorises the Court, in cases of dishonesty, to make an order which prevents payment to the practitioner of any sum deposited in a bank or building society in the relevant practitioner's name without the leave of the court.

Disclosure of documents etc.

22.—(1) Any communication made to or by—
  (a) an independent qualified conveyancer or an executry practitioner in the course of his or its acting as such for a client; or
  (b) a recognised financial institution in the course of providing executry services for a client,
shall in any action or proceedings in any court be protected from disclosure on the ground of confidentiality between client and professional legal adviser in like manner as if the conveyancer, practitioner or institution had at all material times been a solicitor acting for the client.

(2) Any enactment or instrument making special provision in relation to a solicitor or other legal representative as to the disclosure of information, or as to the production, seizure or removal of documents, with respect to which a claim to confidentiality between client and professional legal adviser could be maintained, shall, with any necessary modifications, have effect in relation to—
  (a) an independent qualified conveyancer;
  (b) an executry practitioner; and
  (c) a recognised financial institution in relation to the provision of executry services,
as it has effect in relation to a solicitor.

GENERAL NOTE

This section grants privilege on grounds of confidentiality to communications between independent qualified conveyancers, executry practitioners, recognised financial institutions which offer executry services and their clients to the same extent as applies between solicitor and client. It also ensures that any statute or statutory instrument which makes special provision for a solicitor on ground of confidentiality as to the disclosure of information or the production, seizure or removal of documents will also apply to independent qualified conveyancers, executry practitioners and recognised financial institutions which offer executry services.

Interpretation of sections 16 to 22

23. In sections 16 to 22 of this Act and this section, except where the context otherwise requires—
  "the Board" means the Scottish Conveyancing and Executry Services Board;
  "conveyancing services" means the preparation of writs, contracts and other documents in connection with the transfer of heritable property and loans secured over such property, and services ancillary thereto, but does not include any services—

　　　　(a) relating to the arranging of loan; or
　　　　(b) falling within section 1(1)(a) of the Estate Agents Act
　　　　1979;
"executry practitioner" means a person registered under section 18 in
　　　the register of executry practitioners;
"executry services" means the drawing and preparation of papers on
　　　which to found or oppose an application for a grant of confirmation
　　　of executors and services in connection with the administration,
　　　ingathering, distribution and winding up of the estate of a deceased
　　　person by executors, but does not include anything which consti-
　　　tutes investment business within the meaning of the Financial
　　　Services Act 1986;
"inadequate professional services" means professional services which
　　　are in any respect not of the quality which could reasonably be
　　　expected of a competent practitioner; and references to the provi-
　　　sion of inadequate professional services shall be construed as
　　　including references to not providing professional services which
　　　such a practitioner ought to have provided;
"independent qualified conveyancer" means a person registered as
　　　such under section 17(7) in the register of qualified conveyancers;
"practitioner" means an executry practitioner or a qualified
　　　conveyancer;
"qualified conveyancer" means a person registered under section 17 in
　　　the register of qualified conveyancers; and
"recognised financial institution" has the meaning given to it in section
　　　19(2).

Rights of audience

Rights of audience in the Court of Session, the House of Lords, the Judicial Committee of the Privy Council and the High Court of Justiciary

24. After section 25 of the 1980 Act there shall be inserted the following
section—

**"Rights of audience in the Court of Session, the House of Lords, the
Judicial Committee of the Privy Council and the High Court of
Justiciary**
　　25A.—(1) Without prejudice to section 250 (right of audience of
solicitor before single judge) of the Criminal Procedure (Scotland)
Act 1975 and section 48(2)(b) (extension of rights of audience by act
of sederunt) of the Court of Session Act 1988, a solicitor who—
　　　　(a) seeks a right of audience in, on the one hand, the Court of
　　　　　　Session, the House of Lords and the Judicial Committee of the
　　　　　　Privy Council or, on the other hand, the High Court of Justici-
　　　　　　ary; and
　　　　(b) has satisfied the Council as to the requirements provided for in
　　　　　　this section,
shall have a right of audience in those courts or, as the case may be,
that court.
　　(2) The requirements mentioned in subsection (1), in relation to
the courts or, as the case may be, the court in which a solicitor seeks a
right of audience, are that—
　　　　(a) he has completed, to the satisfaction of the Council, a course of
　　　　　　training in evidence and pleading in relation to proceedings in
　　　　　　those courts or that court;
　　　　(b) he has such knowledge as appears to the Council to be appro-
　　　　　　priate of—

(i) the practice and procedure of; and
(ii) professional conduct in regard to,
those courts or that court; and
  (c) he has satisfied the Council that he is, having regard among other things to his experience in appropriate proceedings in the sheriff court, otherwise a fit and proper person to have a right of audience in those courts or that court.

(3) Where a solicitor has satisfied the Council as to the requirements of subsection (2) in relation to the courts or, as the case may be, the court in which he seeks a right of audience the Council shall make an appropriate annotation on the roll against his name.

(4) The Council shall make rules under this section as to—
  (a) the matters to be included in, the methods of instruction to be employed in, and the qualifications of the person who will conduct, any course of training such as is mentioned in subsection (2)(a); and
  (b) the manner in which a solicitor's knowledge of the practice and procedure and professional conduct mentioned in subsection (2)(b) is to be demonstrated,
and separate rules shall be so made in relation to, on the one hand, the Court of Session, the House of Lords and the Judicial Committee of the Privy Council and, on the other hand, the High Court of Justiciary,

(5) The Council shall make rules of conduct in relation to the exercising of any right of audience held by virtue of this section.

(6) Where a solicitor having a right of audience in any of the courts mentioned in subsection (1) is instructed to appear in that court, those instructions shall take precedence before any of his other professional obligations, and the Council shall make rules—
  (a) stating the order of precedence of those courts for the purposes of this subsection;
  (b) stating general criteria to which solicitors should have regard in determining whether to accept instructions in particular circumstances; and
  (c) securing, through such of their officers as they think appropriate, that, where reasonably practicable, any person wishing to be represented before any of those courts by a solicitor holding an appropriate right of audience is so represented,
and for the purposes of rules made under this subsection the Inner and Outer Houses of the Court of Session, and the High Court of Justiciary exercising its appellate jurisdiction, may be treated as separate courts.

(7) Subsection (6) does not apply to an employed solicitor whose contract of employment prevents him from acting for persons other than his employer.

(8) Subject to subsection (9) and (10), the provisions of section 34(2) and (3) apply to rules made under this section as they apply to rules made under that section and, in considering any rules made by the Council under subsection (5), the Lord President shall have regard to the desirability of there being common principles applying in relation to the exercising of rights of audience by all practitioners appearing before the Court of Session and the High Court of Justiciary.

(9) The Council shall, after any rules made under subsection (4) have been approved by the Lord President, submit such rules to the Secretary of State, and no such rules shall have effect unless the Secretary of State, after consulting the Director in accordance with section 64A, has approved them.

(10) The Council shall, after any rules made under subsection (5) have been approved by the Lord President, submit such rules to the Secretary of State.

(11) Where the Secretary of State considers that any rule submitted to him under section (10) would directly or indirectly inhibit the freedom of a solicitor to appear in court or undertake all the work preparatory thereto he shall consult the Director in accordance with section 64A.

(12) The Council may bring into force the rules submitted by them to the Secretary of State under subsection (10) with the exception of any such rule which he has, in accordance with section 64B, refused to approve.

(13) Nothing in this section affects the powers of any court in relation to any proceedings—

(a) to hear a person who would not otherwise have a right of audience before the court in relation to those proceedings; or

(b) to refuse to hear a person (for reasons which apply to him as an individual) who would otherwise have a right of audience before the court in relation to those proceedings, and where a court so refuses it shall gives its reasons for that decision.

(14) Where a complaint has been made that a solicitor has been guilty of professional misconduct in the exercise of any right of audience held by him by virtue of this section, the Council may, or if so requested by the Lord President shall, suspend him from exercising that right pending determination of that complaint under Part IV.

(15) Where a function is conferred on any person or body by this section he or, as the case may be, they shall exercise that function as soon as is reasonably practicable.".

GENERAL NOTE

This provision gives statutory effect to the proposal in *The Scottish Legal Profession: The Way Forward* that solicitors who can demonstrate certain prescribed standards of training and experience should be granted rights of audience in the supreme courts. This is achieved by enacting a new s.25A to the Solicitors (Scotland) Act 1980. The section creates a framework by which solicitors can obtain rights of audience by bestowing considerable rule-making powers on the Council of the Law Society. It provides that solicitors who seek rights of audience in the Court of Session, House of Lords or Judicial Committee of the Privy Council, on the one hand, or the High Court of Justiciary, on the other, must undergo a period of training in evidence and pleading and be able to demonstrate a proper knowledge of supreme court practice, procedure and conduct. In addition, any such solicitor must satisfy the Council that he is a fit and proper person to exercise such rights. The precise method and scope of the training will be a matter for the Council to decide, subject to the approval of the Lord President and the Secretary of State. Moreover, the section seeks to ensure that solicitors who obtain rights of audience should not enjoy any advantages over advocates, so much so that the Lord President, when considering the Council's rules, must have regard to the desirability of ensuring common rules for all practitioners before the supreme courts. Just as important, the section also makes clear that a solicitor's instructions to appear in a case in the supreme courts will take precedence over his other business and requires the Council to make rules on the issue of precedence. The clause, which was opposed by the Faculty of Advocates, was also the subject of considerable critical analysis at Committee Stage in the House of Lords by the former Lord President, Lord Emslie, and some of the section's key provisions owe much of their origin to his amendments which were accepted by the Lord Advocate at Committee.

S.25A(1)

This provision bestows rights of audience upon solicitors in the Court of Session, House of Lords and Judicial Committee of the Privy Council or in the High Court of Justiciary so long as they satisfy certain requirements laid down by the Council of the Law Society under powers granted by this section.

S.25A(2)

This provision is based upon an amendment to the Bill which was tabled by Lord Emslie in the House of Lords. It is aimed at ensuring that solicitors who acquire rights of audience have undergone a course of training in evidence and pleading in the supreme courts, have the necessary knowledge in practice and procedure and professional conduct of those courts, and, having regard to their sheriff court experience, are fit and proper persons to obtain rights of audience.

S.25A(3)

A solicitor who obtains rights of audience has the right to have an appropriate annotation made to the roll of solicitors against his name.

S.25A(4) and (5)

These provisions grant rule-making powers to the Council as regards the qualifications, training and examinations for solicitor/advocates and require it to make separate rules in relation to, on the one hand, the Court of Session, etc. and, on the other hand, the High Court of Justiciary. On the matter of training, although this will be a matter for the Council, the Under-Secretary of State, Lord James Douglas-Hamilton, made it clear at the Committee Stage in the House of Commons that solicitors will not necessarily be required to undergo a period of full-time training, nor will they be denied the right to continue to earn other fee income.

S.25A(6)

This provision provides for the creation of a form of cab rank rule for solicitors practising in the supreme courts. It has two main purposes. First, it makes it clear that a solicitor's supreme court work must take precedence over his other professional duties. Second, it authorises the Council to make rules providing for the order of precedence within the supreme courts and places responsibilities upon the whole body of solicitors with rights of audience to represent clients who seek their services by means of directions from the Law Society's officers.

S.25A(7)

The rules of precedence provided for in s.25A(6) do not apply to employed solicitors who can only work for their employers.

S.25A(8)

This provision ensures that when the Council exercises its rule-making functions about rights of audience it must involve the members of the Law Society in this process to the same extent as for other rules and also requires that the rules be approved by the Lord President, who must consider the desirability of ensuring common rules with advocates.

S.25A(9) and (10)

These provisions ensure that any rules which have been approved by the Lord President are also approved by the Secretary of State, who must consult the Director General of Fair Trading so as to discover whether the proposed rules restrict, distort or prevent competition.

S.25A(11)

The Secretary of State is given a specific duty to consult the Director where he considers that a proposed rule will inhibit the freedom of a solicitor to appear in court or to undertake any preparatory work.

S.25A(12)

The Council is given the power to bring the rules into effect, except any rules which the Secretary of State has refused to approve. He may refuse to approve because of the Director's advice, or because the rule is contrary to the interests of justice or because of sheriff court practice requirements.

S.25A(13)

This provision preserves the discretion of the court in relation to persons who seek to appear before it.

S.25A(14)

This provision grants the Council the authority to suspend a solicitor/advocate pending investigation and determination of a complaint of professional misconduct and corresponds closely to the power of interim suspension over advocates which the Dean of the Faculty of Advocates possesses.

S.25A(15)

This is an unusual and, arguably, an unnecessary provision. The Lord Advocate defended the provision in Committee in the House of Lords on the basis that it was merely a reminder to all concerned of the importance of securing in practice solicitors' extended rights of audience. It may also form a basis for judicial review if any person or body fails to exercise functions as soon as is reasonably practicable.

Right to conduct litigation and rights of audience

25.—(1) Any professional or other body may, for the purpose of enabling any of their members who is a natural person to acquire—

(a) rights to conduct litigation on behalf of members of the public; and

(b) rights of audience,

make an application in that regard to the Lord President and the Secretary of State.

(2) An application under subsection (1) above shall include a draft scheme—

(a) specifying—
    (i) the courts;
    (ii) the categories of proceedings;
    (iii) the nature of the business; and
    (iv) the rights to conduct litigation and the rights of audience,
in relation to which the application is made;

(b) describing—
    (i) the training requirements which the body would impose upon any of their members who sought to acquire any right such as is mentioned in subsection (1) above; and
    (ii) the code of practice which they would impose upon their members in relation to the exercise by those members of any rights acquired by them by virtue of this section,
in the event of the application being granted; and

(c) proposing arrangements for—
    (i) the indemnification of members of the public against loss suffered by them through the actings of the body's members in the exercise by those members of any rights acquired by them by virtue of this section; and
    (ii) the treatment by the body of complaints made to them by members of the public in relation to the actings of members of the body exercising rights acquired by virtue of this section,
and shall state that the body have complied with the provisions of Schedule 2 to this Act.

(3) A code of practice such as is mentioned in subsection (2)(b)(ii) above shall include provision with regard to revoking, suspending or attaching conditions to the exercise of any right acquired by a member of the body by virtue of this section in consequence of a breach by that member of that code of practice; and shall in particular include provision enabling the body to comply with the provisions of section 27(4) of this Act.

(4) A draft scheme submitted under this section shall also include the proposals of the body in relation to such other matters as may be prescribed by the Secretary of State in regulations made under this section.

(5) Regulations under this section shall be made by statutory instrument subject to annulment in pursuance of a resolution of either House of Parliament.

(6) Schedule 2 shall have effect in relation to the publication of applications made under subsection (1) above.

GENERAL NOTE

This may well be the most controversial section in the whole Act. It survived the Committee Stage in the House of Commons only on the casting vote of the Chairman. It provides a mechanism by which rights to conduct litigation and rights of audience can be granted to members of a professional or other body. This is achieved by means of a scheme specifying the members' rights of audience, which is drawn up by the body seeking rights of audience for its members and approved by the Lord President and Secretary of State.

The section has been defended by the Government on the basis that it is part of the process of ensuring greater flexibility in the provision of legal services and of increasing client choice. It is supported by such bodies as the Scottish Consumer Council, Citizens Advice Scotland and the Institute of Chartered Accountants in Scotland. Much of the criticism during the debates on the Bill centred upon the meaning of "any professional or other body". The meaning of professional body is straightforward. This would normally be a group of persons who share some sort of common qualification and who subscribe to an association which imposes standards of behaviour upon them which such persons must accept in order to acquire and maintain membership. The difficulty is over the meaning of other body. It would seem to apply to any group of people who have come together because of a common interest. Lord James Douglas-Hamilton has defended the use of this phrase by arguing that it permits persons appearing in court, who are not professionals in the generally understood sense of the word, but who may be able to offer a useful, quality service to people with particular needs. It is clear that a member's rights under a particular scheme can be restricted (and are likely to be so restricted) to certain categories of business in certain courts.

Subs. (1)

This permits any professional or other body to make application to the Lord President and Secretary of State to obtain rights to conduct litigation and rights of audience for their members. There is no definition of "professional or other body" provided in the Act.

Subs. (2)

This is a key provision which specifies the requirements for a scheme granting rights of audience to the members of any body. The draft scheme must cover such matters as the courts, categories of proceedings and nature of the business which the members will perform; the training requirements for members who wish to obtain rights of audience and the provision of a code of practice imposing responsibilities upon members; and arrangements for indemnification of clients and for handling complaints. In addition, the body is also required to publicise the draft scheme in conformity with the arrangements specified in Sched. 2.

Subs. (3)

This provision makes it clear that the code of practice must contain provision permitting the revocation or suspension of or the attachment of conditions to a member's rights of audience following a breach of the code. Moreover, the code must also permit the interim suspension of a member's rights pending the investigation and determination of a complaint.

Subs. (4)

This provision grants a long stop power to the Secretary of State by regulation to prescribe other matters which must be provided for in a draft scheme.

Subs. (5)

Such regulations will be made by means of the negative resolution procedure.

Consideration of applications made under section 25

26.—(1) The Lord President shall consider the provision made in any draft scheme submitted to him under section 25(1) of this Act in relation to the matters mentioned in section 25(2); and the Secretary of State shall, subject to subsection (5) below and to section 40 of this Act, consider the provision so made in section 25(2)(b) and (c).

(2) In considering the code of practice included in the draft scheme by virtue of section 25(2)(b)(ii), the Lord President shall have regard to the desirability of there being common principles applying in relation to the exercising of rights to conduct litigation and rights of audience by all practitioners in relation to the court or, as the case may be, the courts, mentioned in the application.

(3) The Lord President and the Secretary of State shall—

(a) consult each other in considering a draft scheme submitted to them under section 25(1); and

(b) consider any written representations timeously made to them under Schedule 2 to this Act, and may, either jointly or severally, make preliminary observations to the body concerned in relation to that draft; and the body may make such adjustments to the draft as appear to them to be appropriate, and the Lord President and the Secretary of State (who shall, in accordance with section 40, consult the Director in respect of any adjustments made in relation to the matters mentioned in section 25(2)(b) or (c)) shall thereafter consider the draft scheme as so adjusted.

(4) In considering a draft scheme under subsection (1) or (3) above, the Lord President and the Secretary of State shall have regard to whether the provisions of the draft scheme are such as—

    (a) to achieve; and

    (b) to ensure the maintenance of,

appropriate standards of conduct and practice by persons who may acquire rights to conduct litigation or rights of audience in the event of the draft scheme being approved.

(5) In relation to any code of practice such as is mentioned in section 25(2)(b)(ii), the duty of the Secretary of State under subsection (1) above is limited to a consideration of any provision of such a code as would, in his view, directly or indirectly inhibit the freedom of a member of the body concerned to undertake all the work necessary for the preparation of a case or for the presentation of a case before the court, other than such a provision which has that effect only by reason of the provision made in the draft scheme with respect to the matters mentioned in section 25(2)(a).

(6) After they have considered a draft scheme under subsections (1) and (3) above, if the Lord President and the Secretary of State—

    (a) are satisfied with the draft scheme, the Lord President shall grant the application, and shall so inform the body;

    (b) are not satisfied with the scheme, the Lord President shall refuse the application, and shall so inform the body, giving written reasons for the refusal,

and the Lord President shall send a copy of the letter granting or refusing the application to any person who has made representations in relation to the draft scheme under Schedule 2 to this Act.

(7) Where the Lord President has granted an application under subsection (6)(a) above, in relation to—

    (a) civil proceedings, the Court of Session may by act of sederunt; and

    (b) criminal proceedings, the High Court of Justiciary may by act of adjournal,

make such provision of giving effect to the scheme as appears to it to be appropriate.

GENERAL NOTE

This section specifies the arrangements for approving a draft scheme which has been submitted to the Lord President and the Secretary of State for their approval by any professional or other body and outlines the powers and duties of both the Lord President and Secretary of State. Both officials are also required to consult with one another and to ensure that the draft scheme will achieve appropriate standards of conduct and practice by the members of the body concerned.

Subs. (1)

This provision ensures a division of functions in relation to a draft scheme. The Lord President must consider all the matters specified by s.25(2), whereas the Secretary of State is only required to consider the training, code of practice, indemnification and complaints aspects of the draft scheme. However, he must also consult the Director General of Fair Trading to ensure that the draft scheme will not restrict, distort or prevent competition.

Subs. (2)

This provision requires the Lord President, when considering the code of practice, to have regard to the desirability of there being common principles for all practitioners in relation to rights of audience.

Subs. (3)

The Lord President and Secretary of State are required to consult with one another and to consider any written representations made to them as a result of the publication requirements of Sched. 2. They also have the right to make preliminary observations which may lead to adjustments being made to the draft scheme.

Subs. (4)

This provision places specific obligations on both the Lord President and Secretary of State to ensure that the draft scheme will achieve and maintain appropriate standards of conduct and practice by the members of the applicant body.

Subs. (5)

When the Secretary of State is considering the code of practice he is limited to considering whether or not it inhibits the members undertaking all the work necessary for the preparation and presentation of the case.

Subs. (6)

If both the Lord President and Secretary of State are satisfied with the draft scheme it will be for the Lord President to grant the application and to inform the body. If they are not satisfied with the Scheme, the Lord President will refuse it and give written reasons for the refusal. Persons who made representations are also entitled to a copy of the Lord President's letter which grants or refuses the application.

Subs. (7)

Where rights of audience are being granted to a body the scheme will be brought into effect by means of an Act of Sederunt in civil proceedings and an act of Adjournal in criminal matters.

Exercise of rights to conduct litigation and rights of audience

27.—(1) Where an application made under section 25 of this Act has been granted under section 26 of this Act, any member of the body concerned who has complied with the terms of the scheme in relation to the matters mentioned in section 25(2)(b)(i), and who appears to the body to be a fit and proper person, shall have the right to conduct litigation or rights of audience to which that compliance entitles him.

(2) Where a function is, whether expressly or by the implication, conferred on any person or body by section 26 or this section he or, as the case may be, they shall exercise that function as soon as is reasonably practicable.

(3) Nothing in subsection (1) above affects the power of any court in relation to any proceedings—

(a) to hear a person who would not otherwise have a right of audience before that court in relation to those proceedings; or

(b) to refuse to hear a person (for reasons which apply to him as an individual) who would otherwise have a right of audience before that court in relation to those proceedings, and where a court so refuses it shall give its reasons for that decision.

(4) Where a complaint has been made that a person has been guilty of professional misconduct in the exercise of any right to conduct litigation of right of audience held by him by virtue of this section, the body of which he is a member may, or if so requested by the Lord President shall, suspend that person from exercising that right pending determination of that complaint by the body.

(5) Where a person holding a right of audience in any court by virtue of this section is instructed to appear in that court, those instructions shall take precedence before any of his other professional or business obligations, and the code of practice mentioned in section 25(2)(b)(ii) shall include rules—

(a) stating the order of precedence of courts for the purposes of this subsection;

(b) stating general criteria to which members of the body should have regard in determining whether to accept instructions in particular circumstances; and

   (c) securing, through such of their officers as they think appropriate, that, where reasonably practicable, any person wishing to be represented before any court by one of their members holding an appropriate right of audience is so represented,

and, for the purposes of such rules, the Inner and Outer Houses of the Court of Session, and the High Court of Justiciary exercising its appellate jurisdiction, may be treated as separate courts.

   (6) A person exercising any right of audience held by virtue of this section shall have the same immunity from liability for negligence in respect of his acts or omissions as if he were an advocate, and no act or omission on the part of any such person shall give rise to an action for breach of contract in relation to the exercise by him of such a right of audience.

   (7) Any person who wilfully and falsely—

   (a) pretends to have any right to conduct litigation or right of audience by virtue of this section; or

   (b) where he has any such right, pretends to have any further such right which he does not have; or

   (c) takes or uses any name, title, addition or description implying that he has any such right or, as the case may be, any further such right,

shall be guilty of an offence and liable on summary conviction to a fine not exceeding level 4 on the standard scale.

   (8) For the purposes of section 25, section 26 and this section—

     "right of audience" includes, in relation to any court, any such right exercisable by an advocate; and

     "right to conduct litigation" means the right to exercise on behalf of a client all or any of the functions, other than any right of audience, which may be exercised by a solicitor in relation to litigation.

GENERAL NOTE

   This section specifies the rights of a member of a body which has obtained rights of audience. Only members who appear to the body to be fit and proper persons and who have also satisfied the training requirements of the appropriate scheme can obtain rights to conduct litigation or rights of audience. The provision also grants the body concerned the power to suspend a member with rights of audience on an interim basis pending determination of a complaint of professional misconduct against him and makes clear that any instructions to appear in court will take precedence over any of his other professional or business commitments. Moreover, the relevant Code of Practice will also specify the order of precedence as far as practice in particular courts is concerned, the general criteria for accepting instructions and arrangements to ensure that persons wishing to be represented by a member of the appropriate body obtain the necessary representation. A person exercising rights of audience has the same immunity from liability in negligence as has an advocate and cannot be sued for breach of contract as regards the exercise of a right of audience. Finally, subs. (7) creates a number of offences which can be committed by persons who pretend to have rights of audience or pretend to have wider rights than they actually possess or use any name, etc. which implies a right of audience or one wider than the person actually possesses.

Surrender of rights to conduct litigation and rights of audience

   28.—(1) Subject to the provisions of this section, where an application made under section 25 of this Act has been granted under section 26(6) of this Act, the body concerned may apply to the Lord President and the Secretary of State for permission to surrender any entitlement of their members to acquire rights to conduct litigation or rights of audience.

   (2) The Lord President and the Secretary of State shall jointly issue directions as to the requirements with which any body wishing to surrender their members' entitlement will have to comply, and, without prejudice to the generality of the foregoing, any such directions may include provision—

   (a) where members of a body have acquired rights to conduct litigation or rights of audience, as to the arrangements to be made for the completion of any work outstanding at the time the application is made; and

   (b) relating to the particular circumstances of a particular body.

(3) An application under subsection (1) above shall describe the manner in which the body have complied, or will comply, with the directions issued under subsection (2) above.

(4) Where the Lord President and the Secretary of State are satisfied that the body concerned have complied, or will comply, with the directions issued under subsection (2) above, the Lord President shall grant the application, and shall so inform the body.

(5) With effect from the date on which an application under subsection (1) above is granted, any member of the body concerned who has acquired rights to conduct litigation or rights of audience by virtue of the scheme shall cease to hold those rights.

GENERAL NOTE

This section permits a body who has obtained rights of audience for its members to apply to the Lord President and Secretary of State for permission to surrender such rights. Where this is to happen the Lord President and Secretary of State must jointly issue directions as to the requirements for the surrender of members' rights. Such directions may include provision as to the arrangements for completion of any outstanding work at the time of the application. The date on which the application for surrender of rights is granted shall be the date when a member's rights to conduct litigation or rights of audience will cease to exist.

Revocation of rights granted under section 26

29.—(1) Where is appears to the Secretary of State that a body has failed to comply with a direction under section 42(6) of this Act, he may by order made by statutory instrument revoke the grant of the application made by that body under section 25 of this Act.

(2) No instrument shall be made under subsection (1) above unless a draft of the instrument has been laid before and approved by each House of Parliament.

(3) With effect from the date on which an order under subsection (1) above takes effect, any member of the body concerned who has acquired rights to conduct litigation or rights of audience by virtue of the scheme shall cease to hold those rights.

GENERAL NOTE

This provision was added by the Government at Committee Stage in the House of Commons in order to assuage the disquiet expressed by a number of peers in the House of Lords that there was no provision for the termination of a scheme which proved to be unsatisfactory. It gives the Secretary of State the power by order made by statutory instrument to revoke a scheme which the relevant body has refused to amend. Whereas the previous section enabled the body concerned to initiate the procedure for surrender of rights of audience this section grants a power of revocation to the Secretary of State which he can initiate of his own volition. The Secretary of State can only exercise this power, however, when he and the Lord President agree that the terms of the body's existing scheme are not satisfactory; they also must agree on what the terms should be and must have directed the body accordingly, but the body must have refused to comply with the appropriate direction.

Regulation of right of English, Welsh and Northern Irish practitioners to practise in Scotland

30.—(1) The Secretary of State, after consulting the Lord President, may by regulations prescribe circumstances in which, and conditions subject to which, practitioners who are qualified to practise in England and Wales or Northern Ireland may, in such capacity as may be prescribed, exercise in Scotland—

(a) prescribed rights of audience; or

(b) prescribed rights to conduct litigation,

without being entitled to do so apart from the regulations.

(2) The Secretary of State, after consulting the Lord President, may by regulations make provision for the purpose of enabling practitioners who

are entitled to practise in England and Wales or Northern Ireland to become qualified to practise in Scotland on terms, and subject to conditions, corresponding or similar to those on which practitioners who are entitled to practise in member States may become qualified to practise in Scotland.

(3) Regulations made under subsection (1) above may, in particular—

(a) prescribe any right of audience which may not be exercised by a person in Scotland unless he is instructed to act together with a person who has that right of audience there;

(b) prescribe legal services which may not be provided by any person practising by virtue of the regulations;

(c) prescribe the title or description which must be used by any person practising by virtue of the regulations;

(d) provide for the body by whom and the means by which the qualification of any person claiming to be entitled to practise by virtue of the regulations is to be verified; and

(e) provide for such professional or other body as may be prescribed to have power to investigate and deal with any complaint made against a person practising by virtue of the regulations.

(4) Regulations made under subsection (1) or (2) above may modify any rule of law or practice which the Secretary of State considers should be modified in order to give effect to the regulations.

(5) Regulations under this section shall be made by statutory instrument subject to annulment in pursuance of a resolution of either House of Parliament.

(6) In this section "practitioner" means, in relation to England and Wales and Northern Ireland—

(a) a barrister or solicitor; and

(b) any person falling within such category as may be prescribed in regulations made by the Secretary of State after consultation with the Lord President.

GENERAL NOTE

The Council Directive of the European Communities of March 22, 1977 (77/249/EEC) on legal services requires member states to permit a lawyer from another member state to offer legal services within their jurisdictions, subject to certain conditions. This directive was implemented as far as the U.K. is concerned by the European Communities (Services of Lawyers) Order S.I. 1978 No. 1910. However, because the U.K. is a unitary state, the order which entitled lawyers from other member states of the EEC to offer legal services in the U.K. does not operate in relation to U.K. practitioners who practise in one jurisdiction but who may wish to practise in any of the U.K.'s other jurisdictions. Equally, the Council Directive of the European Communities of December 21, 1988, 89/48/EEC on recognition of foreign diplomas, will require member states to recognise equivalent professional qualifications gained elsewhere in the EEC. Once again such an arrangement will not necessarily apply to practitioners, who are qualified in one of the jurisdictions of the U.K., becoming qualified in another jurisdiction. This section seeks to implement both directives as far as Scotland is concerned by giving powers to the Secretary of State to make regulations and there is a reciprocal clause in the Courts and Legal Services Act 1990 as far as the English courts are concerned. It should be noted that for the purposes of the implementation of the two directives in a U.K. context the Act defines a practitioner to include not only barristers or solicitors but also any person who falls within such category as will be prescribed by regulations. This may mean, for example, that English "bare-foot" pleaders might acquire rights of audience in Scotland and that English conveyancing practitioners might be permitted to practise there.

Subs. (1)

This provision seeks to give effect to the legal services directive and gives the Secretary of State the power, after consulting the Lord President, to prescribe by regulations the circumstances, the conditions and the capacities under which English, Welsh and Northern Irish practitioners may acquire rights of audience and rights to conduct litigation in Scotland for the purposes of the regulations alone.

Subs. (2)

This provision gives effect to the diplomas directive by granting to the Secretary of State, after consulting the Lord President, the power to make regulations so as to enable English, Welsh and Northern Irish practitioners to become qualified to practise in Scotland on similar terms and conditions as apply to practitioners from other member states who wish to practise here.

Subs. (3)

This provision specifies the matters which the regulations relating to rights of audience may prescribe or provide for.

Subs. (4)

This provision empowers the Secretary of State when making regulations for both purposes to modify any rule of law or practice which is necessary in order to give effect to the regulations.

Subs. (5)

Any regulations under this section will be made under the negative resolution procedure.

Subs. (6)

The interesting point under this provision is that the definition of "practitioner" is not restricted to barristers or solicitors but may include any person falling within a category which the Secretary of State may prescribe after consultation with the Lord President.

Rules of conduct

Rules of conduct etc.

31.—(1) Any rule, whether made before or after the coming into force of this section, whereby an advocate is prohibited from forming a legal relationship with another advocate or with any other person for the purpose of their jointly offering professional services to the public shall have no effect unless it is approved by the Lord President and the Secretary of State; and before approving any such rule the Secretary of State shall consult the Director in accordance with section 40 of this Act.

(2) Where it appears to the Faculty of Advocates that any rule of conduct in relation to the exercise of an advocate's right of audience in the Court of Session is more restrictive than the equivalent rule in relation to the exercise of the equivalent right in the sheriff court, they may submit that rule to the Secretary of State for his approval, and the Secretary of State shall consult the Director in accordance with section 40 of this Act, and thereafter, having—

(a) considered any advice tendered to him by the Director;

(b) compared the rule applicable in the Court of Session with the equivalent rule applicable in the sheriff court; and

(c) considered whether the interests of justice require that there should be such a rule in the Court of Session,

he may approve or refuse to approve the rule.

(3) In section 34 of the 1980 Act (rules as to professional practice, conduct and discipline)—

(a) at the end of subsection (1A) there shall be inserted—

"and

(f) make such additional or different provision as the Council think fit in relation to solicitors who, or incorporated practices which, are partners in or directors of multi-disciplinary practices."; and

(b) after subsection (3) there shall be inserted—

"(3A) Without prejudice to subsection (3), any rule made, whether before or after the coming into force of this subsection, by the Council under this section or section 35 which has the effect of prohibiting the formation of multi-disciplinary practices shall not have effect unless the Secretary of State, after consulting the Director in accordance with section 64A, has approved it.".

GENERAL NOTE

At present there is a statutory ban against solicitors entering into partnerships with non-solicitors through the provisions of the Solicitors (Scotland) Act 1980, s.27(1), which make it an offence for a solicitor to share with an unqualified person any profits or fees from his business. In the case of advocates there is no statutory ban, but partnerships are prohibited under the Faculty's own rules. This section seeks to end the absolute barrier against advocates entering into partnerships with other advocates or any other person and also removes the statutory barrier against solicitors forming partnerships with non-solicitors. However, the section does not actually impose partnerships upon advocates or multi-disciplinary practices upon solicitors. Instead, it ensures that any rule of the Faculty of Advocates which prohibits partnerships between advocates or with any other person will not be effective unless it has been approved by the Lord President and the Secretary of State, who must consult the Director General. Equally, any rule of the Council of the Law Society which prohibits a solicitor joining a multi-disciplinary practice will have no effect unless it has been approved by the Secretary of State, after consulting the Director General.

If such approval is obtained the relevant rules will be sheltered from scrutiny from the competition authority which the Department of Trade and Industry proposed to create in *Opening Markets: New Policy on Restrictive Trade Practices.* In correspondence between the previous Secretary of State for Scotland and the Law Society which was made available at Committee Stage in the House of Commons it was made clear that he was minded to approve a Law Society rule which will prohibit multi-disciplinary practices so long as it is done in conformity with this Act. This may mean that any rule against multi-disciplinary practices will be more secure after the introduction of this Act than it would be if s.31 were never enacted.

The other important matter in this section is dealt with in subs. (2), which creates a mechanism whereby any rule applying to an advocate's rights of audience in the Court of Session which is more restrictive than the equivalent rule in the sheriff court can be referred by the Faculty of Advocates to the Secretary of State so as he can approve it or reject it. The purpose of this provision is to ensure that the professional rules of the Faculty of Advocates are treated on exactly the same basis as rules made by the Council of the Law Society which govern the conduct of solicitors with rights of audience in the supreme courts.

Multi-national practices

Multi-national practices

32. Before section 61 of the 1980 Act shall be inserted the following section—

"Multi-national practices

60A.—(1) Subject to the provisions of this section, solicitors and incorporated practices may enter into multi-national practices with registered foreign lawyers.

(2) The Council shall maintain a register of foreign lawyers, and may make rules with regard to registration; and, without prejudice to the generality of the foregoing, such rules may include provision as to—

(a) the manner in which applications for registration are to be made;

(b) the fees payable in respect of such applications;

(c) conditions which may be imposed in respect of registration; and

(d) the period for which any such registration is to run.

(3) Section 34(2) and (3) apply to rules made under subsection (2) as they apply to rules made under that section.

(4) Any foreign lawyer may apply to the Council to be registered as such for the purposes of this section and the Council shall, if they are satisfied that the legal profession of which the applicant is a member is so regulated as to make it appropriate for him to be allowed to enter into a multi-national practice with solicitors or incorporated practices, enter his name on the register.

(5) Subject to subsection (6), the Secretary of State may by order made by statutory instrument provide that any enactment or instrument—

(a) passed or made before the commencement of this section;

(b) having effect in relation to solicitors; and
(c) specified in the order,
shall have effect with respect to registered foreign lawyers as it has
effect with respect to solicitors.

(6) Before making any order under subsection (5), the Secretary of
State shall consult the Council.

(7) An order under subsection (5) may provide for an enactment or
instrument to have effect with respect to registered foreign lawyers
subject to such additions, omissions or other modifications as the
Secretary of State specifies in the order.

(8) No order shall be made under subsection (5) unless a draft of
the order has been approved by both Houses of Parliament."

GENERAL NOTE

This section was added at Report Stage in the House of Commons. S.30 already permits
non-Scottish practitioners to practise in Scotland and European Community practitioners will
be able to do so on the basis of the two Council Directives. This provision makes it clear that
Scottish solicitors will be entitled to enter into multi-national practices with foreign lawyers and
adds a new s.60A to the Solicitors (Scotland) Act 1980. It is largely an enabling measure
granting regulation-making powers to the Secretary of State to apply existing statutes and
statutory instruments to foreign lawyers practising in Scotland or in partnerships with Scottish
solicitors. That power can only be exercised after consultation with the Council of the Law
Society and is subject to affirmative resolution in both Houses of Parliament. The section also
places duties on the Council of the Law Society to maintain a register of foreign lawyers and to
make rules with regard to registration. By an addition to s.65 of the 1980 Act which is made by
Sched. 8, para. 29(15)(a) of this Act, a foreign lawyer is defined as a person who is not a solicitor
or an advocate but who is a member, and entitled to practise as such, of a legal profession
regulated within a jurisdiction outwith Scotland.

Complaints in relation to legal services

Complaints in relation to legal services

33.—(1) Where any person with an interest has made a complaint (a
"conduct complaint") to a professional organisation that a practitioner
has—
(a) been guilty of professional misconduct; or
(b) provided inadequate professional services,
the organisation shall investigate the matter, and shall thereafter make a
written report to the complainer and the practitioner concerned of—
(i) the facts of the matter as found by the organisation; and
(ii) what action the organisation propose to take, or have taken, in the
matter.

(2) The organisation shall ensure that the procedures adopted by them for
the purpose of dealing with any conduct complaint are not such as to inhibit
them from taking further action in the matter following consideration by
them of such a report as is mentioned in subsection (4) below.

(3) The organisation shall comply with any request made to them by the
Scottish legal services ombudsman under section 34 of this Act for information or, as the case may be, a report as soon as is reasonably practicable.

(4) On receipt of any report made to them by the ombudsman under
section 34(4) of this Act in relation to a handling complaint the organisation
shall—
(a) consider whether any further action requires to be taken in relation to
the conduct complaint the treatment of which formed the subject-
matter of the ombudsman's investigation; and
(b) report the results of the consideration mentioned in paragraph (a)
above to the person who made the handling complaint and the
ombudsman; and, without prejudice to the foregoing, any such report
shall include an account of what further action they have taken, or
propose to take, in the matter.

(5) For the purposes of this section—
 "professional organisation" means—
  (a) the Faculty of Advocates;
  (b) the Council of the Law Society of Scotland;
  (c) the Scottish Conveyancing and Executry Services Board established under section 16 of this Act; and
  (d) a body which has made a successful application under section 25 of this Act; and
 "practitioner" means, in relation to—
  (a) the Faculty of Advocates, an advocate;
  (b) the Council, a solicitor;
  (c) the Scottish Conveyancing and Executry Services Board, a practitioner within the meaning of section 23 of this Act; and
  (d) a body which has made a successful application under section 25 of this Act, any person exercising—
   (i) a right to conduct litigation; or
   (ii) a right of audience;
 acquired by virtue of section 27 of this Act.

GENERAL NOTE
Before the enactment of this statute only the Law Society had a specific statutory duty to investigate complaints about a solicitor as regards the provision of inadequate professional services. (See the powers of the Council and the Scottish Solicitors' Discipline Tribunal as provided for in ss.42A and 53A of the Solicitors (Scotland) Act 1980, which were added by the Solicitors (Scotland) Act 1988, ss.1 and 3.) It is also the case that it is the practice of the Faculty of Advocates to investigate complaints. This section places responsibilities upon a wide range of professional organisations (and not just the Law Society and Faculty of Advocates but also upon the Board and any professional or other body which has obtained rights of audience for its members) to investigate and to make a written report in relation to a conduct complaint made against a practitioner. All these professional organisations are now put under a specific statutory duty by this section to investigate and to report to both the complainer and the practitioner about their findings and proposed course of action in relation to a complaint. Their complaints arrangements are also the subjects of scrutiny by the Scottish legal services ombudsman who is entitled to report on a complaint by a member of the public concerning the organisation's handling of a complaint about a practitioner's conduct and the relevant organisation may be required to reconsider its action in the light of the report.

Subs. (1)
 This section defines a conduct complaint as a complaint made by any person with an interest and places responsibilities on the professional organisation to investigate and report where the complainer alleges that the practitioner has been guilty of professional misconduct or has provided inadequate professional services. The organisation must make a written report to the complainer and practitioner about the facts as found and any action which it intends to take in the matter.

Subs. (2)
 This provision requires that the organisation introduces flexible complaints arrangements so that it is not inhibited from taking further action after it has considered a report from the Scottish legal services ombudsman about the way the complaint was handled.

Subs. (3)
 This provision requires the organisation to comply with a request from the ombudsman for information or, in certain circumstances, for a report.

Subs. (4)
 This provision implements the proposal in *The Scottish Legal Profession: The Way Forward* that there should be a mechanism for the reconsideration of a case following upon a report from the ombudsman. It ensures that when an organisation receives a report from the ombudsman concerning its handling of a complaint it must consider whether any further action requires to be taken and report the results of such consideration to the original complainer, practitioner, person who made the handling complaint and the ombudsman.

Subs. (5)
 This provision makes it clear that the complaints procedures apply not only to the Law

Society, Faculty of Advocates and a professional or other body whose members have rights of audience but also to the Board in relation to the conduct of qualified conveyancers and executry practitioners.

Scottish legal services ombudsman

Scottish legal services ombudsman

34.—(1) The Secretary of State may, after consultation with the Lord President, and subject to subsection (9) below, appoint a person, to be known as the Scottish legal services ombudsman, to examine any written complaint (a "handling complaint") made by or on behalf of a member of the public concerning the treatment by a professional organisation within the meaning of section 33 of this Act of a conduct complaint such as is mentioned in that section made by that member of the public or on his behalf.

(2) The ombudsman shall make such investigation of any handling complaint as seems to him to be appropriate; and for that purpose he may request the organisation concerned to provide him with such information as he may reasonably require.

(3) Where the organisation concerned have not completed an investigation under section 33(1) of this Act within such period as the Secretary of State may from time to time determine, the ombudsman may request a report from them on the progress of the investigation.

(4) The ombudsman—

(a) may, at any stage in the investigation of a handling complaint, make an interim report in relation to that investigation; and

(b) shall, at the conclusion of such an investigation, report the result of that investigation,

to the complainer and to the organisation concerned.

(5) The ombudsman may—

(a) if so requested by any person appointed to carry out equivalent functions in relation to the provision of legal services in England and Wales, investigate a complaint against a professional body in England and Wales on that person's behalf; and

(b) request any person appointed as mentioned in paragraph (a) above to investigate a complaint against an organisation in Scotland on his behalf.

(6) The Secretary of State may by regulations extend the jurisdiction of the ombudsman by providing for this section to apply, with such modifications (if any) as he thinks fit, in relation to the investigation by the ombudsman of such categories of handling complaints as may be specified in the regulations with respect to the provision of executry services by persons other than executry practitioners within the meaning of section 23 of this Act.

(7) Without prejudice to the generality of subsection (6) above, regulations under that subsection may make provision for the investigation of handling complaints with respect to particular persons or categories of person.

(8) Regulations under subsection (6) above shall be made by statutory instrument subject to annulment in pursuance of a resolution of either House of Parliament.

(9) The following shall not be eligible to be appointed as the ombudsman—

(a) advocates;

(b) solicitors;

(c) members and officers of the Scottish Conveyancing and Executry Services Board established by section 16 of this Act;

(d) subject to paragraph (e) below, executry practitioners within the meaning of section 23 of this Act;

(e) where any such executry practitioner is a partnership or a body corporate, the partners or, as the case may be, the directors, secretary or other similar officers;

(f) the directors, secretary or other similar officers of any recognised financial institution within the meaning of section 19(2) of this Act;

(g) qualified conveyancers within the meaning of section 23 of this Act or;

(h) any member or employee of a professional or other body any of whose members has acquired any right to conduct litigation or right of audience by virtue of section 27 of this Act.

(10) Schedule 3 to this Act shall have effect in relation to the ombudsman.

GENERAL NOTE

In the policy statement *The Legal Profession: The Way Forward* the Secretary of State made it clear that he intended to extend the office of the Lay Observer which is presently regulated by the Solicitors (Scotland) Act 1980, s.49, as far as solicitors are concerned. Such an extension was intended to ensure that his area of responsibility was not simply restricted to solicitors and it was proposed to rename the post "Legal Complaints Ombudsman". This section gives effect to this proposal by creating the office of Scottish legal services ombudsman and by giving the ombudsman the power to examine handling complaints made by members of the public against professional organisations who have investigated complaints about the conduct of a practitioner.

Subs. (1)

This provision gives the Secretary of State the power, after consultation with the Lord President, to appoint a person as Scottish legal services ombudsman to examine any written complaint (a handling complaint) made by or on behalf of a member of the public concerning the way in which a professional organisation has dealt with a conduct complaint.

Subs. (2)

The ombudsman is given the power to make his own arrangements when investigating a handling complaint and to require a professional organisation to provide him with such information as he may reasonably require.

Subs. (3)

The ombudsman is also given the power to request a report from the professional organisation in relation to the progress of a particularly lengthy investigation.

Subs. (4)

This provision gives the ombudsman the power to make an interim report and a final report on the results of the investigation which must be sent to the complainer and the professional organisation concerned.

Subs. (5)

This provision gives the Scottish ombudsman, when so requested by the Legal Services Ombudsman for England and Wales, the right to conduct an investigation into a complaint against a professional organisation situated there and places reciprocal investigative powers for professional bodies in Scotland upon the ombudsman for England and Wales.

Subss. (6)–(8)

These provisions give the Secretary of State the power, by regulation, to extend the jurisdiction of the ombudsman to cover handling complaints in relation to executry services provided by persons other than executry practitioners. Such regulations can be restricted to particular persons or categories of person and will be made by the negative resolution procedure.

Subs. (9)

This provision is intended to protect the independence and integrity of the ombudsman by excluding from appointment to the post any person who is entitled to provide legal services, officers and directors of financial institutions who provide executry services, members and officers of the Board and members and employees of a professional or other body whose members enjoy rights of audience.

Subs. (10)

Sched. 3 specifies the administrative duties of the ombudsman and gives the Secretary of

State the power, with the consent of the Treasury, to determine his terms and conditions of service.

Judicial appointments

Judicial appointments

35.—(1) Paragraphs 1 to 3 of Schedule 4 to this Act shall have effect in relation to the eligibility of sheriffs principal, sheriffs and solicitors to be appointed as judges of the Court of Session.

(2) Paragraph 4 of the said Schedule shall have effect in relation to the appointment of—

(a) members of the Inner House of the Court of Session; and

(b) a Lord Ordinary of that Court to be the Lord Ordinary in exchequer causes.

(3) Notwithstanding any provision in any enactment, if it appears expedient to the Secretary of State he may, in accordance with the provisions of paragraphs 5 to 11 of the said Schedule, and after consulting the Lord President, appoint persons to act as temporary judges of the Court of Session.

(4) Section 3 (constitution of Scottish Land Court) of the Small Landholders (Scotland) Act 1911 shall have effect subject to the amendments mentioned in paragraph 12 of the said Schedule.

GENERAL NOTE

Subs. (1)

In *The Scottish Legal Profession: The Way Forward* the Secretary of State made it clear that he considered that the general principle underlying all judicial appointments should be that eligibility should depend not on the particular branch of the legal profession to which an individual belongs but on the relevance to the work of the post of an individual's qualifications, abilities and experience. Given that the policy statement also recommended that solicitors should be entitled to acquire rights to practise in the supreme courts (a proposal implemented by s.24 of this Act) the Secretary of State also recommended that solicitors with full rights of audience should be eligible for appointment as Senators of the College of Justice. This right was also to be extended to sheriffs principal and sheriffs who were originally solicitors. This section and paras. 1 to 3 of Sched. 4 give effect to these proposals and ensure that a sheriff or sheriff principal, who has held office as such for a continuous period of not less than five years and who is not otherwise eligible for appointment to the Court of Session bench, can be appointed as a judge of the Court of Session. Equally, solicitors who have enjoyed rights of audience in both the Court of Session and High Court of Justiciary for a continuous period of not less than five years are eligible for appointment as judges of the Court of Session.

It is interesting that the minimum period of continuous practice for a solicitor with rights of audience to be eligible for appointment as a judge of the Court of Session is five years. In art. XIX of the Act of Union it is declared that advocates or principal clerks of session are eligible for appointment as ordinary lords of session if they have served in the college of justice for a period of five years. On the other hand, writers to the signet must have practised for 10 years and are not eligible for appointment until they have undergone a private and public trial on the civil law before the Faculty of Advocates and be found by them to be qualified for office for a period of two years before appointment. It has been argued that the effect of this Act is to reduce the qualification for appointment for solicitors from 12 to five years. However, the Lord Advocate made it clear in Committee in the House of Lords that the five years qualification was chosen so as to create a symmetry between the requirements for advocates and those solicitors with rights of audience in the supreme courts. In any case, as the Lord Advocate also pointed out, it would be just as unrealistic for a solicitor who has exercised his rights of audience for five years to be appointed as a judge of the Court of Session as it is, at present, for an advocate with five years' practice.

Subs. (2)

This provision, along with Sched. 4, para. 4, fulfils three functions. First, it amends the Court of Session Act 1988, s.2(3), by no longer requiring that the senior judge should preside in the Inner House when an extra Division is convened. Instead, it is for the Lord President to direct one of the judges hearing the case to preside. Second, in a significant change which it is surprising to find in a Schedule, it will no longer be the case that a vacancy in the Inner House will be filled by the automatic appointment of the senior Lord Ordinary in the Outer House. Para. 4(2)(b) enacts a new s.2(6) to the 1988 Act so that in future a vacancy will be filled by a joint appointment by the Lord President and Lord Justice Clerk of any Lord Ordinary. Such appointment requires the consent of the Secretary of State and must be made after consultation with those judges whom it is appropriate to consult in the circumstances. These latter requirements are intended to dispel any possible suspicion of favouritism towards the successful candidate. Finally, this provision and para. 4(3) replace the previous arrangement whereby the Lord Ordinary in Exchequer Causes was appointed by Act of Sederunt. This was thought to be a cumbersome procedure and so in future the appointment will be made by the Lord President.

Subs. (3)

The Law Reform (Miscellaneous Provisions) (Scotland) Act 1985, s.22(1), permits the Lord President, with the consent of the Secretary of State, and, where it is expedient as a temporary measure, to appoint retired Court of Session judges or Lords of Appeal in Ordinary who have not yet reached the age of 75 years. This provision takes this process a stage further by permitting the *Secretary of State*, after consulting the Lord President, to appoint persons eligible for appointment as a judge of the Court of Session (including persons made eligible by this Act) as a temporary judge. Such persons would sit as judges in the Court of Session or High Court of Justiciary when required. The Lord Advocate at the Committee Stage in the House of Lords suggested that a person who is appointed as a temporary judge would not previously have received any commission from the Crown, so that temporary judges will not be selected from among the ranks of retired judges. It is interesting that para. 11(b) makes it clear that a person's appointment as a temporary judge is without prejudice to his continuing with any business or professional occupation not inconsistent with his acting as a judge.

Subs. (4)

This provision permits advocates, sheriffs principal and sheriffs, and solicitors with rights of audience to be eligible for appointment as Chairman of the Scottish Land Court so long as in every case they have 10 years' experience.

Solicitors' and counsel's fees

Solicitors' and counsel's fees

36.—(1) An advocate and the person instructing him may agree, in relation to a litigation undertaken on a speculative basis, that, in the event of the litigation being successful, the advocate's fee shall be increased by such percentage as may, subject to subsection (2) below, be agreed.

(2) The percentage increase which may be agreed under subsection (1) above shall not exceed such limit as the court may, after consultation with the Dean of the Faculty of Advocates, prescribe by act of sederunt.

(3) After section 61 of the 1980 Act there shall be inserted the following section—

"Solicitors' fees

61A.—(1) Subject to the provisions of this section, and without prejudice to—

(a) section 32(1)(i) of the Sheriff Courts (Scotland) Act 1971; or

(b) section 5(h) of the Court of Session Act 1988,

where a solicitor and his client have reached an agreement in writing as to the solicitor's fees in respect of any work done or to be done by him for his client it shall not be competent, in any litigation arising out of any dispute as to the amount due to be paid under any such agreement, for the court to remit the solicitor's account for taxation.

(2) Subsection (1) is without prejudice to the court's power to remit a solicitor's account for taxation in a case where there has been no written agreement as to the fees to be charged.

(3) A solicitor and his client may agree, in relation to a litigation undertaken on a speculative basis, that, in the event of the litigation being successful, the solicitor's fee shall be increased by such a percentage as may, subject to subsection (4), be agreed.

(4) The percentage increase which may be agreed under subsection (3) shall not exceed such limit as the court may, after consultation with the Council, prescribe by act of sederunt.".

(4) In section 33 of the Legal Aid (Scotland) Act 1986 (fees and outlays of solicitors and counsel who have provided services under that Act) there shall be added at the end the following subsection—

"(6) It shall not be competent, in any litigation arising out of any dispute as to the amount of—

(a) any fees or outlays to be paid to a solicitor; or

(b) any fees to be paid to an advocate,

under or by virtue of this Act, for the court to remit the account concerned for taxation.".

GENERAL NOTE

Subs. (1)

In *The Scottish Legal Profession: The Way Forward* the Secretary of State made it clear that he would not support a system of contingency fees whereby a lawyer receives a proportion of the damages awarded. Instead, he proposed that in speculative actions it would be open to the lawyer and the client to agree a percentage uplift in the usual fee in the event of success. This provision gives effect to this proposal as far as advocates are concerned and allows them to charge a percentage increase in the fee to take account of the fact that should the action fail they will receive no fee at all.

Subs. (2)

This provision complies with the proposal in the policy statement which recommended that the Lord President should have the power to prescribe the upper limit on any uplift by authorising the court, after consultation with the Dean, to prescribe the percentage increase by Act of Sederunt.

Subs. (3)

This provision inserts a new s.61A into the Solicitors (Scotland) Act 1980. It deals with two issues: the removal of taxing requirements for agreed fees and the introduction of speculative fees for solicitors. As regards the first point, the Law Society has been keen to relieve its members of the requirement to remit their accounts for taxation, particularly where the solicitor and the client have agreed a fee at the outset. This provision removes the requirement that solicitor's accounts be taxed where the parties have agreed a fee for the work done or to be done by the solicitor. However, the provision also introduces a safeguard for the client by requiring that the agreement be in writing—a suggestion first made by Citizens' Advice Scotland. Moreover, if there is no written agreement as to fees, taxation can still take place. The other provisions of s.61A introduce the same rules for speculative fees for solicitors as will be applied to advocates by s.36(1) and (2) of this Act, save for the requirement that it is the Council of the Law Society which is to be consulted prior to the making of the Act of Sederunt which will specify the maximum percentage increase.

Subs. (4)

This provision abolishes the requirement that fees paid to advocates or solicitors under the legal aid scheme should be taxed. This change is intended to pave the way towards the introduction of an independent arbitration system which will apply where there is a dispute over the level of fees which should be paid by the Scottish Legal Aid Board.

Miscellaneous and supplementary

Admission of solicitors and notaries public

37.—(1) For subsection (2) of section 6 of the 1980 Act (admission of persons as solicitors) there shall be substituted the following subsection—

"(2) Where—

(a) a person has complied with the requirements of subsection (1); but

(b) the Council have not lodged a petition for his admission as a solicitor within one month of his having so complied,

40–65

he may apply by petition to the court for admission as a solicitor; and if he produces the certificate mentioned in paragraph (b) of subsection (1) the court shall make an order admitting him as a solicitor.".

(2) Section 57 of that Act (admission of notaries public) shall be amended as follows—

(a) for subsection (1) there shall be substituted—
"(1) The offices and functions of—
(a) the clerk to the admission of notaries public; and
(b) the keeper of the register of notaries public,
are hereby transferred to the Council.";

(b) in subsection (2), for the words from "grant" to the end there shall be substituted "direct the Council to register him in the register of notaries public.";

(c) after subsection (2) there shall be inserted the following subsections—
"(2A) A petition by the Council under section 6(3A) for the admission of a person as a solicitor may, if the person so requests, include an application for the person's admission as a notary public; and an order on any such petition admitting that person as a solicitor may admit him as a notary public and direct the Council to register him in the register of notaries public.

(2B) A petition by a person under section 6(2) for his admission as a solicitor may include an application for his admission as a notary public; and an order on any such petition admitting that person as a solicitor may admit him as a notary public and direct the Council to register him in the register of notaries public.";

(d) in subsection (4) for the word "solicitor" there shall be substituted "person"; and

(e) for subsection (5) there shall be substituted—
"(5) The Council may charge such reasonable fees as they consider appropriate in respect of the admission of any person as a notary public.".

(3) In section 58 of that Act (removal from and restoration to the register of names of notaries public)—

(a) in subsection (1), for the words from "give" to the end there shall be substituted "strike off or, as the case may be, remove his name from the register of notaries public";

(b) in subsection (2), for the words from "it" to "thereupon" there shall be substituted "the Council shall forthwith";

(c) at the end of that section there shall be added the following subsections—
"(3) Where a person who is both a solicitor and a notary public is suspended from practising as a solicitor under this Act the Council shall forthwith remove the person's name from the register of notaries public.

(4) If the suspension of such a person as is mentioned in subsection (3) is terminated or otherwise comes to an end the Council shall restore the person's name to the register.".

GENERAL NOTE

This section amends the rules in s.6 of the Solicitors (Scotland) Act 1980 as far as admission as a solicitor is concerned by adding an additional requirement for petition to the court by an applicant for membership under s.6(2), *viz.* that the Council should not have lodged a petition within one month of the applicant becoming eligible for membership. This section also simplifies the procedure in s.57 of the 1980 Act for admission as a notary public by transferring the responsibilities of the Clerk to the admission of notaries public and that of Register of Notaries Public to the Council of the Law Society. The section also permits new entrants to the profession to make a joint application for admission as a solicitor and as a notary public, although this is not mandatory, and existing solicitors will still be entitled to seek admission as a notary. These changes fulfil the proposals made by the Secretary of State in *The Scottish Legal Profession: The Way Forward*.

Availability of legal aid in relation to services provided under this Act

38. After section 43 of the Legal Aid (Scotland) Act 1986 there shall be inserted the following section—

> **"Application of Act to services provided under Law Reform (Miscellaneous Provisions) (Scotland) Act 1990**
>
> 43A.—(1) Advice and assistance shall be available, in accordance with the provisions of this Act, in relation to the provision of executry services by executry practitioners and recognised financial institutions and conveyancing services by independent qualified conveyancers, all within the meaning of section 23 (interpretation of sections 16 to 22) of the Law Reform (Miscellaneous Provisions) (Scotland) Act 1990 as they are so available in relation to the provision of the like services by solicitors.
>
> (2) Subject to any act of sederunt or act of adjournal made under subsection (7) of section 26 of that Act (consideration of applications made under section 25) advice and assistance, civil legal aid and criminal legal aid shall be available, in accordance with the provisions of this Act, in relation to the provision of services by persons who have acquired rights to conduct litigation or, as the case may be, rights of audience by virtue of that section as they are so available in relation to the provision of the like services by solicitors and, where appropriate, by advocates.
>
> (3) Where advice and assistance, civil legal aid or criminal legal aid has been made available by virtue of this section, the provisions of this Act shall apply in relation to the person providing those services as they apply in relation to a solicitor or advocate providing like services.".

GENERAL NOTE

This section creates a new s.43A of the Legal Aid (Scotland) Act 1986 and ensures that the legal aid scheme will apply to the different types of practitioner created by this Act. This provision fulfils an undertaking made by the Lord Advocate that these new practitioners should have access to legal aid funds and was added at Committee Stage in the House of Lords. It authorises that the legal advice and assistance scheme will be available for clients who seek advice on the provision of executry services from executry practitioners and from financial institutions who offer executry services or for clients who seek advice on conveyancing services from independent qualified conveyancers. It is also made clear that members of professional or other bodies who have rights of audience will have legal advice and assistance, civil legal aid and criminal legal aid made available to them. Finally, the section declares specifically that the provisions on legal aid should apply in the same way to the person providing the service as they do to a solicitor or advocate providing the same service.

Removal of certain restrictions on the borrowing of the court process.

39. Section 29 of the 1980 Act (which restricts the borrowing of the process relating to any court proceedings to solicitors having a place of business, in relation to the Court of Session, in Edinburgh, and, in relation to the inferior courts, within the jurisdiction of the court concerned) shall cease to have effect.

GENERAL NOTE

At present under s.29 of the Solicitors (Scotland) Act 1980 a solicitor cannot borrow the process in any proceedings depending before the Court of Session unless he has a place of business in Edinburgh and in the inferior courts the right to borrow the process is also restricted to solicitors who have a place of business within the jurisdiction of the relevant court. This section will remove these restrictions by repealing s.29.

Advisory and supervisory functions of the Director

40.—(1) Before—

(a) making any regulations under section 17(11) or 18(10) of this Act; or

(b) approving any rules—
　　　　(i) made under section 17(3); or
　　　　(ii) such as are mentioned in section 31(1) or (2),
　　or this Act; or

(c) considering any provisions of a draft scheme under section 26(1) or (3) of this Act,

the Secretary of State shall first send a copy of the proposed regulations, rules or provisions to the Director.

(2) The Director shall consider whether any such regulations, rules or provisions as are mentioned in subsection (1) above would have, or would be likely to have, the effect of restricting, distorting or preventing competition to any significant extent.

(3) When the Director has completed his consideration he shall give such advice to the Secretary of State as he thinks fit.

(4) The Director may publish any advice given by him under subsection (3) above.

(5) The Director shall, so far as practicable, exclude from anything published under subsection (4) above any matter—

(a) which relates to the affairs of a particular person; and

(b) the publication of which would, or might in the Director's opinion, seriously and prejudicially affect the interests of that person.

(6) For the purposes of the Law of defamation, the publication of any advice by the Director under this section shall be absolutely privileged.

GENERAL NOTE

This section was added to the Bill at Committee Stage in the House of Lords by the Lord Advocate. It seeks to set out the advisory duties of the Director General in relation to regulations made by the Secretary of State for qualified conveyancers and executry practitioners, rules made by the Board regarding the education and training requirements for qualified conveyancers, and the draft scheme which a professional body must make in order to acquire rights of audience for its members. In addition, the Director is also given certain responsibilities in relation to rules prohibiting advocates' partnerships and over rules about their rights of audience. His major task is to consider whether any of the above will have the effect of restricting, distorting or preventing competition to any significant extent and he must advise the Secretary of State on this point.

Investigatory powers of the Director

41.—(1) For the purpose of investigating any matter under section 40 of this Act, the Director may by notice in writing—

(a) require any person to produce to him or to any person appointed by him for the purpose, at a time and place specified in the notice, any documents which are specified or described in the notice and which—
　　　　(i) are in that person's custody or under that person's control; and
　　　　(ii) relate to any matter relevant to the investigation; or

(b) require any person carrying on any business to furnish to him (within such time and in such manner and form as the notice may specify) such information as may be specified or described in the notice.

(2) A person shall not be required under this section to produce any document or disclose any information which he would be entitled to refuse to produce or disclose on the grounds confidentiality between a client and his professional legal adviser in any civil proceedings.

(3) Subsections (5) to (8) of section 85 of the Fair Trading Act 1973 shall apply in relation to a notice under this section as they apply in relation to a notice under subsection (1) of that section.

GENERAL NOTE

This section grants investigatory powers to the Director General over any of the matters in s.40 on which he is required to provide advice to the Secretary of State. He has rights to obtain documents and to be furnished with information. However, a person need not produce documents nor provide information on the grounds of confidentiality between client and adviser.

Review of rules approved by the Secretary of State

42.—(1) Where the Secretary of State has approved—

(a) a rule under section 17(15) or 31(2) of this Act; or

(b) a draft scheme under section 26(6) of this Act,

he may and, where the Lord President, in the case of a draft scheme such as is mentioned in paragraph (b), so requests shall, require the body which made the rule or, as the case may be, the scheme to review its terms.

(2) When they have reviewed a rule or, as the case may be, a scheme, following a requirement made under subsection (1) above, the body concerned may revise the rule or scheme in the light of that review, and shall then submit the rule or scheme as revised or, if they have not revised it, as previously approved—

(a) in the case of a rule such as is mentioned in subsection (1)(a) above, to the Secretary of State; or

(b) in the case of a draft scheme such as is mentioned in subsection (1)(b) above, to the Secretary of State and the Lord President.

(3) Where a rule, whether revised or as previously approved, is submitted to the Secretary of State under subsection (2)(a) above, he may—

(a) approve the rule as submitted to him; or

(b) amend the rule in such manner as he considers appropriate,

and (except where the rule remains in the form previously approved) he may direct the body concerned to bring it into operation as soon as is practicable.

(4) Where the Lord President and the Secretary of State are agreed that the terms of a draft scheme submitted to them under subsection (2)(b) above are satisfactory, the Secretary of State may—

(a) approve the scheme; and

(b) (except where the scheme remains in the form previously approved) direct the body concerned to bring the scheme, as so amended, into force as soon as is practicable.

(5) Where either the Secretary of State or the Lord President is of the view that the terms of any such scheme so submitted to them are not satisfactory, but they do not agree as to what the terms of the scheme should be, the scheme shall continue to have effect as previously approved.

(6) Where the Secretary of State and the Lord President agree both that the terms of a scheme so submitted to them are not satisfactory, and as to what the terms of the scheme should be, the Secretary of State may amend the scheme in such manner as he and the Lord President consider appropriate; and may direct the body concerned to bring the scheme, as so amended, into force as soon as is practicable.

(7) The provisions of section 40(1)(b) and (c) of this Act shall apply to rules and schemes submitted under subsection (2) of this section as they apply to rules submitted under sections 17(15) and 31(2) and schemes submitted under section 25(1) of this Act.

General Note

This section specifies the rights of the Secretary of State to review rules made by the Board about the education and training requirements for qualified conveyancers, practice rules about rights of audience for advocates and a draft scheme made by a professional or other body which seeks rights of audience for its members. In particular, it authorises the Secretary of State to require the body concerned to review the terms of its rules or scheme. The body can then resubmit the rules or draft scheme to the Secretary of State or Secretary of State and Lord President as the case may be. The revised rules or draft scheme can then be approved or amended as required and will be brought into force as soon as practicable.

Functions of Direction in relation to certain rules made under the 1980 Act

43. After section 64 of the 1980 Act there shall be inserted the following sections—

> **"Advisory and supervisory functions of the Director General of Fair Trading**
> 64A.—(1) Before considering any rule—
> (a) made under section 25A(4) or (5); or
> (b) such as is mentioned in section 34(3A),
> the Secretary of State shall send a copy of the proposed rule in question to the Director.
> (2) The Director shall consider whether the rule in question would have, or would be likely to have, the effect of restricting, distorting or preventing competition to any significant extent.
> (3) When the Director has completed his consideration he shall give such advice to the Secretary of State as he thinks fit.
> (4) The Director may publish any advice given by him under subsection (3).
> (5) The Director shall, so far as practicable, exclude from anything published under subsection (4) any matter—
> (a) which relates to the affairs of a particular person; and
> (b) the publication of which would, or might in the Director's opinion, seriously and prejudicially affect the interests of that person.
> (6) For the purposes of the law of defamation, the publication of any advice or report by the Director under this section shall be absolutely privileged.

> **Duty of Secretary of State**
> 64B. When he has received advice under section 64A(3) in relation to a rule made under section 25A(4) or (5) or such as is mentioned in section 34(3A), the Secretary of State may, having considered—
> (a) that advice;
> (b) whether the interests of justice require that there should be such a rule; and
> (c) in relation to a rule made under section 25A(5), any relevant practice obtaining in the sheriff court,
> approve or refuse to approve the rule.

> **Investigatory powers of the Director**
> 64C.—(1) For the purpose of investigating any matter under section 64A, the Director may by notice in writing—
> (a) require any person to produce to him or to any person appointed by him for the purpose, at a time and place specified in the notice, any documents which are specified or described in the notice and which—
> > (i) are in that person's custody or under that person's control; and
> > (ii) relate to any matter relevant to the investigation; or
> (b) require any person carrying on any business to furnish to him (within such time and in such manner and form as the notice may specify) such information as may be specified or described in the notice.
> (2) A person shall not be required under this section to produce any document or disclose any information which he would be entitled to refuse to produce or disclose on the grounds of confidentiality between a client and his professional legal adviser in any civil proceedings.

(3) Subsections (5) to (8) of section 85 of the Fair Trading Act 1973 shall apply in relation to a notice under this section as they apply in relation to a notice under subsection (1) of that section.

Review of rules approved by the Secretary of State
64D.—(1) Without prejudice to the power of the Council to review any rule made by them, where the Secretary of State has approved a rule under section 64B he may, and if so requested by the Lord President shall, require the Council to review its terms.

(2) When they have reviewed a rule following a requirement made under subsection (1), the Council made revise the rule in the light of that review, and shall then submit the rule as revised or, if they have not revised it, as previously approved to the Lord President and the Secretary of State.

(3) Where the Lord President and the Secretary of State are agreed that the terms of rule as submitted to them are satisfactory, the Secretary of State shall approve the rule, and may direct the Council to bring it into force as soon as is practicable.

(4) Where either the Secretary of State or the Lord President is of the view that any rule, as submitted to them, is not satisfactory, but they do not agree as to what the terms of the rule should be, the rule shall continue to have effect as previously approved.

(5) Where the Secretary of State and the Lord President agree both that any rule submitted to them under subsection (2) is not satisfactory, and as to what the terms of the rule should be, the Secretary of State may direct the Council—

(a) to amend the rule in such manner as he and the Lord President consider appropriate; and

(b) to bring the rule, as so amended, into force as soon as is practicable.

(6) The provisions of sections 64A and 64B apply to rules submitted to the Secretary of State under this section as they apply to rules submitted to him under sections 25A(9) or (10) and 34(3A).".

GENERAL NOTE
This adds new ss.64A–64D to the Solicitors (Scotland) Act 1980. Ss.64A and 64C are identical to those enacted for other practitioners by ss.40 and 41 of this Act. S.64D gives the Secretary of State the power either of his own volition or if so requested by the Lord President to require the Council of the Law Society to review any of its rules. The Council may revise that rule in light of the review and where the Lord President and Secretary of State are agreed that the terms of the revised rule are satisfactory will direct the council to bring it into force as soon as practicable. Ultimately, the Secretary of State has the power to direct the Council to amend a revised rule which is still unsatisfactory in such a manner as he and the Lord President consider appropriate.

Interpretation of Part II

44. In this Part of this Act, unless the context otherwise requires—
    "advocate" means a member of the Faculty of Advocates practising as such;
    "the Director" means the Director General of Fair Trading;
    "Lord President" means the Lord President of the Court of Session;
    "solicitor" has the same meaning as in section 65(1) of the 1980 Act; and
    "the 1980 Act" means the Solicitors (Scotland) Act 1980.

PART III

THE LICENSING (SCOTLAND) ACT 1976

Times of opening

Permitted hours
    45.—(1) For section 53 of the Licensing (Scotland) Act 1976 (in this Part

of this Act referred to as "the principal Act") there shall be substituted the following section—

> **"Permitted hours in licensed premises and registered clubs**
> 53.—(1) Subject to the provisions of this Act, the permitted hours in licensed premises, licensed canteens and registered clubs shall be—
>> (a) for days other than Sundays, the period between eleven in the morning and eleven in the evening; and
>> (b) for Sundays, the period between half-past twelve and half-past two in the afternoon and the period between half-past six and eleven in the evening.
>
> (2) Nothing in this section shall authorise the sale or supply of alcoholic liquor of consumption off the premises, being premises in respect of which a refreshment licence, an entertainment licence, a restricted hotel licence, a restaurant licence or a licence under Part III of this Act is in force."

(2) In section 56 of that Act (permitted hours in certain clubs)—
(a) for subsection (1) there shall be substituted the following subsection—

> "(1) A registered club may apply to the sheriff for an order providing that during the winter period the permitted hours in the club on Sundays shall not be those set out in section 53 of this Act, but shall instead be the period between half-past twelve and two in the afternoon and the period between four and nine in the evening; and the sheriff shall, if in his opinion the conditions set out in subsection (2) below are satisfied, make the order applied for,"; and

(b) in subsection (2)(d), for words "section 53(3)" there shall be substituted the words "section 53."

(3) In subsection (2) of section 57 of that Act (extension of permitted hours in the afternoon in certain premises), after "afternoon" there shall be inserted the words "on Sundays".

DEFINITIONS
"entertainment licence": s.9 and Sched. 1 of the 1976 Act.
"licensed canteens": s.139(1) of the 1976 Act.
"licensed premises": s.139(1) of the 1976 Act.
"permitted hours": s.139(1) of the 1976 Act.
"refreshment licence": s.139(1) of the 1976 Act.
"registered clubs": s.139(1) of the 1976 Act.
"restaurant licence": s.9 and Sched. 1 of the 1976 Act.
"restricted hotel": s.9 and Sched. 1 of the 1976 Act.

GENERAL NOTE
This section replaces s.53 of the Licensing (Scotland) Act 1976 (hereinafter referred to as the "1976 Act") and provides new basic permitted hours in licensed premises, licensed canteens and registered clubs. The hours for days other than Sundays are 11 a.m. to 11 p.m., thus abolishing the requirement to apply for an extension of hours on weekday afternoons. On Sunday the permitted hours remain 12.30 p.m. to 2.30 p.m. and 6.30 p.m. to 11 p.m. Premises operated under a public house or refreshment licence may have permitted hours on Sundays only where applications for Sunday opening have been granted in terms of Sched. 4 to the 1976 Act or s.46 *et seq.* In cases of premises operated under hotel, restricted hotel, restaurant or entertainment licences or a registered club, basic permitted hours are the same, *i.e.* 12.30 p.m. to 2.30 p.m. and 6.30 p.m. to 11 p.m., but no application is required for Sunday opening. The new section repeats the express prohibition of Off-Sales on premises where a refreshment, entertainment, restricted hotel, or restaurant licence or a licence under Pt. III of the 1976 Act (Seamen's Canteen) is in force.
Consequent amendment is made to s.56 of the 1976 Act to allow application to the sheriff for alternative permitted hours for athletic clubs on Sundays. The alternative hours are 12.30 p.m. to 2 p.m. and 4 p.m. to 9 p.m.

S.57 of the 1976 Act is amended to refer to Sundays only, as there is no longer a requirement to apply in respect of weekday afternoons.

Subs. (2)

This replaces s.56(1) of the 1976 Act, taking account of the change in weekday permitted hours, and allows sports clubs to have alternative permitted hours on a Sunday. In order to qualify for alternative permitted hours, the club must fulfil the conditions set out in subs. (2) of s.56 of the 1976 Act. The procedure is by application to the sheriff for an order granting alternative permitted hours on a Sunday (see s.56(c) of the 1976 Act).

Subs. (3)

Permitted hours. This is defined in s.139(1) of the 1976 Act. The effect of the application of the section to premises is to extend the permitted hours on a Sunday afternoon to 4 p.m. for consumption of alcoholic liquor ancillary to a table meal, in premises suitably adapted for the provision of meals. "Table meal" is defined in s.139(1) of the 1976 Act.

Sunday opening of licensed premises

46.—(1) The amendment by section 45 of this Act of section 53 of the principal Act shall not permit the opening for sale or supply of alcoholic liquor during the permitted hours on a Sunday of premises for which there is in force a public house licence or a refreshment licence unless—

(a) the grant, provisional grant or renewal of such licence was in response to an application which stated that it was the intention of the applicant that the premises should be open for the sale or supply of alcoholic liquor during the permitted hours on a Sunday; or

(b) before such a licence has been renewed, the licensing board has granted an application for Sunday opening in respect of the premises in accordance with the provisions of Schedule 4 to the principal Act,

and, subject to subsection (8) below, the said Schedule 4 shall continue to have effect until all such licences in force at the commencement of this Act have been renewed or have ceased to have effect.

(2) In section 10 of the principal Act (applications for licences)—

(a) after subsection (3) there shall be added the following subsection—

"(3A) In the case of an application for the grant, the provisional grant or the renewal of a public house licence or a refreshment licence, the application shall state whether the applicant intends the premises to be open for the sale or supply of alcoholic liquor during the permitted hours on a Sunday."; and

(b) after subsection (7) there shall be added the following subsection—

"(8) A notice as mentioned in subsection (2) above and notice under subsection (5) above shall include a statement as to whether the applicant intends the premises to be open for the sale or supply of alcoholic liquor during the permitted hours on a Sunday.".

(3) In section 12 of that Act (publication of list of applications), at the end of subsection (2) there shall be added the following paragraph—

"(f) in the case of an application for a public house licence or a refreshment licence, whether the applicant intends the premises to be open for the sale or supply of alcoholic liquor during the permitted hours on a Sunday.".

(4) In section 17 of that Act (grounds for refusal of application)—

(a) after subsection (2) there shall be inserted the following subsection—

"(2A) A licensing board shall refuse to grant or renew a public house or a refreshment licence in respect of the permitted hours on a Sunday if it finds that the opening and use on a Sunday of the premises to which the application relates would cause undue disturbance or public nuisance in the locality, but the refusal of an application on the ground alone shall not prevent the licensing board from granting the application in respect of days other than Sundays.".

(b) in subsection (4), after the words "transfer the licence" there shall be inserted the words "or to grant the licence in respect of the permitted hours on Sunday".

(5) In section 59 (restaurants in public houses to have permitted hours on Sundays), for the words "an application for Sunday opening has not been granted under Schedule 4 to this Act" there shall be substituted the words "there are no permitted hours on a Sunday".

(6) In section 60 (other extensions of permitted hours on Sundays), for the words "an application for Sunday opening has been granted under Schedule 4 to this Act" there shall be substituted the words "there are permitted hours on Sundays in accordance with section 53 of this Act".

(7) In section 64 (extensions to permitted hours), for subsection (4) there shall be substituted the following subsections—

"(4) A licensing board shall not grant an application from the holder of a public house licence for an occasional or regular extension of permitted hours on Sundays except—

(a) as respects premises to which section 59 of this Act applies and for the purposes of that section; and

(b) in the case of other premises, as respects any period or periods after half-past two in the afternoon,

and the board shall refuse to grant such an application if it finds that the extension of permitted hours would cause undue disturbance or public nuisance in the locality.

(4A) Nothing in subsection (4) above shall prevent the granting of an application for an occasional or regular extension of permitted hours on a Saturday for a period which continues into Sunday morning."

(8) In Schedule 4 to the principal Act (provision for Sunday opening of premises with a public house or refreshment licence)—

(a) in paragraph 1, the words "as mentioned in section 53(2) of this Act" shall cease to have effect;

(b) in paragraph 15, the words "or 12 above" shall cease to have effect;

(c) after paragraph 15 there shall be inserted the following paragraph—

"15A. If an application for renewal of a public house licence or a refreshment licence includes a statement that the applicant intends that the premises should be open for the sale or supply of alcoholic liquor during the permitted hours on a Sunday and if there is currently in force the grant of an application for Sunday opening, that grant shall continue to have effect—

(a) until the renewal application is granted by the board;

(b) if the renewal application is refused by the board, or refused in respect of Sunday opening, until the time within which an appeal may be made has elapsed, or if an appeal has been lodged until the appeal has been abandoned or determined."; and

(d) paragraphs 12 to 14, 16 and 17 shall cease to have effect.

(9) Expressions used in this section and in the principal Act shall have the same meaning as in the Act.

GENERAL NOTE

This section requires, despite the amendment of s.45, that premises operated under a public house licence or a refreshment licence may only have permitted hours on a Sunday (12.30 p.m. to 2.30 p.m. and 6.30 p.m. to 11 p.m.) where the applicant for the grant, provisional grant or renewal of such a licence has stated the intention that the premises be opened for the sale or supply of alcoholic liquor on a Sunday or where an application for Sunday opening in accordance with Sched. 4 of the 1976 Act has been granted. The existing Sched. 4 procedure continues to have effect until existing licences for Sunday opening are renewed or cease to have effect. Thereafter a new procedure will simplify Sunday opening applications by allowing the applicant simply to state an intention to open on a Sunday on the application for grant, provisional grant or renewal of a public house or refreshment licence. The new provisions allow application for Sunday opening by a person who is not yet a licence-holder, which was not the former position: see *Ginera* v. *City of Glasgow District Licensing Board*, 1982 S.L.T. 136. The statement of intention will also be published and appear on site notices and notices to neighbouring proprietors if the case is a new grant only. The grounds for refusal of permitted hours on a Sunday, that the grant would cause undue disturbance or public nuisance, are the same grounds as those in Sched. 4 to the 1976 Act. Public houses are given the opportunity to apply for occasional or regular extensions of permitted hours on a Sunday for the first time. The application must be for premises to which s.59 of the 1976 Act applies, namely premises structurally adapted and bona fide used for provision of meals or, in the case of premises to which s.59 does not apply, must be for hours in the afternoon and evening only; see also para. 12 of Sched. 8 to this Act for regular extension of permitted hours for refreshment licence. S.64 of the 1976 Act is further amended to clarify the position when an extension of hours is granted on a Saturday evening which extends into Sunday mornings. In the past certain Boards have not allowed such an extension to go beyond midnight; however, the sub-section confirms that such an extension is permissible.

Subs. (1)

This allows for Sched. 4 to the 1976 Act to continue to have effect until all licences with Sunday opening in force at the commencement of the Act have been renewed or have ceased to have effect. Thereafter a simplification of the procedure is envisaged.

Subs. (2)

New subs. (3A). This amends s.10 of the 1976 Act. An applicant for the grant, provisional grant or renewal of a public house or refreshment licence shall state an intention to open on a Sunday for the sale or supply of alcoholic liquor in the context of that application, without the need to make a separate application in terms of Sched. 4. If such an intention is stated then new subs. (8) of s.10 of the 1976 Act requires that Notices in terms of ss.10(2) and 10(5) of the 1976 Act shall include a statement as to whether the applicant intends the premises to be opened on Sundays.

Subs. (3)

S.12 of the 1976 Act is also amended in consequence, to the effect that where an application for a public house licence or a refreshment licence is advertised by the Clerk of a licensing board, the intention to be open for the sale or supply of alcoholic liquor should also be advertised.

Subs. (4)

S.17 of the 1976 Act is amended by the addition of subs. (2A), which requires the Licensing Board to refuse to grant permitted hours on a Sunday in circumstances where it considers that the grant of permitted hours on a Sunday to premises operating a public house or refreshment licence, would cause undue disturbance or public nuisance in the locality. However, the refusal to grant or renew the permitted hours on a Sunday alone shall not prevent the licensing board from granting the application in respect of days other than Sundays. S.17(4) is amended to allow the refusal of permitted hours on a Sunday to be appealed to the Sheriff.

Subs. (5)

The wording of s.59 of the 1976 Act is amended to include reference to permitted hours on a Sunday granted other than in terms of an application under Sched. 4 of the 1976 Act.

Subs. (6)

A similar amendment to that in subs. (5) is made to s.60 of the 1976 Act.

Subs. (7)

S.64(4) of the 1976 Act is replaced by a new subsection which allows a holder of a public house licence to apply for an occasional or regular extension of permitted hours on a Sunday but only in respect of premises to which s.59 of the 1976 Act applies, namely premises permitted to open on a Sunday during permitted hours of which all or part is structurally adapted and bona fide used for providing meals at midday or in the evening and which do not have a bar counter; or in respect of other premises to which s.59 does not apply, only for periods after 2.30 p.m. A licensing board must refuse the application if it finds that such an extension of hours would cause undue disturbance or public nuisance in the locality. The new s.64(4) applies a stricter test than that which applies to other applications under the section. This subsection applies a different test from that which applies to the other applications under the section, where the test in terms of s.64(8) of the 1976 Act requires the licensing board to refuse if *it considers* the extension is *likely* to cause undue public nuisance or to be a threat to public order or safety.

New subs. (4A). This clarifies the position as regards an extension granted on Saturday evening which extends into Sunday morning. In the past certain boards have interpreted s.64(4) as a prohibition of the extended hours on a Sunday altogether in public houses and have not allowed a Saturday evening extension to go beyond midnight. The addition of the new subsection confirms that a Saturday evening extension granted in respect of premises with a public house licence can continue into the Sunday following.

Subs. (8)

Sched. 4 to the 1976 Act is amended to take account of the new s.10 procedure, namely that an applicant need no longer make a separate application for Sunday opening. Notice does not require to be given in terms of s.10(2)(b) and (5) when renewing a Public House or Refreshment Licence in respect of Sunday opening. New subs. (15A) states that where there is already a Sched. 4 grant of Sunday opening, it continues until the renewal of the licence by the board or if renewal is refused, or renewal of Sunday opening refused, until the time has elapsed for the making of an appeal under s.39 of the 1976 Act, or that appeal is determined. Thereafter a statement of intention to open on a Sunday for the sale or supply of alcoholic liquor will suffice.

Regular extensions of permitted hours

47.—(1) A licensing board shall not grant an application under section 64 of the principal Act for an extension of permitted hours unless it is satisfied by the applicant, taking account of the factors mentioned in subsection (3) of that section—

    (a) that there is a need in the locality in which the premises in respect of which the application is made are situated for a regular extension of the permitted hours; and

    (b) that such an extension is likely to be of such benefit to the community as a whole as to outweigh any detriment to that locality.

(2) In determining whether to grant an application for a regular extension to permitted hours in respect of any premises it shall not be a relevant consideration for the licensing board to have regard to whether any application relating to any other premises in its area has, at any time, been granted or refused or the grounds on which any such application has been granted or refused.

(3) Expressions used in this section and in the principal Act shall have the same meaning as in the Act.

GENERAL NOTE

This section extends the criteria to be taken into account by the licensing board when considering an extension of permitted hours in terms of s.64 of the 1976 Act. The wide discretion given to licensing boards in respect of their consideration of occasional and regular extensions has been restricted by the new wording, which states that a Board "shall not" grant an application unless satisfied, by the applicant, having regard to the social circumstances of the locality and to activities taking place in that locality (s.64(3)) that there is a need for an extension of permitted hours *and* that an extension is likely to be of such benefit to the community as a whole as to outweigh any detriment.

Subs. (1)

This places the onus on the applicant to place before the board sufficient material upon which it may be satisfied with regard to the requirements set out in the 1976 Act.

Subs. (2)

This reinforces the requirement that each application for regular extension of permitted hours be considered on its own individual merits, and makes it irrelevant to consider that (1) other premises in the board's area may have been granted or refused extended hours or that (2) the grounds upon which an application in respect of other premises was granted or refused. (For refusal see s.64(8) and Sched. 8, para. 12, to this Act.)

Restriction orders

48.—(1) Section 65 of the principal Act (restriction on the permitted hours) shall be amended in accordance with the following provisions of this section.

(2) For subsection (1) there shall be substituted the following subsections—

"(1) Where, on a complaint being made to a licensing board by any person mentioned in section 16(1) of this Act in respect of any licensed premises or registered club, the board is satisfied that—

(a) the sale or supply of alcoholic liquor in the afternoon or in the evening in licensed premises or in a registered club is the cause of undue public nuisance or constitutes a threat to public order or safety; or

(b) the use of licensed premises is the cause of undue disturbance or public nuisance having regard to the way of life in the locality on a Sunday,

the board may make an order, in this section referred to as an "afternoon restriction order" or "evening restriction order" in the case of the grounds mentioned in paragraph (a) above or as a "Sunday restriction order" in the case of the grounds mentioned in paragraph (b) above; and, in this section, "restriction order" includes any such order.

(1A) The effect of an afternoon restriction order in that the permitted hours between half-past two and five in the afternoon shall be reduced by such a time and for such a period as may be specified in the order.

(1B) The effect of an evening restriction order is that the permitted hours in the evening shall be reduced by such a time and for such a period as may be specified in the order but no such order shall restrict the permitted hours before ten in the evening.

(1C) The effect of a Sunday restriction order is that there shall be no permitted hours on Sunday for such period as may be specified in the order or that the permitted hours on Sunday shall be reduced by such a time and for such a period as may be so specified."

(3) At the end of subsection (3) there shall be inserted the words "provided that no restriction order shall be made in respect of premises in respect of which no complaint has been made".

GENERAL NOTE

This section extends the provisions of s.65 of the 1976 Act to take account of the new and extended permitted hours on weekdays and Sunday (see ss.45, 46 and para. 12 of Sched. 8.to this Act) for the restriction of permitted hours for the sale of liquor in premises or registered clubs where such sale is the cause of undue public nuisance or constitutes a threat to public safety or order or the use of the premises is the cause of disturbance or a threat to public order or safety, on a Sunday. The phrase "any person entitled to object to the grant of a licence" in terms of s.16(1) of the 1976 Act, is amended by para. 5 of Sched. 8 to this Act. The section distinguishes between difficulties arising as a result of a sale or supply of alcoholic liquor in the afternoon, in the evening and on Sundays. The restriction order which the board is authorised to make must now relate to the particular part of the day in which the board considers that undue nuisance or threat to public order or safety occurs. Previously the only restriction order which could be made related to permitted hours in the evening and such an order could restrict to a time not earlier than 10 p.m. The same restriction now relates to an "evening restriction order" only. A board may also impose an "afternoon restriction order", reducing the permitted hours from 2.30 p.m. to 5 p.m. as they see fit, if they are satisfied that the sale or supply of alcoholic liquor in the afternoon is the cause of undue public nuisance, etc. Further, the board may impose a "Sunday restriction order" if satisfied that "the use of licensed premises" (more general than sale or supply of alcoholic liquor in afternoon and evening restrictions) is the cause of undue disturbance or public nuisance having regard to the "way of life" in the locality, a further distinction in respect of Sunday, charging the licensing board to consider the particular locality in which the premises are situated and the habits of those who live there. See note to s.65 in Allan and Chapman, *The Licensing (Scotland) Act 1976* (2nd ed.), p. 94.

Subs. (3)

Subs. (3) of s.65 of the 1976 Act is amended with the addition of a proviso that a restriction order can only be made in respect of premises which are the subject of a complaint. S.65(3) of the 1976 Act allows the Board to make a restriction order in relation to individual premises or in relation to a group of premises in respect of which the same type of licence is held. The subsection makes it clear, in respect of a group of premises, that only those premises specifically complained of may be the subject of a restriction order.

Children's certificates

Children's certificates

49.—(1) The holder of a public house licence or an hotel licence in respect of any premises or an applicant for the grant, provisional grant or renewal of such a licence may apply to the licensing board, in accordance with this section, for the grant of a children's certificate in respect of the premises or any part or parts of the premises specified in the application for the certificate.

(2) A licensing board may grant a certificate (in this section and section 50 of this Act referred to as a "children's certificate") in respect of any premises or, as the case may be, part or parts of any premises if it is satisfied—

(a) that the premises or, as the case may be, the part or parts of the premises constitute an environment in which it is suitable for children to be present; and

(b) that there will be available for sale or supply for consumption in the part of the premises in respect of which the certificate is to apply meals and beverages other than alcoholic liquor within the meaning of the principal Act.

(3) Where a children's certificate is in force in respect of any part of any premises, notwithstanding section 69 of the principal Act, and, subject to the provisions of this section, it shall be lawful for a person under 14 years of age accompanied by a person of not less then 18 years of age to be present in such part at any time when the premises are open to the public between eleven in the morning and eight in the evening for the purpose of the consumption of a meal sold or supplied on the premises.

(4) When granting a children's certificate, the licensing board may attach such conditions to the grant of the certificate, including conditions restricting the hours during which and days on which children may be present in any premises or part of premises to which the certificate relates, as appear to the board to be appropriate.

(5) There shall be displayed at all times in any premises or part of such premises to which a children's certificate applies a notice of the fact that a children's certificate has been granted in respect of such premises or part.

(6) Any person who is the holder of a licence in respect of any premises to which or part of which a children's certificate applies or any employee or agent of such a person who contravenes this section or any condition attached to a children's certificate shall be guilty of an offence and liable on summary conviction to a fine not exceeding level 3 on the standard scale.

(7) The following provisions of the principal Act shall apply as regards an offence under subsection (6) above—

(a) subsections (2) and (3) of section 67, as if an entry relating to that offence appeared respectively in columns 3 and 4 of Schedule 5 to that Act; and

(b) section 71.

(8) Schedule 5 to this Act shall have effect as regards the procedure to be followed for the purposes of an application for a children's certificate.

(9) A children's certificate shall be valid—

(a) where is is granted at the same time as the grant, provisional grant or renewal of a licence, for the period of the licence;

(b) where it is granted at any other time, until the end of the period for which the licence to which it relates has effect in pursuance of section 30 of the principal Act.

(10) Where a licence is transferred in pursuance of section 25 of the principal Act, any children's certificate in respect of the premises or any part of the premises to which the licence relates shall be transferred to the new licence holder subject to the same conditions as were applied to the original grant of the certificate.

(11) Expressions used in this section and section 50 of this Act and in the principal Act shall have the same meaning as in the principal Act.

DEFINITIONS
"bar": s.139(1) of the 1976 Act.

GENERAL NOTE
See also Sched. 1 to the 1976 Act.

This section introduces a Clayson recommendation and permits the holder of a public house or a hotel licence to apply for a children's certificate either in the context of an application for a grant or a provisional grant or renewal of the licence or in terms of the new Sched. 5 procedure in this Act in respect of a suitable part or all of the premises. The grant of a certificate is discretionary: the board needs to be satisfied that the premises or the part to which the application relates constitute an environment in which it is suitable for children to be present and that meals and non-alcoholic beverages will be available. Where a children's certificate is in force, despite the terms of s.69 of the 1976 Act, children under the age of 14 years are allowed to be present in the bar if accompanied by a person over 18 years during the hours from 11 a.m. to 8 p.m. or such others as may be specified by the board (see *infra*) for the consumption of a meal sold or supplied on the premises. S.69 of the 1976 Act prohibits persons under 14 to be in the bar of any premises during permitted hours, however, it does not apply where the premises have been considered suitable and granted a children's certificate. The board, in granting a children's certificate, may attach conditions as it sees fit, including conditions restricting the hours during which or days on which children may be allowed on the premises. A notice intimating that a children's certificate is in force must be displayed at all times in the part of the premises to which it relates. Contravention of this section or any condition attached to the certificate is a criminal offence, for which the licence-holder can be vicariously liable, and which can result in disqualification. S.71 of the 1976 Act provides the statutory defence of due diligence. For discussion of vicarious liability and due diligence see pp. 25 and 26 of the Introduction to Allan and Chapman, *The Licensing (Scotland) Act 1976* (2nd ed.). The procedure for applying for a children's certificate is set out in Sched. 5 to this Act. The certificate is valid if granted at the same time as the licence, for the period of the licence, or, if granted at any other time, until the end of the validity of the licence in terms of s.30 of the 1976 Act, *i.e.* the balance of its three years. The children's certificate, once granted, will transfer in respect of an application in terms of s.25 of the 1976 Act with the main licence, subject to the same conditions, if any, as attach to the original grant.

Suspension of children's certificate

50.—(1) Where a licensing board considers that the premises or part of the premises to which a children's certificate relates no longer constitute an environment in which it is suitable for children to be present they shall decide whether or not to hold a hearing for the purpose of determining whether to suspend the certificate.

(2) Where the licensing board decides to hold a hearing as mentioned in subsection (1) above—
  (a) the clerk of the board shall serve on the holder of the children's certificate, not less than 21 days before the hearing, a notice that the board proposes to hold a hearing, specifying the grounds upon which suspension of the certificate may be made;
  (b) the clerk of the board shall give notice of the hearing to the chief constable;
  (c) the chief constable may, not less than 7 days before the hearing, lodge notice with the clerk of the board that he wishes to be heard in support of suspension of the children's certificate specifying the grounds on which he seeks such suspension, and any such notice shall be intimated by the chief constable to the holder of the licence;
  (d) the board shall not order suspension of a children's certificate without hearing the holder thereof unless, after receiving due notice of the hearing, the holder fails to appear.

(3) The period of the suspension of a children's certificate under this section shall be a fixed period not exceeding one year or the unexpired portion of the duration of the certificate, whichever is the less, and the effect

of the suspension is that the certificate shall cease to have effect during the period of the suspension.

(4) Where

(a) a children's certificate has been suspended under this section, or further suspended under this subsection; and

(b) it appears to the licensing board that the grounds upon which the suspension or further suspension was made continue to obtain,

the licensing board may, not more than one month before the expiry of the period of the suspension or, as the case may be, further suspension, determine that the suspension shall be continued for a further period of not more than one year, and this section shall have effect as regards any such further suspension as it has for the purposes of an initial suspension.

GENERAL NOTE

This section allows the licensing board to decide whether or not to hold a hearing to consider the suspension of a children's certificate when the premises to which the certificate relates no longer constitute an environment suitable for children. The decision to hold a hearing does not need to be made in respect of a complaint, and the terms of the section are similar to the provisions of s.32 of the 1976 Act which gives a licensing board power to make a closure order in respect of premises it considers no longer suitable or convenient for the sale of alcoholic liquor. The procedure for intimation of the hearing is also similar to the terms of s.32 of the 1976 Act, and similarly requires notice to be given to the Chief Constable. Such notice by the Clerk to the Chief Constable should allow the Chief Constable sufficient time to intimate that he wishes to be heard not less than seven days before the hearing. The Chief Constable may give notice not less than seven days before the hearing that he wishes to be heard in support of the suspension and he must specify the grounds on which he seeks suspension. The Chief Constable must intimate that notice, specifying the grounds, to the licence-holder before the hearing. If the licence-holder fails to appear at the hearing, the licensing board may suspend the certificate, but if the licence-holder appears, he must be given the opportunity of being heard. The period of suspension must be fixed and must not exceed one year or the unexpired portion of the duration of the certificate, whichever is less; the effect of suspension is that the certificate ceases to have effect (for discussion of "cease to have effect" see *Argyll Arms (McManus)* v. *Lorn,* Mid-Argyll, Kintyre and Islay Divisional Licensing Board, 1988 S.L.T. 290). During the suspension, if the circumstances which led to suspension continue, the licensing board may, not more than one month before the expiry of the suspension, determine that the suspension continue, apparently without need for a further hearing, although natural justice would require a board to give a licence-holder an opportunity to make representations to the board before a decision is made on continuation of the suspension. The further period of suspension must not exceed one year.

Transfer of licences

Transfer of licences

51.—(1) In section 5 of the principal Act (arrangements for discharge of functions by licensing boards), at the end of subsection (2) there shall be added the following paragraph—

"(m) confirming, under section 25(4) of this Act, the transfer of a licence transferred by virtue of subsections (2) or (3) of that section."

(2) In subsection (1) of section 25 of that Act (transfer of licences)—

(a) after "behalf," there shall be inserted "temporarily"; and

(b) after "or" there shall be inserted the words "to a new or existing."

(3) After subsection (1) of that section there shall be added the following subsection—

"(1A) Subject to subsection (1C) below, a temporary transfer made under subsection (1) above shall have effect until the appropriate meeting of the licensing board which shall be—

(a) the next meeting of the board; or

(b) in the case of a temporary transfer made within the period of six weeks before the first day of the next meeting of the board, the next following meeting of the board.

(1B) At an appropriate meeting of the licensing board, within the meaning of subsection (1A) above, and on an application being made for the permanent transfer of the licence, the board shall make a decision on the permanent transfer of the licence.

(1C) If the licensing board refuses to make a permanent transfer of a licence under subsection (1B) above, the person to whom the licence had been transferred temporarily may appeal to the sheriff against that refusal and the licence shall have effect until the time within which an appeal may be made has elapsed or, if an appeal has been lodged, until the appeal has been abandoned or determined."

(4) For subsection (4) of that section there shall be substituted the following subsections—

"(4) A licence transferred by virtue of subsection (2) or (3) above shall have effect until the next meeting of the licensing board, which, on an application for confirmation of the transfer of the licence, shall consider whether it is satisfied that the person to whom the licence has been transferred is a fit and proper person to be the holder of a licence and—

(a) if it is so satisfied, it shall confirm the transfer of the licence; and;

(b) if it is not so satisfied, it shall refuse to confirm the transfer.

(4A) In considering the fitness of the person to whom the licence has been transferred, the licensing board may have regard to any misconduct on his part, whether or not constituting a breach of this Act or any byelaw made thereunder, which in its opinion has a bearing on his fitness to hold a licence.

(4B) If the transfer of a licence has been confirmed under subsection (4) above, the licence shall have effect, in accordance with subsections (4) and (5) of section 30 of this Act, until the quarterly meeting of the licensing board three years after the meeting at which the licence was originally granted or renewed by a licensing board.

(4C) If a licensing board refuses to confirm the transfer of a licence under subsection (4) above, the person to whom the licence had been transferred may appeal to the sheriff against that refusal and the licence shall have effect until the time within which an appeal may be made has elapsed or, if an appeal has been lodged, until the appeal has been abandoned or determined."

(5) In section 64 of that Act (occasional and regular extensions of permitted hours), after subsection (3) there shall be inserted the following subsection—

"(3A) Where a licence has been transferred by virtue of section 25 of this Act and an application under subsection (1) above has been granted under subsection (2) or (3) above to the previous holder of the licence, the reference in subsections (2) and (3) above to the person whose application has been granted shall include a reference to the person to whom the licence has been transferred."

(6) For subsection (7) of that section there shall be substituted the following subsection—

"(7) References in this Act to the permanent transfer of a licence shall be construed as references to the transfer of a licence by virtue of subsection (1B) above."

GENERAL NOTE

Transfer of licences

This section amends s.25 of the 1976 Act to provide for an initial temporary transfer of the licence, which may be applied for at any time between board meetings. Such a temporary transfer will be effected administratively under the delegated powers given by s.5(1) of the 1976 Act. A temporary transfer then needs to be confirmed by the licensing board at a subsequent meeting, upon an application being made to the board for a permanent transfer. The section makes consequential amendments to other sections of the 1976 Act. This amendment remedies the lacuna in s.25, where the permanent transfer of a licence could only be effected at a quarterly board meeting, which put purchasers or new tenants in difficulty if their date of entry was at a date between board meetings. The amendment appears to preclude an application for a permanent transfer being made, without there first having been an application for a temporary transfer. This has implications in contracts for the sale of licensed premises; see *infra*.

Subs. (5) amends s.64 of the 1976 Act, so that grants of occasional and regular extensions automatically go with the temporary or permanent transfer of the licence, which clarifies the conflicting decisions in *Archyield* v. *City of Glasgow District Licensing Board* 1987 S.L.T. 547 and *CRS Leisure* v. *Dumbarton District Licensing Board* 1990 S.L.T. 200 and corrects an obvious injustice if *Archyield* was correctly decided.

Purchase and sale of licensed premises
Under the previous statutory provisions it was suggested (see Allan and Chapman, *The Licensing (Scotland) Act 1976* (2nd ed.), p. 58) that offers should be conditional on the licences being permanently transferred by the licensing board. A temporary transfer, which appears to be a mandatory preliminary to a permanent transfer, makes difficulties for such a condition, because the new acquirer has to take entry, before or at the time of a temporary transfer. As the decision on whether or not the temporary transfer will be made permanent might not be made for four and a half months after the temporary transfer, if that was made less than six weeks from the next board (new subs. (1A)(b)) it might be difficult, at that stage, to undo a contract.

Any seller would be wise to insist that the buyer, who has to satisfy the board on applying for a permanent transfer under the terms of s.17(1)(a) of the 1976 Act, that he is a fit and proper person to hold a licence, takes the risk of failing to get a permanent transfer after taking entry upon a temporary transfer. This may well make for difficulties with lenders, who may be unwilling to release funds until a temporary transfer has been made permanent. It may be possible to devise a contract whereby the intended purchaser takes entry as under a licence to occupy, upon which he obtains a temporary transfer, with the contract being purified, when the permanent transfer is granted. Such a scheme would have dangers for the seller, who would be bound to cede occupation, at least in part, to the intended purchaser. As the issue of a temporary transfer is an administrative act under the delegated powers, careful liaison will be required with the Clerk of the Board, to ensure that the temporary transfer takes place at the same date as entry. See "Licensing Nightmare" 1990 S.L.T. (News) 374 and "Licensing Transfers" 1991 S.L.T. (News) 58.

Subs. (2)
This subsection amends s.25(1) of the 1976 Act to the effect that the initial transfer is a temporary transfer. Subs. (2)(b), by the insertion of "to a new or existing" occupant, corrects a difficulty focused upon in *Chief Constable of Tayside* v. *Angus District Licensing Board* 1980 S.L.T. (Sh. Ct.) 31, which held that in a reorganisation of responsibility between a husband and wife the wife could not take a transfer, as "new" qualified both tenant and occupant and she was neither a new tenant nor a new occupant.

Subs. (3)
This subsection inserts new subss. (1A), (1B) and (1C) to s.25 of the 1976 Act. Subs. (1A) provides that the temporary transfer granted under s.25(1) as amended is only effective "until the appropriate meeting" of the board, which is either (a) the next meeting of the board or (b) if the temporary transfer was made within the period of six weeks before the first day of the next meeting, to the next following meeting of the board. Subs. (1B) requires the temporary transferee to make an application in terms of s.10 of the 1976 Act to the appropriate board meeting for a permanent transfer. At the appropriate meeting, the board are required to make a decision on the application for a permanent transfer in terms of s.17(1)(a) of the 1979 Act. Subs. (1C) provides that where a board refuse a permanent transfer, the person to whom the temporary transfer has been made may appeal to the sheriff (under s.39 of the 1976 Act) against that refusal and that the licence will continue in force until the time for an appeal has lapsed or, if an appeal has been lodged, it has been abandoned or determined.

Subs. (4)
This subsection substitutes new subss. (4), (4A), (4B), and (4C) for subs. (4), making new provisions for the former temporary transfers, which could be effected by executors, etc. of deceased persons and trustees, etc. of persons who had become bankrupt or incapable during the currency of the licence. New subs. (4) provides that the temporary transfer under subss. (2) and (3) shall have effect until the next board meeting (and not the appropriate board meeting as in a temporary transfer under subs. (1)) and spells out the requirement, which was considered to be implied in the former subs. (4), that the board, on an application for confirmation of the temporary transfer, shall consider whether it is satisfied that the person to whom the licence has

been transferred is a fit and proper person to be the holder of the licence and, if so satisfied, (a) shall confirm it, or (b) if not so satisfied, shall refuse to confirm the transfer. In considering whether a transferee is a "fit and proper person" the board are to take account of the factors set out in subs. (4B), which echoes s.17(3) of the 1976 Act. Subs. 4(C) provides for an appeal to the sheriff against a refusal to confirm the temporary transfer and that the licence shall continue in force until the time for an appeal has lapsed, or, if an appeal has been lodged, it has been abandoned or determined.

Subss. (5) and (6)
These subsections provide that grants of occasional or regular extensions under s.64 of the 1976 Act follow the transfer automatically, which overrules the decision in *Archyield* v. *City of Glasgow District Licensing Board* 1987 S.L.T. 547 that a grant of a regular extension fell on the transfer of a licence under s.25. The correctness of that decision was questioned in *CRS Leisure* v. *Dumbarton District Licensing Board* 1990 S.L.T. 200.

Wholesale selling of alcoholic liquor

Wholesale selling of alcoholic liquor

52.—(1) After section 90 of the principal Act there shall be inserted the following section—

"**Wholesale selling of alcoholic liquor**
90A.—(1) A wholesaler or his employee or agent who barters, sells, or exposes or offers for sale alcoholic liquor shall be guilty of an offence unless—
(a) he does so from premises which are used exclusively for whole-sale trading (whether solely of alcoholic liquor or not); or
(b) he does so from licensed premises, a licensed canteen or a registered club during the hours in respect of which it is lawful to sell alcohol by retail from or in these premises, that canteen or that club.
(2) A wholesaler or his employee or agent who sells alcoholic liquor to a person under 18 shall be guilty of an offence.
(3) A wholesaler or his employee or agent who causes or permits a person under 18 to sell alcoholic liquor without that sale having been specifically approved by a person of or over 18 shall be guilty of an offence.
(4) Section 67 of this Act (penalties for offences) shall apply in respect of offences under this section as if references in that section to a licence-holder were references to a wholesaler.
(5) Section 71 of this Act (defence of due diligence) shall apply to any person charged with an offence under this section as if the reference in that section to a licence-holder were a reference to a wholesaler.
(6) In this section—
"licence-holder" includes the holder of a licence under Part III of this Act; and
"wholesale" and "wholesaler," insofar as they relate to the sale of alcoholic liquor, have the meaning given in section 4(1) of the Alcoholic Liquor Duties Act 1979 in relation to dealing in alcoholic liquor."

(2) In Schedule 5 to that Act, after the entry relating to section 90(c) there shall be inserted—

"Section 90A(1)	Dealing wholesale other than from permitted premises	Yes — Level 5 on the standard scale.
Section 90A(2)	Wholesaler selling liquor to person under 18	Yes — level 3 on the standard scale.
Section 90A(3)	Wholesaler permitting person under 18 to sell alcohol without approval	Yes — level 1 on the standard scale."

DEFINITIONS
"licensed canteen": s.139(1) of the 1976 Act.
"licensed premises": s.139(1) of the 1976 Act.
"registered club": s.139(1) of the 1976 Act.

GENERAL NOTE
This section was introduced to remedy the anomaly which arose from the repeal by the
Finance Act 1981 of the excise licence requirements for wholesalers of alcohol and s.94 of the
1976 Act, which had the effect that wholesalers of alcohol were no longer subject to any
controls. Concern had been expressed that anyone could set up as a "wholesaler" and, provided
that they sold alcoholic liquor in wholesale quantities, they could sell from any premises to any
age group: see *Hansard*, H.C. Vol. 177, col. 1143.
The section introduces a new s.90A to the 1976 Act, which makes it an offence for a
wholesaler or his employee or agent to barter, sell or expose or offer for sale alcoholic liquor
unless he does so from (a) premises which are used exclusively for wholesale trading, whether
solely of alcoholic liquor or not, or (b) he does so from licensed premises, a licensed canteen or
registered club during the hours in which it is lawful to sell alcohol in those premises. The
section also makes it an offence for a wholesaler to sell alcohol to a person under the age of 18 or
for a person under the age of 18 to sell alcohol unless the sale is specifically approved. The
defence of "due diligence" is made available by subs. (5).

Subs. (1)
This subsection adds a new s.90A to the 1976 Act which makes the wholesaler or his
employee or agent guilty of an offence if they barter, sell, or expose or offer for sale alcoholic
liquor unless (a) they do so from premises which are exclusively used for wholesale trading
(whether solely of alcoholic liquor or not), or (b) they do so from licensed premises, a licensed
canteen or a registered club during the hours in respect of which it is lawful to sell alcohol by
retail from those premises. For a general discussion of the "vicarious liability" of the licence-
holder in statutory crimes, with reference to the 1976 Act, see Introduction to Allan and
Chapman, *The Licensing (Scotland) Act 1976* (2nd ed.), p. 25, and G.H. Gordon, *Criminal
Law of Scotland* (2nd ed.), p. 295 *et seq.*, and in relation to vicarious liability for a "sale" see
p. 299. In *British Car Auctions* v. *Wright* [1972] 1 W.L.R. 1519 (*q.v.*, and the cases there cited) a
distinction was drawn between an "offer to sell", which was an offence, and an "invitation to
treat", which was not an offence. A flick-knife exposed in a shop window with a price tag on it
was not "an offer to sell", but an "invitation to treat" and accordingly not an offence: *Fisher* v.
Bell [1961] 1 Q.B. 394.

New subs. (2)
The sale by the wholesaler or his employee or agent of alcoholic liquor to a person under the
age of 18 is an offence. The prosecution will need to prove that the person is under the age of 18
by corroborated evidence: *Lockwood* v. *Walker* 1909 2 S.L.T. 400. Evidence of impression that
a person is under 18 is not corroboration of a young person's admission of their age: *Paton* v.
Wilson, 1988 S.L.T. 634.

New subs. (3)
The subsection makes provisions similar to those of the new s.97A apply to wholesalers, so
that a sale by a person under the age of 18 years, unless specifically approved, is an offence: see
note to s.54 (*infra*).

New subs. (4)
This subsection makes wholesalers liable to the same penalties which apply to any licence-
holder under the 1976 Act. See note to s.67 in Allan and Chapman, *The Licensing (Scotland)
Act 1976* (2nd ed.), p. 96.

New subs. (5)
This subsection provides that s.71 of the 1976 Act shall apply in respect of offences under this
section. The defence of "due diligence" is available to a person accused under this section. For a
general discussion of that defence, see Allan and Chapman, *The Licensing (Scotland) Act 1976*
(2nd ed.), Introduction, p. 26. The defence need only be proved on a balance of probabilities:
H.M.A. v. *Mitchell*, 1951 J.C. 53; *Neish* v. *Stevenson*, 1969 S.L.T. 229.

New subs. (6)
By making "licence-holder" include the holder of a licence under Pt. III of the 1976 Act, the

section expands the definition of licence-holder given in s.139(1) to include the holder of a licence for a Seamen's Canteen to take account of permitted sales from licensed canteens under subs. (1)(b).

Wholesale. This is defined by ss.4(1) and 65(8) of the Alcoholic Liquor Duties Act 1979 (c.4) in the terms: "dealing wholesale means the sale at any one time to any one person of quantities not less than the following, namely—(a) in the case of spirits, wine or made-wine, 2 gallons or 1 case; or (b) in the case of beer, 4½ gallons or 2 cases". Words including "case", "spirits", "wine", "made-wine" and "beer" are defined by ss.1 and 4 of the 1979 Act.

Subs. (2)

This subsection amends Sched. 5 to the 1976 Act to provide that a penalty of level 5 applies to an offence under subs. (1), level 3 applies to an offence under subs. (2) and level 1 to an offence under subs. (3).

Observations by Chief Constable

Observations by chief constable in relation to applications

53.—(1) After section 16 of the principal Act (objections in relation to applications), there shall be inserted the following section—

"Observations by chief constable in relation to applications

16A.—(1) Without prejudice to section 16 of this Act, in considering an application—

(a) for the grant (including the provisional grant), renewal or permanent transfer of a licence;

(b) the regular extension of permitted hours under section 64 of this Act; or

(c) the grant of a children's certificate under section 49 of the Law Reform (Miscellaneous Provisions) (Scotland) Act 1990,

a licensing board shall have regard to any observations on the application submitted by the chief constable in accordance with the following provisions of this section.

(2) Where the chief constable intends to submit observations in relation to any application, he shall, not later than seven days before the meeting of the licensing board at which the application is to be considered—

(a) lodge with the clerk of the board a written notice of his observations; and

(b) intimate his observations to the applicant in the manner provided by subsection (3) below,

and observations shall not be entertained by the licensing board unless it is proved or admitted that such observations were intimated to the applicant as aforesaid.

(3) Observations shall, for the purposes of paragraph (b) of subsection (2) above, be intimated to the applicant—

(a) by delivering to him a copy of the observations lodged with the licensing board under paragraph (a) of that subsection; or

(b) by sending him a copy of the said observations by registered post or by recorded delivery in a letter addressed to him at his proper address; or

(c) by leaving a copy of the said observations for him at his proper address;

and, for the purposes of paragraphs (b) and (c) of this subsection, the proper address of an applicant shall be as provided for in subsection (3) of section 16 of this Act.

(4) Notwithstanding anything in the foregoing provisions of this section, it shall be competent for the licensing board to entertain observations from the chief constable, lodged at any time before the hearing of an application, if the board is satisfied that there is sufficient reason why due notice and intimation of the observations could

not be given, and in such a case the chief constable shall cause his observations to be intimated to the applicant before the hearing.

(5) The licensing board shall have regard to any observations submitted by the chief constable in accordance with this section whether or not they are relevant to one or more grounds on which, by virtue of section 17 of this Act, an application may be refused."

(2) In section 31 of that Act (suspension of licences), after subsection (5) there shall be inserted the following subsection—

"(5A) Where the licensing board decides to hold a hearing as mentioned in subsection (4) above in respect of a complaint under this section which was made by a person or body other than the chief constable, the chief constable may, not less than 7 days before the hearing, lodge with the clerk of the board observations in respect of the proposed suspension of the licence, and any such observations shall be intimated by the chief constable to the holder of the licence."

GENERAL NOTE

This section inserts a new s.16A to the 1976 Act and amends s.31 of that Act (suspension of licences). S.16A provides that licensing boards are to have regard to any observations (as distinct from objections made under s.16 of the 1976 Act) made by the Chief Constable and provides for the procedure for lodging and intimation of such observations by the Chief Constable. It had become commonplace for Chief Constables to make "observations" upon applications at board meetings, which were said not to amount to an objection. The board would take those observations into account, while the applicant or his agent might have been prejudiced by the lack of notice. The requirement for this section arose from the decision in *Centralbite* v. *Kincardine and Deeside District Licensing Board*, 1990 S.L.T. 231, where the Lord Ordinary held that an "observation" by the Chief Constable amounted to an objection and that as it had not been intimated in terms of s.16 it could not be taken into account.

Subs. (1)

This subsection inserts the new s.16A, which provides (16A(1)) that a licensing board shall have regard to any observations made by the Chief Constable in relation to an application made to the board for (a) the grant (including the provisional grant), renewal or permanent transfer of a licence; (b) the regular extension of permitted hours (but not an application for an occasional extension); or (c) the grant of a children's certificate.

New subss. (2) and (3)

The terms of these subsections, which are identical to the provisions on lodging and intimation in s.16(2) and (3) of the 1976 Act, provide that observations have to be lodged with the Clerk and intimated to the applicant in terms of subs. (3), not later than seven days before the board meeting. "Not later than" means at least seven clear days before the meeting and would exclude the day of the notice and the day on which the board met: see *Main* v. *City of Glasgow District Licensing Board*, 1987 S.L.T. 305.

New subs. (4)

Subs. (4), which is in the same terms as s.16(4) of the 1976 Act, gives the board a limited discretion to dispense with timeous lodging and intimation, provided that the observations are in fact intimated before the hearing. See in general the notes to s.16 in Allan and Chapman, *The Licensing (Scotland) Act 1976* (2nd ed.), p. 49.

New subs. (5)

This subsection provides that the board are to have regard to the observations, whether or not they are relevant to one of the grounds on which the application may be refused under s.17 of the 1976 Act. This provision is bound to lead to difficulty in that, if the board take into account an observation which is not relevant to one of the grounds upon which they may refuse the licence, and refuse the application on that ground, then it might be said that they have reached their decision on irrelevant grounds and so it should be reduced. It is suggested that such observations, which are not relevant to a ground of refusal, might be relevant in considering what conditions might be attached to a licence, when the application is granted.

Subs. (2)

This subsection inserts a new subsection (5)(A) to s.31 of the 1976 Act. The new subsection allows the Chief Constable, where he is not the complainant under s.31(4) seeking the suspension of the licence, to make observations in respect of the proposed suspension, for consideration by the board. The observations have to be lodged not less than seven days before the hearing with the Clerk of the board. Although "not later than" is not used, the effect of the wording is the same (see *supra*). Such observations have to be intimated to the holder of the licence. No timetable is given for intimation to the holder of the licence, but the intimation would have to be before the hearing (see note to subs. (1), *supra*).

Supervision of sales by persons over 18

Supervision of sales of liquor in off-sale premises by persons 18 or over

54.—(1) After section 97 of the principal Act there shall be inserted the following section—

> **"Supervision of sales of liquor in off-sale premises**
> 97A. A holder of a licence in respect of—
> (a) any off-sale premises; or
> (b) the off-sale part of any other premises,
> or any employee or agent of his, who causes or permits a person under 18 to sell on these premises alcoholic liquor without that sale having been specifically approved by the licence holder or by a person of or over 18 acting on his behalf shall be guilty of an offence."

(2) In section 71 of that Act (defence of due diligence), for the words "or 70" there shall be substituted the words ", 70 or 97A."

(3) In Schedule 5 to that Act, after the entry relating to section 97(4) there shall be inserted—

"Section 97A	Permitting person under 18 to sell alcohol without approval	Yes	Yes	level 3 on the standard scale."

DEFINITIONS

"alcoholic liquor": s.139(1).
"off-sale premises": s.139(1).

GENERAL NOTE

This section makes provision for the sale of alcoholic liquor in off-sale premises to be supervised by the licence-holder or a person over the age of 18 years acting on his behalf, by making it an offence for a licence-holder, his employee or agent to cause or permit the sale of alcoholic liquor by a person under the age of 18 years, without the sale having been specifically approved by the licence-holder or a person over the age of 18 years acting on his behalf. The provision is a watered-down version of the Licensing Amendment (Scotland) Bill introduced in 1989. The section has been introduced upon a promise that if the Bill was dropped it would be included in this Act. There was public concern that persons under the legal age to buy alcohol were able to buy it without difficulty in off-sale premises from other under-18-year-olds working in the shop, particularly in a general store, with an off-sales part, which was not properly supervised.

Subs. (1)

This subsection introduces the new s.97A to the 1976 Act, which makes it an offence for the holder of a licence in respect of any off-sale premises or off-sale part of a premises, or any employee or agent of his to cause or permit a person under the age of 18 years to sell alcoholic liquor without that sale having been specifically approved by the licence-holder or by a person of or over 18 acting on his behalf. For a general discussion of the "vicarious liability" of the licence-holder in statutory crimes, with reference to the 1976 Act, see Allan and Chapman, *The Licensing (Scotland) Act 1976* (2nd ed.), p. 25, and G.H. Gordon, *Criminal Law of Scotland* (2nd ed.), p. 295 *et seq*. For a discussion of the meaning of "causes or permits" in statutory offences, see Gordon, *op. cit.*, p. 311 *et seq*. The prosecution will need to prove that the person is under the age of 18 by corroborated evidence: *Lockwood* v. *Walker*, 1909 2 S.L.T. 400. Evidence of impression that a person is under 18 is not corroboration of a young person's admission of their age; *Paton* v. *Wilson*, 1988 S.L.T. 634.

Subs. (2)

By adding a reference to s.97A to s.71 of the 1976 Act, the section provides that the defence of "due diligence" is available. For a general discussion of that defence, see Allan and Chapman, *The Licensing (Scotland) Act 1976* (2nd ed.), Introduction, p. 26. The defence need only be proved on a balance of probabilities: *H.M.A.* v. *Mitchell*, 1951 J.C. 53; *Neish* v. *Stevenson*, 1969 S.L.T. 229.

Subs. (3)
   This subsection provides that the fine is level 3.

Presumption as to contents of containers

Presumption as to contents of containers

   55.—(1) In section 127 of the principal Act (presumptions as to the contents of containers) for subsections (2) to (6) there shall be substituted the following subsections—
   "(2) Any liquid found in a container (sealed or open) shall, subject to the provisions of this section, be presumed to conform to the description of the liquid on the container.
   (3) An open container which is found to contain—
      (a) no liquid; or
      (b) insufficient liquid to permit analysis,
but which when sold or supplied to a person was sealed shall, subject to the provisions of this section, be presumed to have contained at the time of the sale or supply liquid which conformed to the description of the liquid on the container.
   (4) Subject to subsection (5) below, in any trial of a person for an offence under this Act, he may rebut the presumption mentioned in subsection (2) or (3) above by showing that, at the time of the sale or supply, the liquid in the container did not conform to the description of the liquid on the container.
   (5) A person shall not be entitled to lead evidence for the purpose of rebutting a presumption as mentioned in subsection (4) above unless, not less than 7 days before the date of the trial, he has given notice to the prosecutor of his intention to do so."
   (2) Nothing in this section shall apply to the prosecution of any person for an offence committed before the commencement of this section.

GENERAL NOTE
   This section amends the law set out in s.127 of the 1976 Act in relation to the presumption that any liquid found in a container (sealed or open) shall "be presumed to conform to the description of the liquid on the container". The principal effects of the amendment are (1) to allow the presumption to apply to open containers containing no liquid or insufficient liquid to permit analysis, which the prosecution can prove were sold or supplied sealed; (2) to remove the requirement that the prosecution had to give 14 days' notice that they intended to rely on the presumption, which will now apply automatically in any relevant prosecution; and (3) to delete the provision regarding service of notices under this section by recorded delivery and the presumptions arising therefrom as to date of intimation. The defence still have to give at least seven days' notice before the trial, that they intend to rebut the presumption. The defence will have to prove that they gave seven clear days' notice, excluding the day of intimation of the notice and the day of the trial; see note to s.53, *supra*. The rebuttal of the presumption will have to be proved on a balance of probabilities. For a general discussion regarding this presumption see note to s.127 in Allan and Chapman, *The Licensing (Scotland) Act 1976* (2nd ed.), p. 138.

Subs. (2)
   This subsection provides that the amended law on presumptions does not apply retrospectively to an offence committed before the commencement of the section, even if the trial commences after the section comes into force.

PART IV

MISCELLANEOUS REFORMS

Evidence by children in criminal trials

Evidence of children through television link in criminal proceedings

56.—(1) Subject to subsections (2) and (3) below, where a child has been cited to give evidence in a trial, the court may, on an application being made to it, authorise the giving of evidence by the child by means of a live television link.

(2) The court may grant an application under subsection (1) above only on cause shown having regard in particular to—

    (a) the possible effect on the child if required to give evidence, no such application having been granted; and

    (b) whether it is likely that the child would be better able to give evidence if such application were granted.

(3) In considering whether to grant an application under subsection (1) above, the court may take into account, where appropriate, any of the following—

    (a) the age and maturity of the child;

    (b) the nature of the alleged offence;

    (c) the nature of the evidence which the child is likely to be called on to give; and

    (d) the relationship, if any, between the child and the accused.

GENERAL NOTE

Ss.56–60 implement some of the recommendations of the Scottish Law Commission in its *Report on the Evidence of Children and Other Potentially Vulnerable Witnesses* (Scot. Law. Comm. No. 125). In particular, these provisions are only concerned with evidence by children in criminal trials. In Scots law a child of any age is a competent witness in a criminal trial but the presiding judge must satisfy himself that a child of tender years knows the difference between telling the truth and telling lies and, if the judge is so satisfied, he must admonish the child to tell the truth: see *Rees* v. *Lowe*, High Court of Justiciary, November 7, 1989. However, particularly where the child has been the victim of an offence, a child may find the appearance in court distressing. These provisions have therefore been introduced to minimalise such distress while at the same time ensuring fairness to the accused. It should be stressed that these provisions are *additional* to existing conventional steps which can be taken to reduce the trauma for the child of an appearance in court, for example, the removal of wigs and gowns, positioning the child in the well of the court rather than the witness box, allowing the child to be supported by a relative or adult or closing the court to persons not directly involved in the trial. These matters are left to the discretion of the presiding judge in the light of a memorandum of guidance issued by the Lord Justice General.

Subs. (1)

    Child. A child is a person under the age of 16: s.59.

    Trial. Trial means a trial under solemn or under summary procedure: s.59. The provision is restricted to the citation of the child as a witness in a criminal trial.

    The court. The court is the High Court of Judiciary or the sheriff court: s.59.

    May, on an application being made to it, authorise. There must be an application to the court before the provision operates: it would appear that the court cannot make the authorisation *ex proprio motu*. Where an application has been made, the court has discretion whether or not to make the authorisation.

    By means of a live television link. It is envisaged that the child will give evidence by means of a live closed circuit television system. The child will give evidence in a room near the courtroom, accompanied by a relative or other supporting adult. There is no need for camera operators or technicians to be present, as the camera is concealed in an ordinary domestic set, on which appears the person in court who is speaking to the child. In the court, there are three different kinds of monitor: for the jury, the accused and the public there are large screens which simply show the face of the child: for counsel, small monitors which, on split screens, show the child and the person questioning the child; for the judge, a monitor which shows not only what can be seen by counsel but also a view of the whole room where the child is. The admission as evidence of video recordings of earlier interviews with the child has been rejected on the ground that the absence of an opportunity to cross-examine the child would cause great prejudice to the accused.

Subs. (2)
   Only on cause shown. The court is empowered to grant an application only on cause shown. While it is unusual for a statute to give guidance on how the court should exercise a statutory discretion, this subsection provides that the court should have regard in particular to (a) the possible effect on the child of giving evidence if the application is *not* granted and (b) whether the child would be better able to give evidence if the application is granted.

Subs. (3)
   In addition to the matters in subs. (2), this subsection provides four further factors which the court may take into consideration in determining whether or not cause has been shown, *viz.* the age and maturity of the child; the nature of the alleged offence; the nature of the evidence which the child is likely to be called upon to give; and the relationship between the child and the accused. These factors need only be taken into account where appropriate. These (and those in subs. (2)) are, of course, not intended to be exhaustive and the judge can have regard to any factor which appears relevant in a particular case.

Transfer of cases in which child's evidence is to be given through television link

57.—(1) Where a sheriff to whom an application has been made under section 56 of this Act would have granted the application but for the lack of accommodation or equipment necessary to achieve the purpose of the application, he may by order transfer the case to any sheriff court which has such accommodation and equipment available, being a sheriff court in the same sheriffdom.

(2) The sheriff court to which a case is transferred under this section shall be deemed to have granted an application under that section in relation to the case.

GENERAL NOTE
   It is not envisaged that closed circuit television systems will be installed in every sheriff court. This section provides that where a sheriff would have granted an application under s.56 but does not have the necessary equipment in his court, he may by order transfer the case to another sheriff court within the same sheriffdom where such equipment has been installed. The sheriff court to which a case has been transferred shall be deemed to have granted the application under s.56 in relation to the case.

Identification of accused by child

58. Where a court has, or is deemed to have, granted an application made under section 56 of this Act in relation to a child cited to give evidence in a trial, and the child gives evidence that he recalls having identified, prior to the trial, a person alleged to have committed an offence, the evidence of a third party as to the identification of that person by the child prior to the trial shall be admissible as evidence as to such identification.

GENERAL NOTE
   The identification by a witness of the accused as the perpetrator of an offence is an essential matter which the prosecution requires to establish in the course of a trial. This is still necessary even though a previous identification parade has taken place. The obligation to look at and point to the accused may be upsetting for a witness, in particular a child witness who has been the victim of the alleged offence. This provision attempts to limit the incidence of such distress, by rendering admissible evidence of a third party that the child had identified the accused prior to the trial, thus eliminating the need for the child to identify the accused at the trial. However, before the section is applicable, the court must have granted an application under s.56, *i.e.* there must be cause shown under s.56(2) and (3). At the pre-trial identification, the accused will have the right to legal representation: if his representative wishes to challenge the identification at the trial he is free to do so and can examine the child on the identification procedures using the live closed circuit television technique.

Court. This means the High Court of Justiciary or the sheriff court: s.59.
Child. This means a person under the age of 16: s.59.
Trial. This means a trial under solemn or summary procedure: s.59.

Interpretation of sections 56, 57 and 58

59. In sections 56, 57 and 58 of this Act, unless the contrary intention appears—
"child" means a person under the age of 16 years;
"court" means the High Court of Justiciary or the sheriff court; and
"trial" means a trial under solemn or under summary procedure.

GENERAL NOTE
See notes to ss.56 and 58. The reference to s.57 appears otiose.

Sheriff court jurisdiction

Criminal jurisdiction of sheriff court

60. The following subsection shall be inserted at the end of each of sections 3 and 288 of the Criminal Procedure (Scotland) Act 1975 to form subsection (4) and subsection (5) respectively of these sections—
"( ) Where an offence is alleged to have been committed in one district in a sheriffdom, it shall be competent to try that offence in a sheriff court in any other district in that sheriffdom."

GENERAL NOTE
A sheriff has jurisdiction in all districts of the sheriffdom for which he is appointed: s.7 of the Sheriff Courts (Scotland) Act 1971. However, it does not necessarily follow that a sheriff sitting in one sheriff court district can competently try a crime which has been committed in another sheriff court district, even although it is in the same sheriffdom: see *Kilbane* v. *HMA*, 1989 S.C.C.R. 313; *cf.* Renton & Brown, *Criminal Procedure* (5th ed.), paras. 1–30. For the avoidance of doubt, this provision amends ss.3 and 288 of the Criminal Procedure (Scotland) Act 1975 to ensure that it is competent for an offence committed in one district of a sheriffdom to be tried in a sheriff court in any other district in that sheriffdom. While general in its effect, this provision is important in the context of a transfer of a case under s.57.

Treatment of offenders

Probation and community service orders and supervision and care of persons on probation or released from prison etc.

61.—(1) Sections 183 and 384 of the Criminal Procedure (Scotland) Act 1975 (probation) shall be amended as follows—
(a) at the beginning of subsection (1) of each section there shall be inserted "Subject to subsection (1A) below,";
(b) after subsection (1) of each section there shall be inserted the following subsection—
"(1A) A court shall not make a probation order under subsection (1) above unless it is satisfied that suitable arrangements for the supervision of the offender can be made by the local authority in whose area he resides or is to reside."; and
(c) in subsection (4) of each section—
(i) for the words "necessary for" there shall be substituted "conducive to"; and
(ii) for the word "for" in the second place where it occurs there shall be substituted "to."
(2) In subsection (1) of each of sections 186 and 387 of that Act (failure to comply with probation order)—
(a) after the word "from" there shall be inserted "(a)"; and
(b) after the word "probationer" where it first occurs there shall be inserted—
"(b) the director of social work of the local authority whose officer is supervising the probationer; or
(c) an officer appointed by the director of social work to act on his behalf for the purposes of this subsection,".

(3) In section 1(1) of the Community Service by Offenders (Scotland) Act 1978 (community service orders), for the words "dealing with him in any other way" there shall be substituted "imposing on him a sentence of, or including, imprisonment or any other form of detention."

(4) In section 27 of the Social Work (Scotland) Act 1968 (supervision and care of persons on probation or released from prison etc)—

(a) at the end of subsection (1) there shall be added—

"; and

    (c) the provision of advice, guidance and assistance for persons in their area who, within 12 months of their release from prison or any other form of detention, request such advice, guidance or assistance."; and

(b) after paragraph (a) of subsection (3) there shall be inserted the following paragraph—

"(aa) the matters to be included in such a report;".

(5) In section 27A of that Act (grants in respect of community service facilities)—

(a) at the beginning there shall be inserted "(1)"; and

(b) for the words from "for the purposes" to the end there shall be substituted—

"(a) for the purposes mentioned in section 27(1) of this Act; and

    (b) for such other similar purposes as the Secretary of State may prescribe.

(2) Before exercising his power under subsection (1)(b) above the Secretary of State shall consult local authorities and such other bodies as he considers appropriate.".

(6) In section 27B of that Act (grants in respect of hostel accommodation for certain persons)—

(a) at the beginning there shall be inserted "(1)"; and

(b) for the words from "sub-paragraphs (i) and (ii)" to the end there shall be substituted—

"subsection (2) below.

(2) The persons referred to in subsection (1) above are—

(a) persons mentioned in section 27(1)(b)(i) and (ii) of this Act;

(b) persons who have been charged with an offence and are on bail;

(c) persons who have been released from prison or any other form of detention but do not fall within section 27(1)(b)(ii) of this Act; and

(d) such other classes of persons as the Secretary of State may prescribe.

(3) Before exercising his power under subsection (2)(d) above the Secretary of State shall consult local authorities and such other persons as he considers appropriate.".

(7) In section 94(1) of that Act (interpretation), in paragraph (c) of the definition of "prescribed," after the word "sections" there shall be inserted "27A, 27B,".

GENERAL NOTE

Subs. (1)

This subsection amends ss.183 and 384 of the Criminal Procedure (Scotland) Act 1975 to ensure that a court shall not make a probation order unless satisfied that suitable arrangements can be made for the supervision of the offender by the local authority in whose area he resides or is to reside: in addition, the court can make requirements in the probation order which are merely conducive to the good conduct of the offender and could prevent a repetition of the offence or the commission of other offences.

Subs. (2)

Where information is given on oath that a probationer has failed to comply with any of the requirements of a probation order, the court may issue a warrant for his arrest: ss.186 and 387 are amended so that the director of social work or an officer appointed by him can give the information in addition to the officer supervising the probationer.

Subs. (3)

This amendment makes it clear that a community service order is intended to be an alternative to a custodial sentence or other form of detention.

Subs. (4)(a)

This amendment makes it a function of a local authority to provide advice, guidance and assistance for persons released from prison who request it.

Subs. (4)(b)

A protection and community scheme must now make provision in relation to the matters to be included in social background reports requested by the courts.

Subs. (5)

This provision extends the range of local authority services for which grants can be obtained by the authority in respect of expenditure incurred: they include the provision of social background reports, help for persons subject to supervision or community service orders and the new service in relation to "after prison" advice, guidance or assistance.

Subs. (6)

This extends the range of persons in respect of whom a local authority can receive a grant in relation to expenditure incurred by the authority in providing them with residential accommodation. These include persons under supervision, on bail or released from prison or other detention but not subject to any supervision requirement.

Supervised attendance orders as alternative to imprisonment on fine default

62.—(1) A court may make a supervised attendance order in the circumstances specified in subsection (3) below.

(2) A supervised attendance order is an order made by a court with the consent of an offender requiring him—

(a) to attend a place of supervision for such time, being 10, 20, 30, 40, 50 or 60 hours, as is specified in the order; and

(b) during that time, to carry out such instructions as may be given to him by the supervising officer.

(3) The circumstances are where—

(a) the offender is of or over 16 years of age; and

(b) having been convicted of an offence, he has had imposed on him a fine which (or any part or instalment of which) he has failed to pay and either of the following sub-paragraphs applies—

(i) the court, prior to the commencement of this section, has imposed on him a period of imprisonment under paragraph (a) of subsection (1) of section 407 of the Criminal Procedure (Scotland) Act 1975 (power of court, when imposing a fine, to impose also imprisonment on default) but he has not served any of that period of imprisonment;

(ii) the court, but for this section, would also have imposed on him a period of imprisonment under that paragraph or paragraph (b) of that subsection (power of court to impose imprisonment when a person fails to pay a fine or any part or instalment thereof); and

(c) the court considers a supervised attendance order more appropriate than the serving of or, as the case may be, imposition of such a period of imprisonment.

(4) Where, in respect of an offender, a court makes a supervised attendance order in circumstances where sub-paragraph (i) of paragraph (b) of subsection (3) above applies, the making of that order shall have the effect of discharging the sentence of imprisonment imposed on the offender.

(5) Schedule 6 to this Act has effect for the purpose of making further and qualifying provision as to supervised attendance orders.

(6) In this section—

"local authority" means a regional or islands council;

"place of supervision" means such place as may be determined for the purposes of a supervised attendance order by the supervising officer; and

"supervising officer," in relation to a supervised attendance order, means a person appointed or assigned under Schedule 6 to this Act by the local authority whose area includes the locality in which the offender resides or will be residing when the order comes into force.

GENERAL NOTE

Under s.407 of the Criminal Procedure (Scotland) Act 1975 (as amended by para. 27(3) of Sched. 8 to this Act) (a) when imposing a fine, a court of summary jurisdiction may impose a period of imprisonment in default of payment; or (b) when no order has been made under (a) and the person fails to pay a fine, or any part or instalment of a fine, by the time ordered, the court may impose a period of imprisonment for such failure either with immediate effect or upon failure to pay by some future date which the court may order. Where the person is over the age of 16, if a sentence has been imposed under (a) but no part of the sentence has been served or the court would have imposed a sentence under (b) for non-payment, s.62 gives the court the power to make a supervised attendance order, if appropriate, as an alternative to prison. A supervised attendance order can only be made with the consent of the offender. The details of a supervised attendance order are to be found in Sched. 6. This provision is clearly aimed at reducing the number of persons serving custodial sentences.

Drug trafficking confiscation orders

Registration and enforcement of external confiscation orders

63. The following sections shall be substituted for section 30 of the Criminal Justice (Scotland) Act 1987—

"Enforcement of other external orders

30.—(1) Her Majesty may by Order in Council—

(a) direct in relation to a country or territory outside the United Kingdom designated by the order ("a designated country") that, subject to such modifications as may be specified, this Part of this Act shall apply to external confiscation orders and to proceedings which have been or are to be instituted in the designated country and may result in an external confiscation order being made there;

(b) make—

(i) such provision in connection with the taking of action in the designated country with a view to satisfying a confiscation order; and

(ii) such provision as to evidence or proof of any matter for the purposes of this section and section 30A of this Act; and

(iii) such incidental, consequential and transitional provision,

as appears to Her Majesty to be expedient; and

(c) without prejudice to the generality of this subsection, direct that in such circumstances as may be specified proceeds which arise out of action taken in the designated country with a view to satisfying a confiscation order shall be treated as reducing the amount payable under the order to such extent as may be specified.

(2) In this Part of this Act—

"external confiscation order" means an order made by a court in a designated country for the purpose of recovering payments or other rewards received in connection with drug trafficking or their value; and

"modifications" includes additions, alterations and omissions.

(3) An Order in Council under this section may make different provision for different cases or classes of case.

(4) The power to make an Order in Council under this section includes power to modify this Part of this Act in such a way as to confer power on a person to exercise a discretion.

(5) An Order in Council under this section shall not be made unless a draft of the Order has been laid before Parliament and approved by a resolution of each House of Parliament.

Registration of external confiscation orders

30A.—(1) On an application made by or on behalf of the Government of a designated country, the Court of Session may register an external confiscation order made there if—

(a) it is satisfied that at the time of registration the order is in force and not subject to appeal;

(b) it is satisfied, where the person against whom the order is made did not appear in the proceedings, that he received notice of the proceedings in sufficient time to enable him to defend them; and

(c) it is of the opinion that enforcing the order in Scotland would not be contrary to the interests of justice.

(2) In subsection (1) above "appeal" includes—

(a) any proceedings by way of discharging or setting aside a judgment; and

(b) an application for a new trial or a stay of execution.

(3) The Court of Session shall cancel the registration of an external confiscation order if it appears to the court that the order has been satisfied by payment of the amount due under it or by the person against whom it was made serving imprisonment in default of payment or by any other means."

GENERAL NOTE

Pt. I of the Criminal Justice (Scotland) Act 1987 introduced important measures to recover the proceeds of drug trafficking. In particular, the High Court of Justiciary can make a confiscation order requiring a person convicted of drug trafficking to pay what the Court assessed to be the value of the proceeds of his involvement in drug trafficking. The new s.30 provides a framework for the registration and enforcement of confiscation orders made outside Scotland. On the application of the government of a designated country, an external confiscation may be registered by the Court of Session, whereupon Pt. I of the Act is applicable as if the external confiscation order were a confiscation order made by the High Court of Justiciary. Registration is not automatic but subject to the provisions of the new s.30A.

Matrimonial interdicts

Matrimonial interdicts

64. In section 15 of the Matrimonial Homes (Family Protection) (Scotland) Act 1981 (powers of arrest attached to matrimonial interdicts)—

(a) in subsection (2), after the words "such interdict" there shall be inserted "together with the attached power of arrest"; and

(b) in subsection (4)—

(i) after the word "interdict" in the second place where it occurs there shall be inserted "together with the attached power of arrest"; and

(ii) at the end there shall be added "and, where the application to attach the power of arrest to the interdict was made after the

interdict was granted, a copy of that application and of the interlocutor granting it and a certificate of service of the interdict
together with the attached power of arrest."

GENERAL NOTE

Where a power of arrest has been attached to a matrimonial interdict, it does not have effect
unless the interdict is served on the non-applicant spouse: s.15(2) of the Matrimonial Homes
(Family Protection) (Scotland) Act 1981. Moreover, by s.15(4) of the 1981 Act, if a power of
arrest is attached to a matrimonial interdict, the applicant must ensure that (i) the Chief
Constable of the police area in which the matrimonial home is situated and the Chief Constable
of the police area where the applicant spouse resides, if different, receive a copy of the
application for the interdict, the interlocutor granting the interdict together with a certificate of
service of the interdict. By s.64, (i) s.15(2) is amended to make it clear that the non-applicant is
served not only with the interdict but also the attached power of arrest; (ii) s.15(4) is amended
so that where the application for a power of arrest has been made after the interdict has been
granted, the relevant Chief Constable receives a copy of the application, the interlocutor
granting the power of arrest and a certificate of service of the interdict together with the
attached power of arrest. There is therefore no need to deliver a copy of the interdict until a
power of arrest has been attached. This removes any possible ambiguity arising from the
original wording of s.15 of the 1981 Act.

Homelessness

Homelessness

65.—(1) Section 24 of the Housing (Scotland) Act 1987 (definition of
homelessness and persons threatened with homelessness) shall be amended
as follows.

(2) After subsection (2) there shall be inserted the following subsections—
    "(2A) A person shall not be treated as having accommodation unless
it is accommodation which it would be reasonable for him to continue to
occupy.
    (2B) Regard may be had, in determining whether it would be reason-
able for a person to continue to occupy accommodation, to the general
circumstances prevailing in relation to housing in the area of the local
authority to whom he has applied for accommodation or for assistance
in obtaining accommodation."

(3) In subsection (3), after paragraph (b) there shall be inserted—
    "(bb) it is probable that occupation of it will lead to—
        (i) violence; or
        (ii) threats of violence which are likely to be carried out,
    from some other person who previously resided with that
    person, whether in that accommodation or elsewhere, or."

GENERAL NOTE

A person is homeless if he has no accommodation in Scotland, England or Wales: s.24(1) of
the Housing (Scotland) Act 1987. By s.24(2), a person is to be treated as having no accommodation if he or she has no right to occupy accommodation. In *Pulhofer* v. *Hillingdon L.B.C.* [1986]
1 A.C. 484 the House of Lords held that Parliament had not qualified the expression "accommodation" and accordingly a person had accommodation if he or she had a right to reside there
even although the accommodation was unfit for human habitation or was overcrowded. This
led to amendment of the Housing Act 1985 by the Housing (Planning) Act 1986 to the effect
that a person *entitled* to occupy premises was to be regarded as having no accommodation for
the purpose of homelessness unless it was reasonable for him or her to continue to reside there.
S.65(2) makes a similar amendment to the Housing (Scotland) Act 1987.

S.24(3) of the 1987 Act provides that a person is also homeless, even where he or she has
accommodation, if (a) he cannot secure entry to it or (b) he or she is likely to be a victim of
violence from a person currently residing there or (c) when the accommodation is moveable
property, there is no place where it can be placed and (d) the accommodation is overcrowded
within the meaning of s.135 of the Act and occupation may endanger the health of the occupant.
S.65(3) adds a further ground, *viz.* where a person is likely to be a victim of violence from a
person who previously resided with that person.

New subs. (2A)

It is thought that the general aim of this provision is to ensure that a person is not to be treated as having accommodation unless it is reasonable for that person to continue to live there. The most obvious instances when it would be unreasonable to continue to occupy property are when the property is seriously dilapidated or unfit for human habitation or overcrowded. It can be unreasonable for a person to continue to occupy premises on the basis of overcrowding even though the property is not overcrowded within the meaning of Pt. VII of the 1987 Act: see *R.* v. *Westminster City Council,* ex p. *Alouat* (1989) 21 H.L.R. 477. However, the reasonableness criterion is not restricted to the quality of the housing and it has been held that the likelihood of the person being a victim of violence *outside* the home, as opposed to in the accommodation itself, is a relevant consideration: see *Hammell* v. *Royal Borough of Kensington and Chelsea* (1988) 20 H.L.R. 666; *R.* v. *Broxbourne Borough Council,* ex p. *Willmoth* (1989) 21 H.L.R. 415.

New subs. (2B)

In considering the reasonableness criterion, a local authority can consider the general housing situation in its area. This would be important where, for example, dampness or other dilapidations affected much of its housing stock or overcrowding was common in its area. Reasonableness is not an objective test, but must be considered in the context of the housing conditions existing in the local authority's area.

New subs. (6b)

Other person who previously resided with that person, whether in that accommodation or not. The violence or threat of violence must emanate from a person who previously resided with the applicant: however, there is no need for that person to have resided with the applicant in his or her current accommodation. It is envisaged that the violence would take place inside the accommodation.

The Act still does not cover violence from a person who has *never* resided with the applicant or violence which is likely to occur in the area but outside the accommodation: it is thought that where this arises the victim will be treated as having no accommodation by virtue of s.24(2A), *viz.* it would not be reasonable for him or her to continue to occupy the property.

Arbitration

UNCITRAL Model Law on International Commercial Arbitration

66.—(1) In this section, "the Model Law" means the UNCITRAL Model Law on International Commercial Arbitration as adopted by the United Nations Commission on International Trade Law on June 21, 1985.

(2) The Model Law shall have the force of law in Scotland in the form set out in Schedule 7 to this Act (which contains the Model Law with certain modifications to adapt it for application in Scotland).

(3) The documents of the United Nations Commission on International Trade Law and its working group relating to the preparation of the Model Law may be considered in ascertaining the meaning or effect of any provision of the Model Law as set out in Schedule 7 to this Act.

(4) The parties to an arbitration agreement may, notwithstanding that the arbitration would not be an international commercial arbitration within the meaning of article 1 of the Model Law as set out in Schedule 7 to this Act, agree that the Model Law as set out in that Schedule shall apply, and in such a case the Model Law as so set out shall apply to that arbitration.

(5) Subsection (4) above is without prejudice to any other enactment or rule of law relating to arbitration.

(6) Subject to subsections (7) and (8) below, this section shall apply in relation to an arbitration agreement whether entered into before or after the date when this section comes into force.

(7) Notwithstanding subsection (6) above, this section shall not apply with respect to any arbitration which has commenced but has not been concluded on the date when this section comes into force.

(8) The parties to an arbitration agreement entered into before the date when this section comes into force may agree that the foregoing provisions of this section shall not apply to that arbitration agreement.

GENERAL NOTE

This section, together with Sched. 7, gives effect within Scotland to the UNCITRAL Model

Law on International Commercial Arbitration (subject to a few revisions to adapt it to operate within a Scottish framework). A detailed analysis of the Model Law is to be found in the note to Sched. 7.

The Model Law
In March 1984 the Working Group on International Contract Practice of the United Nations Commission on International Trade Law (UNCITRAL) adopted a draft of a Model Law on International Commercial Arbitration. UNCITRAL itself met in June 1985 to consider the draft text, approving a final text on June 21, 1985.

The General Assembly of the UN on December 11, 1985 requested the Secretary General to transmit the text of the Model Law to governments, arbitral institutions and other interested bodies, recommending that all States give due consideration to the Model Law (General Assembly Resolution No. 40/72).

The U.K. and the Model Law
From the very beginning the U.K. favoured the concept of the Model Law and was a very active member of the Working Group. In March 1985 the Secretary of State for Trade and Industry set up a Departmental Advisory Committee on the law of international commercial arbitration under the chairmanship of Mustill L.J. Initially, the Committee was required to consider what modification the U.K. should propose to the draft Model Law, but following the approval of the final text of the Model Law on June 21, 1985, it was charged, *inter alia*, with advising the Secretary of State upon whether, and if so to what extent, the provisions of the Model Law should be implemented in England and Wales, Scotland or Northern Ireland, and upon what measures should be taken for that purpose, or what arrangements should be taken to examine any aspects of this question, notably those which may have different implications for the system of arbitration in the three law districts.

It soon became clear that both the law of arbitration and its underlying philosophy were quite different in Scotland as compared to the two other law districts. Accordingly, in July 1986 the Lord Advocate set up a Scottish Advisory Committee under the chairmanship of John Murray Q.C. (now Lord Dervaird), "to advise on whether and if so to what extent the provisions of the draft Model Law adopted by a Working Group of the United Nations Commission on International Trade Law in February 1984 should be implemented in Scotland and what measures should be taken for that purpose".

The two Committees prepared a joint consultative document (October 1987) on the implications of adopting the Model Law. Following the consultation exercise, each committee prepared its final report. The Mustill Committee came out against the adoption of the Model Law in England, Wales and Northern Ireland (Departmental Advisory Committee on Arbitration Law—Report on UNCITRAL Model Law (June 1989) paras. 89–90). However, the Dervaird Committee recommended its adoption within Scotland (Scottish Advisory Committee on Arbitration Law—Report to the Lord Advocate on the UNCITRAL Model Law (May 1989) paras. 1–7). Sched. 7 contains the text of the Model Law subject, by and large, to amendments suggested by the Dervaird Committee to enable it to function properly in the Scottish context.

The Importance of the Travaux Preparatoires
The language employed by the Model Law is at times extremely general, if not actually vague, testifying to the difficulties inherent in drafting such a measure through the medium of a large multi-national committee, representing a considerable diversity of legal cultures and drafting techniques. The language used had to be sufficiently indefinite to be capable of being adapted to a wide variety of legal environments, and the expressions which are employed are often chosen not because they convey exactly the drafter's meaning, but because they are the only words which can be made intelligible in each of the six official languages of the Model Law (English, French, Spanish, Russian, Chinese and Arabic). The lengthy drafting process did, fortunately, yield extremely extensive travaux preparatoires which indicate in considerable detail the meaning and scope of each of the Articles of the Model Law. The Dervaird Committee recognised the importance of the travaux preparatoires and expressed the view that parties should be entitled to refer to them "in order that any matter of doubt or ambiguity can be resolved in accordance with the spirit of the Model Law" (para. 2.1), adding (*ibid.*) "that some legislative reference should be made to this matter in order to avoid the doubts generally in Scots Law as to the extent to which regard may properly be had to such matters in construing legislation". The result is, of course, s.66(3).

It may be noted that reference to the travaux preparatoires is, nevertheless, not mandatory. Thus a court or arbitral tribunal which feels uncomfortable in dealing with material of such a voluminous and discursive nature may choose not to stray beyond the boundaries of the legislation in seeking assistance in interpretation, perhaps electing to reject the interpretation suggested by the travaux preparatoires on the basis that the plain words of the Model Law are perfectly clear. It remains to be seen exactly how adventurous the use of the travaux preparatoires will be. Yet a conservative approach would be regrettable since, for the reasons mentioned above, the true significance of many of the provisions of the Model Law can only be discovered by consulting the travaux preparatoires.

What are the Travaux Preparatoires?

The travaux preparatoires represent the material which emerges from the drafting process considered above, the various reports, notes and comments made by UNCITRAL, its Secretariat, the Working Group and the various governments and organisations involved in the drafting of the Model Law.

Contracting into the Model Law (s.66(4))

The Model Law applies to international commercial arbitrations within the meaning of Art. 1. However, s.66(4) clearly permits parties to arbitrations which would otherwise fall outwith the scope of the Model Law to invoke its application. Thus parties to purely domestic arbitrations may choose to enjoy the benefits of the Model Law, as can parties to arbitrations which are international but not commercial. There is no requirement that the agreement that the Model Law should apply need take any particular form, or be reached at any particular time. Thus such agreement may be found in the original contract, or in the agreement to refer, or may even be reached once the arbitration has commenced.

Effect of Invoking the Model Law—s.66(5)

What is the effect of this provision? Its meaning is far from obvious. It cannot mean that the right to contract into the Model Law is restricted by statutory or common law rules which dictate that certain types of disputes cannot be referred to arbitration or must be referred subject to specific statutory rules, since that effect is already secured by Art. 1(5). It may mean that since the Model Law is a partial law, it applies, when invoked, against a background of common law and statutory rules which continue to govern those matters not governed by the Model Law. This would be the most helpful interpretation. A third interpretation, however, would be that while invocation of the Model Law confers the benefit of the procedures laid down by the Model Law, the parties continue to be bound by current mandatory rules of Scots law. Yet, if this interpretation is correct, it creates a number of problems, since not all the provisions of the Model Law are consistent with current Scots law. Considerations of space preclude an exhaustive account of the instances where the Model Law conflicts with Scots law, and the relationship of individual provisions to existing Scots law is discussed throughout. Nevertheless, one striking example of the difficulties which would be created by such an interpretation is the fact that the Model Law (a) specifically directs that the court will not intervene in the arbitral process except where the Model Law so directs; (b) dictates that an action for setting aside is to be the exclusive recourse against an award; and (c) does not include the commission of errors of law as one of the grounds for setting aside, whereas Scots law under the Administration of Justice (Scotland) Act 1972, s.3, provides for, in effect, an appeal against an award on a point of law under the stated case procedure (unless the parties have agreed to the contrary in the agreement to refer). Does s.66(5) mean that where parties have chosen to be governed by the Model Law, s.3 of the 1972 Act still applies to the arbitration? Such an interpretation would be most unfortunate.

The Coming into Effect of the Model Law—s.66(6)–(8)

The provisions of the Model Law do not apply to any arbitration which is actually under way on January 1, 1991. However, they will apply to any arbitration which commences on or after that date, notwithstanding that the agreement to refer is entered into before that date. Yet if the agreement to refer is entered into before that date it is open to the parties to agree, whether in the agreement to refer or otherwise, that the arbitration will not be governed by the Model Law.

Judicial factors

Further provision as to discharge of judicial factors

67. After section 34 (discharge of factors, tutors and curators) of the Judicial Factors Act 1849 there shall be inserted the following section—

> **"Further provision as to discharge of factors, tutors and curators**
> 34A. The Court may by act of sederunt make provision for the discharge of factors, tutors and curators by means other than the

presentation of a petition under section 34 of this Act where the factory, tutory or curatory is terminated by reason of the recovery, death or coming of age of the ward, or by reason of the exhaustion of the estate.".

GENERAL NOTE

This section provides that where a factory, tutory or curatory is terminated by (i) recovery of the ward, (ii) death of the ward, (iii) majority of the ward, or (iv) the exhaustion of the estate, the factors, tutors or curators may be discharged by means other than petition to the court. The procedure is to be determined by Act of Sederunt. The aim is to save the expense of a petition in these circumstances. The section came into force on January 1, 1991: s.75(3)(b).

Avoidance of civil liability by non-contractual notice

Amendment of Unfair Contract Terms Act 1977

68.—(1) The Unfair Contract Terms Act 1977 shall be amended in accordance with this section.

(2) In section 15(1) (scope of Part II), the words "applies only to contracts," shall cease to have effect.

(3) In section 16 (liability for breach of duty)—

(a) in subsection (1)—

(i) at the beginning there shall be inserted the words "Subject to subsection (1A) below,";

(ii) after the word "contract" in the first place where it occurs there shall be inserted ", or a provision of a notice given to persons generally or to particular persons,";

(iii) after the word "term" in the second place where it occurs there shall be inserted "or provision"; and

(iv) at the end of paragraph (b) there shall be inserted the words "or, as the case may be, if it is not fair and reasonable to allow reliance on the provision";

(b) after subsection (1) there shall be inserted the following subsection—

"(1A) Nothing in paragraph (b) of subsection (1) above shall be taken as implying that a provision of a notice has effect in circumstances where, apart from that paragraph, it would not have effect."; and

(c) in subsection (3)—

(i) after the word "contract" there shall be inserted "or a provision of a notice"; and

(ii) after the word "term" in the second place where it occurs there shall be inserted "or provision."

(4) In section 24 (the "reasonableness" test)—

(a) after subsection (2) there shall be inserted the following subsection—

"(2A) In determining for the purposes of this Part of this Act whether it is fair and reasonable to allow reliance on a provision of a notice (not being a notice having contractual effect), regard shall be had to all the circumstances obtaining when the liability arose or (but for the provision) would have arisen.";

(b) in subsection (3)—

(i) after the word "contract" in the first place where it occurs there shall be inserted "or a provision of a notice";

(ii) after the word "contract" in the second place where it occurs there shall be inserted "or whether it is fair and reasonable to allow reliance on the provision";

(iii) after the word "above" there shall be inserted "in the case of a term in a contract"; and

(iv) in paragraph (a), after the word "term" there shall be inserted "or provision"; and

(c) in subsection (4), after the word "contract" there shall be inserted "or that it is fair and reasonable to allow reliance on a provision of a notice."

(5) In section 25 (interpretation of Part II)—

(a) in subsection (1), after the definition of "hire-purchase agreement" there shall be inserted—

" "notice" includes an announcement, whether or not in writing, and any other communication or pretended communication"; and

(b) subsections (3)(d) and (4) shall cease to have effect.

(6) This section shall have effect only in relation to liability for any loss or damage which is suffered or or after the date appointed for its coming into force.

GENERAL NOTE

Pt. II of the Unfair Contract Terms Act 1977 contains provisions regulating exemption clauses in Scots law. Unlike Pt. I, the Scottish provisions only apply to exemption clauses in contracts. The exclusion of statutory controls over exemption clauses in non-contractual notices could give difficulties in two situations. First, an occupier of business premises could attempt to exclude or limit liability by way of a non-contractual notice to persons entering his property. However, under s.2(1) of the Occupier's Liability (Scotland) Act 1960, liability under that Act can only be excluded or limited by *agreement*: a non-contractual notice would not suffice. It is difficult to see how such an agreement could be made which did not form part of a contract—given that a bilateral gratuitous contract is recognised in Scots law: accordingly, an exemption clause in such an agreement would already be subject to regulation under s.16 of the 1977 Act: see Woolman, *An Introduction to the Scots Law of Contract* (1987) pp. 114 *et seq.*

Second, and more importantly, Scots law now recognises liability for economic loss arising from negligent misrepresentation where there is a special relationship between the parties: see, for example, *Martin* v. *Bell-Ingram*, 1986 S.L.T. 575. The essence of the liability is that it was reasonable (i) for the pursuer to rely on the statement and (ii) that the defender should know that such reliance would be made. Because of the importance of reliance, it was held that a defender could exclude or limit liability by virtue of a non-contractual disclaimer, provided that notice of the disclaimer was given to the pursuer *before* he relied on the statement: *Hedley Byrne & Co.* v. *Heller & Partners* [1964] A.C. 468; *Robbie* v. *Graham and Sibbald*, 1989 S.L.T. 870, *cf. Martin* v. *Bell-Ingram*, 1986 S.L.T. 575 (disclaimer arrived after the misrepresentation and after pursuer had relied upon it to his detriment). In *Smith* v. *Eric S. Bush* and *Harris* v. *Wyre Forest D.C.* [1989] 2 W.L.R. 790, the House of Lords held that while such a disclaimer did not prevent a duty of care arising, it could nevertheless exclude or limit liability if the fair and reasonable test under the Unfair Contract Terms Act 1977 was satisfied. Since Pt. II of the Unfair Contract Terms Act 1977 does not apply to non-contractual notices, such disclaimers could still be effective under Scots law to exclude or limit liability, as outlined above, even though it was not fair and reasonable in the circumstances to do so. S.68 amends Pt. II of the Unfair Contract Terms Act 1977 to bring non-contractual notices within the statutory controls, thus bringing Scots law into line with the English position.

Subs. (2)

This removes the restriction of Pt. II of the Unfair Contract Terms Act 1977 to contractual terms.

Subs. (3)

This amends s.16 of the Unfair Contract Terms Act 1977 so that it is applicable to provisions which purport to exclude or limit delictual liability where the exemption takes the form of a non-contractual notice as well as a contract term. Thus a notice purporting to exclude or restrict liability for death or personal injuries is void (s.16(1)(a)): any notice purporting to exclude or restrict liability for economic loss is not effective unless it was fair and reasonable to do so. It should be emphasised that s.16 is only applicable in respect of delictual liability arising in the course of business or occupation of premises used for business purposes.

New subs. (1A)

This ensures that the inclusion of non-contractual notices within s.16 does not result in a notice being effective when it would not otherwise be effective under existing law: for example, non-contractual notices purporting to exclude or limit liability under the Occupier's Liability (Scotland) Act 1960 (see note *supra*).

New subs. (2A)

This provision makes it clear that in applying the fair and reasonable test to a non-contractual notice, regard must be made to all the circumstances obtaining when the liability arose—and not circumstances arising later. This parallels s.24(1), where, in relation to a contract term, the relevant circumstances are those known—or which ought reasonably to have been known—to the parties at the time the contract was made.

Subs. 5
Notice. While notice is broadly defined, it remains at least arguable that where a statement excluding or limiting liability is part of a *pollicitatio* or unilateral promise, it may still be outwith the scope of the Act being neither a contractual term *stricto sensu* nor a non-contractual notice.

Subs. 6
The amendments are not retrospective.

Liability in respect of services to injured persons

Future services to injured person

69.—(1) For subsection (2) of section 8 of the Administration of Justice Act 1982 (services rendered to injured person) there shall be substituted the following subsections—

"(2) The injured person shall be under an obligation to account to the relative for any damages recovered from the responsible person under subsection (1) above.

(3) Where, at the date of an award of damages in favour of the injured person, it is likely that necessary services will, after that date, be rendered to him by a relative in consequence of the injuries in question, then, unless the relative has expressly agreed that no payment shall be made in respect of those services, the responsible person shall be liable to pay to the injured person by way of damages such sum as represents—

(a) reasonable remuneration for those services; and

(b) reasonable expenses which are likely to be incurred in connection therewith.

(4) The relative shall have no direct right of action in delict against the responsible person in respect of any services or expenses referred to in this section."

(2) Without prejudice to Parts II and III of the Prescription and Limitation (Scotland) Act 1973, this section shall apply to rights accruing both before and after the date appointed for its coming into force, but shall not affect any proceedings commenced before that date.

GENERAL NOTE
Where a person has suffered personal injuries, by s.8 of the Administration of Justice Act 1982, the injured person can recover damages which amount to reasonable remuneration for necessary services rendered to him by a relative as a result of the injuries. The injured person then accounts to the relative for any damages so recovered. In *Forsyth's Curator Bonis* v. *Govan Shipbuilders* 1988 S.L.T. 321 it was held that damages could only be recovered in respect of services provided by a relative up to the date of the action and that damages could not be awarded in respect of services to be provided by the relative in the future. S.58(1) amends s.8 to allow the court to make an award of damages to the injured person which represents reasonable remuneration for the relative's services in the future and reasonable expenses likely to be incurred, provided that the relative has not expressly agreed that no payment is to be made in respect of those services.

New subs. (3)
It should be noted that there is no equivalent of s.8(2) obliging the injured person to account to the relative for any damages awarded under s.8(3). This is explicable in that the injured person is receiving damages in respect of remuneration and expenses for services yet to be rendered by the relative; nevertheless, there appears to be no statutory mechanism whereby the relative can actually obtain from the injured person reasonable remuneration and expenses once the services have in fact been rendered. It may be that in order to succeed under s.8(3), the injured person may have to establish that he has undertaken to pay reasonable remuneration

and expenses to the relative in respect of services in the future, and the relative could then sue the injured person on that undertaking if reasonable remuneration and expenses were not forthcoming.

New subs. (4)

This emphasises that the injured person and not the relative has title to sue in delict in respect of services given or to be given in the future: *cf. Robertson* v. *Turnbull* 1982 S.L.T. 96 (common law).

Blood and other samples in civil proceedings

Blood and other samples in civil proceedings

70.—(1) In any civil proceedings to which this section applies, the court may (whether or not on application made to it) request a party to the proceedings—

  (a) to provide a sample of blood or other body fluid or of body tissue for the purpose of laboratory analysis;

  (b) to consent to the taking of such a sample from a child in relation to whom the party has power to give such consent.

(2) Where a party to whom a request under subsection (1) above has been made refuses or fails—

  (a) to provide or, as the case may be, to consent to the taking of, a sample as requested by the court, or

  (b) to take any step necessary for the provision or taking of such a sample,

the court may draw from the refusal or failure such adverse inference, if any, in relation to the subject matter of the proceedings as seems to it to be appropriate.

(3) In section 6 of the Law Reform (Parent and Child) (Scotland) Act 1986 (determination of parentage by blood sample)—

  (a) in subsection (1), for the words "blood sample" there shall be substituted "sample of blood or other body fluid or of body tissue"; and

  (b) in each of subsections (2), (3) and (4), for the words "a blood" there shall be substituted "such a."

(4) This section applies to any civil proceedings brought in the Court of Session or the sheriff court—

  (a) on or after the date of the commencement of this section; or

  (b) before the said date in a case where the proof has not by that date begun.

GENERAL NOTE

In *Torrie* v. *Turner* 1990 S.L.T. 718 an Extra Division of the Inner House confirmed that at common law a court has no power to compel an adult to provide a blood sample for the purpose of determining paternity either through blood tests or DNA profiling. Similarly, an adult cannot be compelled to consent to blood samples to be taken from a pupil in relation to whom he has power to consent, for the same purpose. In spite of dicta to the contrary (see *Docherty* v. *McGlynn* 1985 S.L.T. 645, *per* Lord Cameron at 650) it would also appear that a court cannot make a direction that a blood sample be taken and draw adverse inferences if the direction was not obtempered.

This section implements the recommendations of the Scottish Law Commission (SLC No. 120). First, it empowers a court to request a party to civil proceedings to provide a sample of blood or other body fluid or tissue or consent to such a sample being taken from a child in respect of whom he has power to consent. Second, if the party refuses to obtemper the direction, the court has the power to draw adverse inferences from the refusal. Third, it amends s.6 of the Law Reform (Parent and Child) (Scotland) Act 1986 to encompass samples of body fluid or other tissue as well as blood samples.

These provisions will therefore facilitate the acquisition of evidence from blood tests or DNA profiling in civil proceedings. While a party still cannot be compelled to provide samples, refusal could lead to appropriate adverse inferences being drawn.

However, where the proceedings relate to parental rights, it is submitted that in exercising its power to make a direction, the court must regard the welfare of the child as the paramount consideration: s.3(2) of the Law Reform (Parent and Child) (Scotland) Act 1986.

Subs. (1)

(*Whether or not on application made to it*). The court has the power to make a request not only when there is an application for such an order but also *ex proprio motu.*

A party to the proceedings. Only a party to the proceedings may be called upon to provide a sample or consent to a sample being taken from a child.

For the purpose of laboratory analysis. The samples can be used for traditional blood tests or for DNA profiling.

A child in relation to whom the party has power to give consent. At common law a pupil's tutor has power to consent on his behalf. If the application is made for the purpose of determining parentage in civil proceeding by a party or a *curator ad litem*, this power can be exercised by any person having custody or care of the child as well as the tutor: s.6(2) of the Law Reform (Parent and Child) (Scotland) Act 1986. At common law a minor has capacity to consent on his or her own behalf.

Subs. (2)

This provides that adverse inferences can be drawn when a party fails to provide a sample or consent to such a sample being taken from a child.

Subs. (3)

This subsection amends s.6 of the Law Reform (Parent and Child) (Scotland) Act 1986 so that its provisions are applicable not only in relation to samples of blood but also samples of other body fluid or tissue. It should be noted that s.6 applies only where the sample is sought to determine parentage in civil proceedings by a party to the proceedings or a *curator ad litem*: in particular, the court's restricted power to consent where there is no person entitled to consent on behalf of a child or where that person's consent cannot be obtained, is restricted to such applications: s.6(3). This could be important if the court were to make a request *ex proprio motu* under s.70(1), *i.e.* s.6 would not be applicable and only the child's tutor would be able to consent if a party to the proceedings: the court could *not* consent under s.6(3).

Subs. (4)

These provisions are retrospective to the extent that they apply to proceedings instituted before the date of commencement, provided that proof has not yet begun. The section came into force on January 1, 1991: s.75(3)(b).

Powers of attorney

Effect of mental incapacity on powers of attorney etc.

71.—(1) Any rule of law by which a factory and commission or power of attorney ceases to have effect in the event of the mental incapacity of the granter shall not apply to a factory and commission or power of attorney granted on or after the date on which this section comes into force.

(2) In subsection (1) above, "mental incapacity" means, in relation to a person, that he is incapable of managing his property and affairs by reason of mental disorder within the meaning of section 1 of the Mental Health (Scotland) Act 1984.

GENERAL NOTE

In Scots law, it is generally thought that a factory and commission or power of attorney will lapse in the event of the insanity of the granter, provided that the insanity is not merely temporary: *Wink* v. *Mortimer* (1849) 11D 995. This rule of law has been a source of difficulty for families where a person has obtained a factory and commission or power of attorney on behalf of a close relative, who subsequently becomes mentally incapacitated. While a *curator bonis* could be appointed, it is expensive and is only suitable for large estates. This provision changes the common law so that the factory and commission or power of attorney will continue on the subsequent mental incapacity of the granter.

Subs. (1)

Granted on or after the date on which this section comes into force. The provision is not retrospective. It only affects a factory and commission or power of attorney granted after the provision has come into force. This section came into force on January 1, 1991: s.75(3)(b).

Execution of documents by companies

Execution of documents by companies

72.—(1) For section 36B of the Companies Act 1985 (execution of documents: Scotland) there shall be substituted the following section—

"Execution of documents: Scotland

36B.—(1) This section has effect in relation to the execution of any document by a company under the law of Scotland on or after July 31, 1990.

(2) For any purpose other than those mentioned in subsection (3) below, a document is validly executed by a company if it is signed on behalf of the company by a director or the secretary of the company or by a person authorised to sign the document on its behalf.

(3) For the purposes of any enactment or rule of law relating to the authentication of documents under the law of Scotland, a document is validly executed by a company if it is subscribed on behalf of the company by—

(a) two of the directors of the company;

(b) a director and the secretary of the company; or

(c) two persons authorised to subscribe the document on behalf of the company,

notwithstanding that such subscription is not attested by witnesses and the document is not sealed with the company's common seal.

(4) A document which bears to be executed by a company in accordance with subsection (3) above is, in relation to such execution, a probative document.

(5) Notwithstanding the provisions of any enactment (including an enactment contained in this section) a company need not have a common seal.

(6) For the purposes of any enactment providing for a document to be executed by a company by affixing its common seal of referring (in whatever terms) to a document so executed, a document signed or subscribed on behalf of the company by—

(a) two directors of the company;

(b) a director and the secretary of the company; or

(c) two persons authorised to sign or subscribe the document on behalf of the company,

shall have effect as if executed under the common seal of the company.

(7) In this section "enactment" includes an enactment contained in a statutory instrument.

(8) Subsections (2) and (3) above are—

(a) without prejudice to any other method of execution of documents by companies permitted by any enactment or rule of law; and

(b) subject to any other enactment making express provision, in relation to companies, as to the execution of a particular type of document."

(2) Where, on or after July 31, 1990 and prior to the coming into force of this section, a document was signed or subscribed, in accordance with section 36B(2) of the Companies Act 1985 (as inserted by section 130(3) of the Companies Act 1989), by—

(a) a company; or

(b) a body corporate to which section 36B of the 1985 Act (as so inserted) applied by, under or by virtue of any enactment,

that document shall be deemed to have been validly executed by the company or body corporate in accordance with subsection (2) of section 36B of the 1985 Act as substituted by subsection (1) above.

(3) Where, on or after July 31, 1990 and prior to the coming into force of this section, the presumption in section 36B(3) of the Companies Act 1985 (as inserted by section 130(3) of the Companies Act 1989) applied in relation to a document, that document shall be deemed to have been validly executed in accordance with subsection (3) of section 36B of the 1985 Act as

substituted by subsection (1) above, and subsection (4) of that section as so substituted shall apply to the document as if it bore to be so executed.

(4) For the avoidance of doubt, in determining, for the purposes of subsection (3) above, whether the presumption in section 36B(3) of the Companies Act 1985 (as inserted by section 130(3) of the Companies Act 1989) applied in relation to a document, the reference in section 36B(2)(b) of the 1985 Act (as so inserted) to the last page shall be construed as a reference to the last page of the document excluding any inventory, appendix, schedule, plan or other document annexed to the document.

(5) Any reference to section 36B of the Companies Act 1985 (however expressed) in any enactment (including an enactment contained in a statutory instrument) shall be construed as a reference to section 36B of that Act as substituted by subsection (1) above.

GENERAL NOTE

The Requirements of Writing (Scotland) Bill was intended radically to reform the law in relation to the execution of deeds, by introducing a new and comprehensive legal régime. When the Bill was lost, the provisions concerned with the execution of deeds by companies were transferred to the Companies Act 1989: this amended s.36 of the Companies Act 1985 by adding a new s.36B. This provided in s.36B(2) how documents were to be signed and subscribed by a company. However, because s.36B was not a comprehensive code on the *execution* of deeds, doubt arose whether s.36B(2) would be effective validly to execute a deed, which required witnesses in order to be formally valid under the authentication statutes: for full discussion see Kenneth G.C. Reid, *Execution of Deeds by Companies*, 1990 S.L.T. (News) 241; *cf.* J. Murray, *Execution of Deeds by Companies* (1990) 35 J.L.S.S. 358; D.A. Bennett, *The Companies Act 1989* (1990) 35 J.L.S.S. 396. By s.36B(3) a document subscribed on behalf of a company and authenticated by a witness or the company's seal was presumed to have been subscribed by the company, *i.e.* it was a probative document. But since s.36B(3) only created a presumption that the document was *subscribed* by the company, a deed remained only formally valid where properly executed, and, if the deed fell within the authentication statutes, this still required two witnesses. S.72 substitutes a new s.36B of the Companies Act 1985 to remove the difficulties which have arisen as a result of the infelicities in the drafting of the original s.36B. On the new s.36B, see generally Kenneth G.C. Reid, *Execution of Deeds by Companies*, 1990 S.L.T. (News) 369.

New subs. (1)

On or after 31 July 1990. The old s.36B came into effect on July 31, 1990. It will be clear that the new s.36B is retrospective: s.72 came into force on December 1, 1990. Thus the provisions of the new s.36B cover documents signed or subscribed between the period July 31 and November 30, 1990, as well as after that date.

New subs. (2)

For any purpose other than those mentioned in subsection (3) below. Subs. (3) is concerned with the execution of deeds which fall within the requirements of the authentication statutes in order to be formally valid. Subs. (2) is therefore concerned with all other documents where formal writings are not required.

Validly executed. The old s.36B(2) provided a definition of how a document was signed and subscribed by a company. It was defective where a deed had to be witnessed in order to be validly executed. However, it was perfectly acceptable where witnesses were not required for formal validity. The new s.36B(2) achieves the same result by providing a procedure whereby these documents are validly executed, but it fails to provide a definition of how a company signs or subscribes such a document.

New subs. (3)

For the purposes of any enactment or rule of law relating to the authentication of documents under the law of Scotland. Subs. (3) is concerned with the execution of deeds which fall within the requirements of the authentication statutes in order to be formally valid.

Validly executed. A deed will be validly executed for these purposes if it is subscribed on behalf of a company by two directors of the company, or a director and the secretary of the company or two persons authorised to subscribe the document on behalf of the company. The old s.36B(3) was defective in that while it provided that a deed was to be presumed to have been *subscribed* on behalf of the company if the statutory procedure was followed, it was open to argument that the deed was not validly *executed* unless the authentication statutes were satisfied. By expressly stating that a deed will now be validly executed, a deed signed in accordance with the new s.36B(3) is undoubtedly a validly executed deed for these purposes and accordingly, formally valid.

Two persons authorised to subscribe the document on behalf of the company. This is a new method of execution and care should be taken that existing grants of authority cover subscription for such deeds.

Not attested by witnesses. For the avoidance of doubt, it is expressly provided that witnesses are not required for the deed to be validly executed.

Not sealed with the company's common seal. For the avoidance of doubt, it is expressly provided that sealing with the company's common seal is not required for the deed to be validly executed.

New subs. (4)

This provides that a deed executed under the new s.36B(3) is to be presumed to be a probative deed. The deed is presumed to be formally valid, *i.e.* to have been *subscribed* by two directors of the company, a director and secretary of the company or two persons authorised to subscribe the document on behalf of the company. However, it should be emphasised that this is only a presumption which can be rebutted, for example, by proving that the signatures were forgeries. The onus, of course, rests on the person who questions the validity of the signature to rebut the presumption. Since the presumption of probity only applies in relation to the fact of subscription, it does not apply to the question whether the persons signing were in fact directors of the company, the secretary of the company, or authorised by the company to sign: accordingly, it may be prudent to check that these persons are indeed office bearers or authorised persons.

New subs. (5)

This provides that a company need no longer have a company seal.

New subs. (6)

This is ancillary to new subs. (5).

New subs. (8)(a)

A company remains free to execute documents permitted "by *any enactment or rule of law*". Accordingly, a company is no longer free to make its own special rules on execution in its articles of association. The major alternative method is under the Subscription of Deeds Act 1681. It is not clear how a company signs or subscribes a document at common law. It could, however, do so through an authorised person, but he must sign with two witnesses. Under s.36B(3), an authorised person must sign with another authorised person: no witnesses are required.

Subs. (2)

This is a transitional provision. It provides that documents signed or subscribed by a company in accordance with the old s.36B(2) are to be deemed to have been validly executed in accordance with the new s.36B(2): consequently, it does not apply to deeds which fall within the authentication statutes as these are expressly excluded from the new s.36B(2).

Subs. (3)

This is a transitional provision. It provides that deeds presumed to be probative under the old s.36B(3), *i.e.* those which appear to have been subscribed by a director, or secretary or authorised person *and* a witness or sealed with the common seal of the company, are deemed to have been validly executed in accordance with the new s.36B(3). Accordingly, they are validly executed even if the formalities prescribed by the authentication statutes have not been followed, *viz.* there are not two witnesses. Such deeds will also have the benefit of the presumption of probativity under the new s.36B(4): although deemed to be validly executed, probativity is important to bring the document within statutory provisions which only apply to "probative" deeds.

Where during the transitional period, a deed was executed in accordance with the repealed s.36(3) of the Companies Act 1985, *i.e.* by sealing with the common seal accompanied by the subscriptions of two directors or a director and the secretary, s.72(3) does not apply. However, the new s.36B is retrospective so that the new s.36B(3) applies and this merely requires two signatories for the deed to be validly executed: the presence of the seal does not detract from the validity of the deed under the new s.36B(3).

When during the transitional period, a deed was signed and subscribed in accordance with the old s.36B(2) and two witnesses, it was already validly executed under the Subscription of Deeds Act 1681. It would, of course, also be validly executed under s.72(3).

Subs. (4)

The old s.36B(3) operated when a document was subscribed by the relevant persons. Subscription was defined in the old s.36B(2) as being a signature "at the end of the last page". This raised doubts about whether schedules attached to the document had also to be subscribed to obtain the benefit of the presumption of probativity. This provision removes the doubt by enacting that it is the last page of the document that is relevant for the purposes of s.72(3).

PART V

GENERAL

Finance

73.—(1) There shall be paid out of money provided by Parliament—

(a) the expenses of the Lord Advocate in carrying out his functions under Part I of this Act;

(b) the remuneration and expenses of the Scottish legal services ombudsman appointed under section 34 of this Act and of any staff appointed for the ombudsman under Schedule 3 to this Act;

(c) the remuneration of temporary judges appointed under section 35(3) of this Act;

(d) any grant paid by the Secretary of State to the Scottish Conveyancing and Executry Services Board under section 16 of this Act; and

(e) any increase attributable to the provisions of this Act in the sums payable under any other Act out of money provided by Parliament.

(2) Sums repaid to the Secretary of State under section 16(3) of this Act shall be paid by him into the Consolidated Fund.

Amendments and repeals

74.—(1) The enactments mentioned in Schedule 8 to this Act shall have effect subject to the amendments specified in that Schedule.

(2) The enactments mentioned in Schedule 9 to this Act are hereby repealed to the extent specified in the third column of that Schedule.

Citation, commencement and extent

75.—(1) This Act may be cited as the Law Reform (Miscellaneous Provisions) (Scotland) Act 1990.

(2) Subject to subsections (3) and (4) below, this Act shall come into force on such day as the Secretary of State may appoint by order made by statutory instrument and different days may be appointed for different provisions and for different purposes.

(3) The provisions of—

(a) Part III and section 66 of this Act and so much of section 74 as relates to those provisions; and

(b) sections 67, 70 and 71 of this Act and paragraphs 21 and 34 of Schedule 8 to this Act.

shall come into force at the end of the period of two months beginning with the day on which this Act is passed.

(4) Paragraph 27(3) of Schedule 8 to this Act shall come into force on the day on which this Act is passed.

(5) Subject to subsections (6) and (7) below, this Act extends to Scotland only.

(6) Section 72 of this Act, paragraph 33 of Schedule 8 to this Act and Schedule 9 to this Act so far as relating to the Companies Act 1985 and the Companies Act 1989 extend also to England and Wales.

(7) Paragraph 17 of Schedule 1 to this Act, paragraph 11 of Schedule 3 to this Act and Schedule 9 to this Act so far as relating to the House of Commons Disqualification Act 1975 extend also to England and Wales and Northern Ireland.

SCHEDULES

SCHEDULE 1

SCOTTISH CONVEYANCING AND EXECUTRY SERVICES BOARD

PART I

CONSTITUTION, DUTIES, POWERS AND STATUS

Constitution

1. The Scottish Conveyancing and Executry Services Board shall be a body corporate.

2. The Board shall not be regarded as the servant or agent of the Crown or as enjoying any status, immunity or privilege of the Crown; and the Board's property shall not be regarded as property of, or held on behalf of, the Crown.

3. The Board shall consist of—

(a) a chairman; and

(b) not less than six nor more than nine other members,

appointed by the Secretary of State.

4. In making appointments under paragraph 3 above the Secretary of State shall have regard to the desirability of securing—

(a) that members of the Board have expertise or knowledge of—

(i) the provision of conveyancing and executry services;

(ii) the financial arrangements connected with the purchase and sale of heritable property;

(iii) consumer affairs; and

(iv) commercial affairs; and

(b) that, so far as is reasonably practicable, the composition of the Board is such as to provide a proper balance between the interests of, on the one hand, qualified conveyancers and executry practitioners and, on the other hand, those who make use of their services.

5.—(1) Subject to paragraph 6 below, a member of the Board shall hold and vacate office in accordance with his terms of appointment, but a person shall not be appointed a member of the Board for a period of more than five years.

(2) A person who ceases to be a member of the Board shall be eligible for reappointment.

6.—(1) The chairman or any other member of the Board may resign office by giving notice in writing to the Secretary of State.

(2) The Secretary of State may terminate the appointment of a member of the Board if satisfied that—

(a) his estate has been sequestrated or he has made an arrangement with or granted a trust deed for his creditors;

(b) he is unable to carry out his duties as a Board member by reason of physical or mental illness;

(c) he is failing to carry out the duties of his appointment;

(d) he has been convicted of a criminal offence rendering him unsuitable to continue as a member; or

(e) he is otherwise unable or unfit to discharge the functions of a member of the Board.

Remuneration

7.—(1) The Board may—

(a) pay such remuneration to their members; and

(b) make provision for the payment of such pensions, allowances or gratuities to or in respect of their members,

as the Board may, with the consent of the Secretary of State, determine.

(2) Where a person ceases to be a member of the Board otherwise than on the expiry of his term of office, and it appears to the Board that there are special circumstances which make it right for that person to receive compensation, the Board may, with the consent of the Secretary of State, make a payment to that person of such amount as the Board may, with the consent of the Secretary of State, determine.

Staff

8. The Board may employ such officers and servants as they think fit, on such terms as to remuneration and conditions of service as the Board may, with the consent of the Secretary of State, determine.

9.—(1) The Board shall make, in respect of such of their employees as they may determine, such arrangements for providing pensions, allowances or gratuities (including pensions, allowances or gratuities by way of compensation to or in respect of any such employee who suffers loss of employment) as the Board may, with the consent of the Secretary of State, determine.

(2) Arrangements under sub-paragraph (1) above may include the establishment and administration, by the Board or otherwise, of one or more pension schemes.

Proceedings

10.—(1) The Board may regulate their own proceedings.

(2) The Board may make such arrangements as they consider appropriate for the discharge of their functions, including the delegation of specified functions other than their power to make rules.

(3) The validity of any proceedings of the Board shall not be affected by any vacancy among the members of the Board or by any defect in the appointment of any member.

Performance of functions

11.—(1) Subject to the provisions of this Schedule, the Board may do anything—
(a) which they consider necessary or expedient for securing the discharge of their functions; or
(b) which is calculated to facilitate or is incidental or conducive to the discharge of their functions.

(2) Without prejudice to the generality of sub-paragraph (1) above, the Board shall have power—
(a) to enter into any contract or agreement, including any contract or agreement to acquire or dispose of land;
(b) to invest and borrow money;
(c) to charge such fees as they may determine in respect of the discharge of their functions; and
(d) to apply sums received by them in respect of fees towards repayment of any grant made to them by virtue of section 16(2) of this Act.

12. Neither the Board nor any of their members, officers or servants shall be liable in damages for anything done or omitted in the discharge or purported discharge of their functions unless the act or omission is shown to have been in bad faith.

Accounts

13.—(1) The Board shall, in respect of each financial year, keep proper accounts and proper records in relation to the accounts.

(2) The accounts shall be audited annually by auditors appointed by the Board.

(3) No person shall be qualified to be appointed auditor under sub-paragraph (2) above unless he is a member of—
(a) the Institute of Chartered Accountants of Scotland;
(b) the Institute of Chartered Accountants in England and Wales;
(c) the Chartered Association of Certified Accountants; or
(d) the Institute of Chartered Accountants in Ireland,
but a firm may be so appointed if each of the partners is qualified to be so appointed.

(4) The Board shall send a copy of the audited accounts for each financial year to every practitioner.

(5) The Board shall, on receipt of such fee as they may determine, send a copy of the audited accounts to any person requesting it.

(6) In this paragraph, "financial year" means the period of 12 months ending with March 31, in each year.

Annual report

14. The Board shall, as soon as possible after March 31, in each year, submit a report to the Secretary of State on the exercise of their functions during the preceding 12 months, which the Secretary of State shall lay before each House of Parliament.

Appeals

15.—(1) The Board shall establish a procedure under which they shall, on the application of any aggrieved person, review any relevant decision made by them.

(2) In sub-paragraph (1) above—

"relevant decision" means—
>> (a) a refusal to grant an application for registration as an executry practitioner or a qualified conveyancer;
>> (b) a decision to grant an application for registration as an executry practitioner subject to conditions; or
>> (c) a decision to take any step set out in subsection (2)(a) to (g) of section 20 of this Act; and

"aggrieved person" means the applicant or, as the case may be, the executry practitioner or qualified conveyancer concerned.

Compensation

16.—(1) The Board shall establish and maintain a fund for the purpose of making grants to compensate persons who in the opinion of the Board have suffered pecuniary loss by reason of dishonesty in connection with the provision of—
(a) conveyancing services by or on behalf of an independent qualified conveyancer; or
(b) executry services by or on behalf of an executry practitioner.

(2) The Board may make rules with regard to the operation of the fund mentioned in sub-paragraph (1) above and, without prejudice to the foregoing generality, such rules may make provision as to—
(a) contributions to be paid to the fund by practitioners;
(b) the procedure for making claims against the fund; and
(c) the administration, management and protection of the fund.

Parliamentary disqualification

17. In Part II of Schedule 1 to the House of Commons Disqualification Act 1975 (bodies of which all members are disqualified) the following entry shall be inserted at the appropriate place in alphabetical order—
"The Scottish Conveyancing and Executry Services Board."

Part II

Powers of Investigation

18. The Board may exercise the power conferred by paragraph 19 below for the following purposes—
(a) an inquiry under subsection (1) of section 20 of this Act;
(b) a review of a decision by virtue of subsection (11)(a) of that section; and
(c) consideration by the Board whether to exercise the powers conferred on them by section 21 of this Act.

19. The Board may give notice in writing to a practitioner specifying the subject matter of their investigation and requiring either or both of the following—
>> (a) the production or delivery to any person appointed by the Board, at a time and place specified in the notice, of such documents so specified as are in the possession or control of the practitioner and relate to the subject matter of the investigation; and
>> (b) an explanation, within such period being not less than 21 days as the notice may specify, from the practitioner regarding the subject matter of the investigation.

20. If a practitioner fails to comply with a notice under paragraph 19(a) above, the Board may apply to the Court of Session for an order requiring the practitioner to produce or deliver the documents to the person appointed at the place specified in the notice within such time as the court may order.

General Note
This sets out the constitution, duties, powers and status of the Board. The most significant provision is that contained in para. 4(b) which was only added to the Bill at Report Stage in the House of Commons. It seeks to ensure that there is a proper balance between the interests of qualified conveyancers and executry practitioners and those of clients who make use of their services as regards the composition of the Board. This was an amendment which the Government was under considerable pressure to make throughout the legislative passage of the Act and was one which consumer interests lobbied hard to achieve. It is also a provision which was included in the original provisions of the Courts and Legal Services Bill as far as the composition of the Authorised Conveyancing Practitioners Board is concerned.

Section 25 SCHEDULE 2

Publication of Applications Made Under Section 25

1. Any professional or other body making an application under section 25 of this Act shall, for

a period of six weeks beginning with the date on which the application is submitted to the Lord President and the Secretary of State—

(a) make a copy of the draft scheme referred to in section 25(2) of this Act available for public inspection at a specified place; and

(b) on a request any person—

(i) send him a copy of the draft scheme; or

(ii) make a copy of the draft scheme available for public inspection at a suitable place in his locality.

2. Any person may make written representations concerning any draft scheme submitted under section 25 of this Act, and such representations shall—

(a) be made to both the Lord President and the Secretary of State; and

(b) be delivered to both the Lord President and the Secretary of State before the expiry of the period of six weeks beginning with the date on which the application is made.

3. At the same time as an application under section 25 is submitted to the Lord President and the Secretary of State, the body making the application shall place an advertisement mentioning the matters referred to in paragraph 4 below in the Edinburgh Gazette and in a daily newspaper circulating throughout Scotland.

4. An advertisement such as referred to in paragraph 3 above shall state that—

(a) a copy of the draft scheme referred to in section 25(2) of this Act will be available for public inspection at a specified place for a period of six weeks beginning with the date on which the advertisement appears;

(b) a copy of the draft scheme will be—

(i) sent, free of charge, to any person on request; or

(ii) made available for public inspection at a suitable place in that person's locality;

(c) any person may make written representations concerning the draft scheme to the Lord President and the Secretary of State; and

(d) any such representations are to be delivered within the period of six weeks beginning with the date on which the application is made.

Section 34   SCHEDULE 3

SCOTTISH LEGAL SERVICES OMBUDSMAN

1. The Scottish legal services ombudsman (the "ombudsman") shall hold and vacate his office in accordance with the terms of his appointment and shall, on ceasing to hold office, be eligible for re-appointment.

2. The Secretary of State may give general directions to the ombudsman about the scope and discharge of his functions, and shall publish any such directions.

3.—(1) The Secretary of State may with the consent of the Treasury determine the terms and conditions of service, including remuneration, of the ombudsman.

(2) Where a person appointed to the office of ombudsman ceases to hold that office otherwise than on the expiry of the term of office specified in his appointment, and it appears to the Secretary of State that there are special circumstances which make it right for the person to receive compensation, the Secretary of State may, with the consent of the Treasury, make a payment to that person of such amount as the Secretary of State may, with the consent of the Treasury, determine.

4. The Secretary of State may appoint staff for the ombudsman of such number, on such terms and conditions of service, as he may with the consent of the Treasury determine; and such terms and conditions may include provision as to remuneration, and as to compensation for loss of employment (which may take the form of pensions, allowances or gratuities).

5. Neither the ombudsman nor his staff are, in such capacity, Crown servants.

6. The Secretary of State shall pay the expenses of the ombudsman and of his staff.

7. Without prejudice to section 33(3) of this Act, a professional organisation within the meaning of subsection (5) of that section shall furnish the ombudsman with such information as he may from time to time reasonably require.

8. Every such professional organisation shall, severally, consider any report which they may receive from the ombudsman, and shall notify him of any action which they have taken in consequence.

9. The ombudsman shall make an annual report of the discharge of the functions conferred on him under this Act to the Secretary of State.

10. The Secretary of State shall lay any report made to him under paragraph 9 above before each House of Parliament.

11. In Part III of Schedule 1 to the House of Commons Disqualification Act 1975 (offices disqualifying for membership) there shall be inserted at the appropriate place in alphabetical order the entry "Scottish legal services ombudsman appointed under section 34 of the Law Reform (Miscellaneous Provisions) (Scotland) Act 1990."

　　　　　SCHEDULE 4

JUDICIAL APPOINTMENTS

Appointments of sheriffs principal, sheriffs and solicitors as judges of the Court of Session

1. The following categories of person shall, in accordance with this paragraph and paragraphs 2 and 3 below, be eligible to be appointed as judges of the Court of Session—
    (a) sheriffs principal and sheriffs who have held office as such for a continuous period of not less than five years; and
    (b) solicitors who, by virtue of section 25A (rights of audience) of the Solicitors (Scotland) Act 1980, have for a continuous period of not less than five years had a right of audience in both the Court of Session and the High Court of Justiciary.

2. Paragraph 1(a) above shall not confer any eligibility for appointment as a judge of the Court of Session on a temporary sheriff principal or sheriff appointed under section 11 (temporary sheriffs principal and sheriffs) of the Sheriff Courts (Scotland) Act 1971 who is not otherwise eligible for appointment as a judge of the Court of Session.

3. Paragraphs 1 and 2 above are without prejudice to any eligibility to be appointed as a judge of the Court of Session conferred on any category of persons by any other enactment.

Further provision as to Inner House and exchequer causes

4.—(1) The Court of Session Act 1988 shall be amended as follows.

(2) In section 2 (composition of court)—
    (a) in subsection (3), for the words "the senior judge present shall preside and shall" there shall be substituted the words "shall direct one of those judges to preside and to"; and
    (b) for subsection (6) there shall be substituted the following subsection—
       "(6) Subject to subsection (7) below, where a vacancy arises in a Division of the Inner House the Lord President and the Lord Justice Clerk, with the consent of the Secretary of State and after such consultation with judges as appears to them to be appropriate in the particular circumstances, shall appoint a Lord Ordinary to fill that vacancy.".

(3) In section 3 (exchequer causes), for the words "Court by Act of Sederunt" there shall be substituted the words "Lord President."

Temporary judges

5. Any person who is eligible under—
    (a) paragraph 1 above; or
    (b) any other enactment,
for appointment as a judge of the Court of Session may be appointed as a temporary judge under section 35(3) of this Act for such period as the Secretary of State may determine, but, subject to paragraph 9 below, no such appointment shall extend beyond the date on which the person reaches the age of 75 years.

6. Subject to paragraph 7 below, a person appointed as a temporary judge under the said section 35(3) shall, while so acting, be treated for all purposes as, and accordingly may perform any of the functions of, a judge of the Court in which he is acting.

7. Subject to paragraph 8 below, a person shall not, by virtue of paragraph 6 above, be treated as a judge of the Court of Session for the purposes of any other enactment or rule of law relating to—
    (a) the appointment, tenure of office, retirement, removal or disqualification of judges of that Court, including, without prejudice to the generality of the foregoing, any enactment or rule of law relating to the number of judges who may be appointed; and
    (b) the remuneration, allowances or pensions of such judges.

8. A person appointed to be a temporary judge of the Court of Session shall, by virtue of such appointment, be a temporary Lord Commissioner of Justiciary in Scotland.

9. Notwithstanding the expiry of any period for which a person is appointed under the said section 35(3) to act as a judge—
    (a) he may attend at the Court of Session or the High Court of Justiciary for the purpose of continuing to deal with, giving judgment in, or dealing with any matter relating to, any case begun before him while acting as a judge of either Court; and
    (b) for that purpose, and for the purpose of any proceedings arising out of any such case or matter, he shall be treated as being or, as the case may be, having been, a judge of the relevant Court.

10. The Secretary of State may pay to a person appointed under the said section 35(3) such remuneration as he may, with the consent of the Treasury, determine.

11. The appointment of a person to act as a temporary judge under the said section 35(3) is without prejudice to—

(a) any appointment held by him as a sheriff principal or sheriff; or

(b) his continuing with any business or professional occupation not inconsistent with his acting as a judge.

Amendments to the Small Landholders (Scotland) Act 1911 (c. 49)

12.—(1) The Small Landholders (Scotland) Act 1911 shall be amended as follows.

(2) For subsection (2) of section 3 (constitution of Scottish Land Court) there shall be substituted the following subsections—

"(2) The Chairman shall be a person who at the date of his appointment is—

(a) an advocate of the Scottish Bar of not less than ten years' standing; or

(b) without prejudice to paragraph (a) above, a sheriff principal or sheriff who has held office as such for a continuous period of not less than ten years; or

(c) a solicitor who, by virtue of section 25A (rights of audience) of the Solicitors (Scotland) Act 1980, has for a continuous period of not less than ten years had a right of audience in the Court of Session;

and shall forthwith on his appointment have the same rank and tenure of office as if he had been appointed a judge of the Court of Session.

(2A) Subsection (2)(b) above shall not confer any eligibility for appointment as Chairman on a temporary sheriff principal or sheriff appointed under section 11 (temporary sheriffs principal and sheriffs) of the Sheriff Courts (Scotland) Act 1971 who is not otherwise eligible for such appointment.".

(3) For subsection (5) of section 3 there shall be substituted the following subsections—

"(5) The Secretary of State may appoint any person having the qualification required for holding the office of Chairman as a Deputy Chairman, who shall act in place of the Chairman for such periods as the Chairman may, with the consent of the Secretary of State, direct.

(5A) Where there is a vacancy in the office of Chairman, or where the Chairman is, for whatever reason, unable to act, the Deputy Chairman shall act at the direction of the Secretary of State.

(5B) A Deputy Chairman appointed under subsection (5) above shall, while he is acting as Chairman, have the same powers and perform the same duties as if he were the Chairman.".

Section 49   SCHEDULE 5

APPLICATIONS FOR CHILDREN'S CERTIFICATES

1. Applications may be made to a licensing board in accordance with the provisions of this Schedule for a children's certificate within the meaning of section 49 of this Act.

2. The holder of a public house licence or hotel licence in respect of any premises or the applicant for a new public house or hotel licence or for the renewal of such a licence may make an application for a children's certificate in respect of those premises, and any such application shall be in such form as may be prescribed, shall be completed and signed by the applicant or his agent and shall be lodged with the clerk of the licensing board within whose area the premises are situated not later than five weeks before the first day of the meeting of the board at which the application is to be considered.

3.—(1) On any application for the grant of a children's certificate in respect of only part of any premises, the licensing board may require a plan of the premises to which the application relates to be produced to it and lodged with the clerk.

(2) A plan produced and lodged in accordance with this paragraph shall be such as will enable the board to ascertain to which part of the premises it is proposed the certificate should relate.

4. A copy of every application made under this Schedule shall be sent by the applicant to the chief constable, and if the chief constable desires to object to the grant of a children's certificate he shall, not later than seven days before the meeting of the licensing board at which the application is to be considered—

(a) lodge with the clerk of the board a written notice of his objection specifying the grounds of his objection to the grant of the certificate; and

(b) intimate such objection and grounds to the applicant,

and the chief constable shall be entitled to appear at the meeting of the licensing board which considers the application and make objection to the grant of the certificate.

5. A licensing board shall not, within two years of its refusal of an application made under paragraph 2 above in respect of any premises, entertain another such application in respect of those premises unless it has made a direction to the contrary in respect of that refusal.

6. An application for a new public house licence or hotel licence or for the renewal of such a licence under section 10 of the principal Act shall state whether the applicant is making an application for a children's certificate.

7. The grant of an application for a children's certificate shall come into effect on the making of the grant or, in the case of such an application made with an application for a new public house or hotel licence, on the day on which such licence comes into effect.

8. The grant of an application for a children's certificate made at the time of an application for the renewal of a licence shall come into effect on the renewal of the licence to which the application relates.

9. If an application for a children's certificate is made at the same time as an application for the renewal of a licence, any existing grant of such an application for a children's certificate shall continue to have effect until the first mentioned application is granted or, as the case may be, refused by the board.

10. The grant of an application for a children's certificate shall cease to have effect when the licence to which it relates ceases to have effect.

GENERAL NOTE

Application procedure for a children's certificate
Para. 2
   The holder of a public-house or hotel licence may apply. The applicant for a new public-house or hotel licence or the renewal of the same may also apply. Applications are to be made in the form prescribed (sometimes by regulation in terms of s.37 of 1976 Act). The application must be lodged five weeks before the meeting of the board, but does not need to be considered at a quarterly meeting only.

Para. 3
   Plans may be required of premises to which the application relates. The lodging of plans may be referred to in individual boards' regulations (s.37 of the 1976 Act) and the regulations may require plans to be to a certain scale and that a certain number be lodged. The plans should indicate the parts of premises to which the application relates.

Para. 4
   A copy of the application should be sent to the Chief Constable by the *applicant*. The Chief Constable may, at least seven clear days before the board's meeting, (a) object by lodging a written notice of objection and he must (b) intimate the grounds of his objection to the applicant.

Para. 5
   This provision introduces in respect of children's certificates a similar provision to that which applies to the refusal of an application for a new licence (s.14 of the 1976 Act), namely, that a further application in respect of the same premises cannot be made within two years of the refusal of an application unless the board make a direction to the contrary. Unlike the terms of s.14 of the 1976 Act, this provision does not require that the direction be requested and made at the time of the refusal. If not requested at the time of the refusal, the request should probably be made in writing as soon as practicable thereafter.

Para. 6
   When making an application for a new public-house or hotel licence or renewal of same, the applicant should state whether application is also being made for a children's certificate. (This is similar to the new arrangements for Sunday opening in terms of s.46 of this Act.)

Para. 7
   This provision stipulates when a children's certificate comes into effect, namely, on the making of the grant of the application, or, in respect of a new public-house or hotel licence when the new licence comes into effect. This clarifies the position as regards application for children's certificates by the holder of a provisional licence and does not follow the decision in *Ginera* v. *City of Glasgow District Licensing Board* 1982 S.L.T. 136.

Para. 8
   A children's certificate applied for at the same time as the renewal of a licence comes into effect on the renewal of the licence: see s.30(5) of the 1976 Act.

Para. 9
   An existing grant of a children's certificate remains in effect pending the consideration and grant or refusal of a further application for a children's certificate made at the same time as an application for renewal of a licence: s.30(5) of the 1976 Act.

A children's certificate only subsists while the licence to which it relates continues to have effect.

Section 62   SCHEDULE 6

SUPERVISED ATTENDANCE ORDERS: FURTHER PROVISIONS

1.—(1) A court shall not make a supervised attendance order in respect of any offender unless—
- (a) the court has been notified by the Secretary of State that arrangements exist for persons who reside in the locality in which the offender resides, or will be residing when the order comes into force, to carry out the requirements of such an order.
- (b) the court is satisfied that provision can be made under the arrangements mentioned in paragraph (a) above for the offender to carry out such requirements.

(2) Before making a supervised attendance order, the court shall explain to the offender in ordinary language—
- (a) the purpose and effect of the order and in particular the obligations on the offender as specified in paragraph 3 below;
- (b) the consequences which may follow under paragraph 4 below if he fails to comply with any of those requirements; and
- (c) that the court has, under paragraph 5 below, the power to review the order on the application either of the offender or of an officer of the local authority in whose area the offender for the time being resides.

(3) The Secretary of State may by order direct the subsection (2) of section 62 of this Act shall be amended by substituting, for any number of hours specified in that subsection such other number of hours as may be specified in the order; and an order under this subsection may in making such amendment specify different such numbers of hours for different classes of case.

(4) An order under paragraph (3) above shall be made by statutory instrument, but no such order shall be unless a draft of it has been laid before, and approved by a resolution of, each House of Parliament.

2.—(1) A supervised attendance order shall—
- (a) specify the locality in which the offender resides or will be residing when the order comes into force; and
- (b) require the local authority in whose area the locality specified under paragraph (a) above is situated to appoint or assign a supervising officer.

(2) Where, whether on the same occasion or on separate occasions, an offender is made subject to more than one supervised attendance order, the court may direct that the requirements specified in any of those orders shall be concurrent with or additional to those specified in any other of those orders, but so that at no time shall the offender have an outstanding number of hours during which he must carry out the requirements of these orders in excess of the largest number specified in section 62 of this Act.

(3) Upon making a supervised attendance order the court shall—
- (a) give a copy of the order to the offender;
- (b) send a copy of the order to the director of social work of the local authority in whose area the offender resides or will be residing when the order comes into force; and
- (c) where it is not the appropriate court, send a copy of the order (together with such documents and information relating to the case as are considered useful) to the clerk of the appropriate court.

3.—(1) An offender in respect of whom a supervised attendance order is in force shall report to the supervising officer and notify him without delay of any change of address or in the times, if any, at which he usually works.

(2) Subject to paragraph 5(1) below, instructions given under a supervised attendance order shall be carried out during the period of twelve months beginning with the date of the order; but, unless revoked, the order shall remain in force until the offender has carried out the instructions given under it for the number of hours specified in it.

(3) The instructions given by the supervising officer under the order shall, so far as practicable, be such as to avoid any conflict with the offender's religious beliefs and any interference with the times, if any, at which he normally works or attends a school or other educational establishment.

4.—(1) If at any time while a supervised attendance order is in force in respect of any offender it appears to the appropriate court, on evidence on oath from the supervising officer, that that offender has failed to comply with any of the requirements of paragraph 3 above or of the order (including any failure satisfactorily to carry out any instructions which he has been given by the supervising officer under the order), the court may issue a warrant for the arrest of that offender, or may, if it thinks fit, instead of issuing a warrant in the first instance issue a citation requiring the offender to appear before that court at such time as may be specified in the citation.

(2) If it is proved to the satisfaction of the court before which an offender is brought or appears in pursuance of sub-paragraph (1) above that he has failed without reasonable excuse to comply with any of the requirements of paragraph 3 above or of the order (including any failure satisfactorily to carry out any instructions which he has been given by the supervising officer under the order), the court may—

    (a) revoke the order and impose such period of imprisonment as could, in respect of the original default or failure, have been imposed by the court which made the order if the order had not been made; or

    (b) subject to section 62 of this Act and paragraph 2(2) above, vary the number of hours specified in the order.

(3) The evidence of one witness shall, for the purposes of sub-paragraph (2) above, be sufficient evidence.

5.—(1) Where a supervised attendance order is in force in respect of any offender and, on the application of that offender or of the supervising officer, it appears to the appropriate court that it would be in the interests of justice to do so having regard to circumstances which have arisen since the order was made, that court may—

    (a) extend, in relation to the order, the period of twelve months specified in paragraph 3 above;

    (b) subject to section 62 of this Act and paragraph 2(2) above, vary the number of hours specified in the order;

    (c) revoke the order; or

    (d) revoke the order and impose such period of imprisonment as could, in respect of the original default or failure, have been imposed by the court which made the order if the order had not been made.

(2) If the appropriate court is satisfied that the offender proposes to change, or has changed, his residence from the locality for the time being specified under paragraph 2(1)(a) above to another locality and—

    (a) that court has been notified by the Secretary of State that arrangements exist for persons who reside in that other locality to carry out instructions under supervised attendance orders; and

    (b) it appears to that court that provision can be made under those arrangements for him to carry out instructions under the order;

that court may, and on application of the supervising officer shall, amend the order by substituting that other locality for the locality for the time being specified in the order; and the provisions of section 62 of this Act and of this Schedule shall apply to the order as amended.

(3) Where the court proposes to exercise its powers under sub-paragraph (1)(a), (b) or (d) above otherwise than on the application of the offender, it shall issue a citation requiring him to appear before the court and, if he fails to appear, may issue a warrant for his arrest.

6.—(1) The Secretary of State may make rules for regulating the carrying out of the requirements of supervised attendance orders.

(2) Without prejudice to the generality of subsection (1) above, rules under this section may—

    (a) limit the number of hours during which the requirements of an order are to be met on any one day;

    (b) make provision as to the reckoning of time for the purposes of the carrying out of these requirements;

    (c) make provision for the payment of travelling and other expenses in connection with the carrying out of these requirements;

    (d) provide for records to be kept of what has been done by any person carrying out these requirements.

(3) Rules under this paragraph shall be made by statutory instrument subject to annulment in pursuance of a resolution of either House of Parliament.

7. The Secretary of State shall lay before Parliament each year, or incorporate in annual reports he already makes, a report of the operation of section 62 of this Act and this Schedule.

8. In section 27 of the Social Work (Scotland) Act 1968 (supervision of persons put on probation, released from prison or subject to community service orders)—

    (a) in subsection (1)(b) there shall be inserted at the end the following "; and

        (iv) without prejudice to paragraphs (i) to (iii) above, persons in their area who are subject to supervised attendance orders under section 62 of the Law Reform (Miscellaneous Provisions) (Scotland) Act 1990.";

    (b) for the words "probation and community service scheme," wherever they occur, there shall be substituted the words "probation, community service and supervised attendance scheme."

9.—(1) In this Schedule—

"the appropriate court," in relation to a supervised attendance order, means the court having jurisdiction in the locality for the time being specified in the order under paragraph 2(1)(a) above, being a sheriff or district court according to whether the order has been made by a sheriff or a district court, but in a case where the order has been made by a district court and there is no district court in that locality, the sheriff court;

"local authority" and "supervising officer" have the same meanings respectively as in section 62 of this Act.

(2) Except where the context otherwise requires, expressions used in this Schedule and in the Criminal Procedure (Scotland) Act 1975 have the same meanings in this Schedule as in that Act.

Section 66   SCHEDULE 7

UNCITRAL

MODEL LAW ON INTERNATIONAL COMMERCIAL ARBITRATION

CHAPTER 1

GENERAL PROVISIONS

Article 1

Scope of application

(1) This Law applies to international commercial arbitration, subject to any agreement in force between the United Kingdom and any other State or States which applies in Scotland.

(2) The provisions of this Law, except articles 8, 9, 35 and 36, apply only if the place of arbitration is in Scotland.

(3) An arbitration is international if:

(a) the parties to an arbitration agreement have, at the time of the conclusion of that agreement, their places of business in different States; or

(b) one of the following places is situated outside the State in which the parties have their places of business:

(i) the place of arbitration if determined in, or pursuant to, the arbitration agreement;

(ii) any place where a substantial part of the obligations of the commercial relationship is to be performed or the place with which the subject-matter of the dispute is most closely connected.

(4) For the purposes of paragraph (3) of this article:

(a) if a party has more than one place of business, the place of business is that which has the closest relationship to the arbitration agreement;

(b) if a party does not have a place of business, reference is to be made to his habitual residence.

(5) This Law shall not affect any other enactment or rule of law in force in Scotland by virtue of which certain disputes may not be submitted to arbitration or may be submitted to arbitration only according to provisions other than those of this Law.

GENERAL NOTE

Para. (1)
International. See note to art. 1(2) below.

Overriding Treaties
Subject to any agreement in force. It is a fundamental principle of the Model Law that its provisions yield to any contrary treaty obligations binding the state in question (Scotland).

Commercial
It will be seen that art. 2(d) states that the term commercial embraces matters arising from all relationships of a commercial nature whether contractual or not. Relationships of a commercial nature are defined as including an extremely wide-ranging set of transactions under art. 2(g).

Para. (2)
Territorial Scope of Application
UNCITRAL eventually agreed that it would be the place of arbitration which determined the applicability of the Model Law.

Exceptions to the Territorial Scope

There are four articles which are not confined by the principle of the territorial scope of application. Under art. 8(1) any court before which an action is brought regarding any matter which is the subject of a valid arbitration agreement, must refer the parties to arbitration. art. 9 establishes the compatibility of an arbitration agreement with a request to a court for an interim measure of protection. Lastly, under arts. 35 and 36 the same régime is applied to the recognition and enforcement of awards made within and outwith Scotland. Aside from these four articles the provisions of Sched. 7 only apply where Scotland is the place of arbitration.

Paras. (3) and (4)

International. An arbitration is international if it falls into any one of the following separate categories:

Firstly, where the parties have, at the time of entering the arbitration agreement, their places of business in different states. It is recognised that a party may have more than one place of business, so that art. 1(4)(a) stipulates that one must focus on that place of business which has the closest relationship to the arbitration agreement. Art. 1(4)(b), moreover, acknowledges that the parties to an arbitration covered by the Model Law need not be commercial individuals or organisations by stating that, if a party does not have a place of business, then reference must be had to his place of habitual residence.

There are of course circumstances, recognised by art. 1(3)(b), where the test of internationality is satisfied even where the parties have their places of business (or place of habitual residence where a party has no place of business) in the same state. The first arises where, under art. 1(3)(b)(i), the place of arbitration is in a different state.

Secondly, the test is satisfied where a substantial part of the obligations is to be performed in a state other than that where the parties have their places of business.

Finally, an arbitration may be international where the parties have their places of business in the same state, if the place with which the subject matter of the dispute is most closely connected is in another state.

By virtue of Art. 2(h) State includes Scotland.

Para. (5)

Arbitrability

This provision makes it clear that the Model Law has no effect on any rule of Scots law whereby certain matters may not be settled by reference to arbitration or may only be settled according to a specific régime.

Article 2

Definitions and rules of interpretation

For the purposes of this Law:
  (a) "arbitration" means any arbitration whether or not administered by a permanent arbitral institution;
  (b) "arbitral tribunal" means an arbitrator or a panel of arbitrators;
  (c) "arbitrator" includes an arbiter;
  (d) "commercial," in relation to an arbitration, includes matters arising from all relationships of a commercial nature, whether contractual or not;
  (e) "country" includes Scotland;
  (f) "court" means a body or organ of the judicial system of a State;
  (g) "relationships of a commercial nature" include, but are not limited to, the following transactions, namely any trade transaction for the supply or exchange of goods or services; distribution agreement; commercial representation or agency; factoring; leasing; construction of works; consulting; engineering; licensing; investment; financing; banking; insurance; exploitation agreement or concession; joint venture and other forms of industrial or business co-operation; carriage of goods or passengers by air, sea, rail or road;
  (h) "State," except in article 1(1), includes Scotland;
  (i) where a provision of this Law, except article 28, leaves the parties free to determine a certain issue, such freedom includes the right of the parties to authorise a third party, including an institution, to make that determination;
  (j) where a provision of this Law refers to the fact that the parties have agreed or that they may agree or in any other way refers to an agreement of the parties, such agreement includes any arbitration rules referred to in that agreement;
  (k) where a provision of this Law, other than in articles 25(a) and 32(2)(a), refers to a claim, it also applies to a counter-claim, and where it refers to a defence, it also applies to a defence to such counter-claim;

(l) article headings are for reference purposes only and are not to be used for purposes of interpretation.

GENERAL NOTE

Introduction
Although headed "Definitions and Rules of Interpretation", this article does not contain an exhaustive list of definitions contained in the Model Law. Moreover, most of the terms which appear are not actually defined as much as clarified in one or more respects.

Subpara. (a)
Arbitration
This is obviously not a definition, merely an acknowledgement that the Model Law applies to both "ad hoc and institutional arbitration".

Subparas. (e) and (h)
Country and *State*. The term country is only employed in the Model Law in arts. 35 and 36 relating to recognition and enforcement of awards, the term State being otherwise employed throughout. The terms are nowhere defined in the Model Law but Scots lawyers in particular should have no difficulty recognising the difference between them, Scotland being a country but not a state. It is therefore quite important that the Model Law deems Scotland to be a State for its purposes.

Subparas. (i) (j) (k) (l)
Rules of Interpretation
Firstly, subpara. (i) makes it clear that where the parties have freedom to determine an issue, *e.g.* number of arbitrators, this freedom includes the right to authorise a third party (including an institution) to determine the issue.
It is made clear by subpara. (j) that where it is open to the parties to agree on any matter, such agreement will be taken to refer to implied agreement through the invocation of arbitration rules, *e.g.* UNCITRAL Arbitration Rules.
Subpara. (k) makes it clear that any reference in the Model Law to a claim or a defence applies *mutatis mutandis* to a counterclaim and a defence thereto.

Article 3

Receipt of written communications

(1) Unless otherwise agreed by the parties:
(a) any written communication is deemed to have been received if it is delivered to the addressee personally or if it is delivered at his place of business, habitual residence or mailing address; if none of these can be found after making a reasonable inquiry, a written communication is deemed to have been received if it is sent to the addressee's last-known place of business, habitual residence or mailing address by registered letter or any other means which provides a record of the attempts to deliver it;
(b) the communication is deemed to have been received on the day it is so delivered.
(2) The provisions of this article do not apply to communications in court proceedings.

GENERAL NOTE
Most arbitrations will witness a considerable amount of correspondence. Difficulties may well arise if any dispute emerges as to whether a communication was properly delivered or received, or when it was received. Art. 3 provides rules to resolve any such difficulties. This is a non-mandatory article in that its provisions will not apply if the parties themselves have chosen to deal with the matter.
It may be noted that art. 3 is couched in terms of deemed reception. It is therefore not necessary that an addressee should actually receive a written communication at all, as long as the rules have been complied with.
The primary requirement of art. 3 is that the communication be delivered to the addressee personally, or at his place of business, habitual residence or mailing address. These are alternatives and none is preferred to any other.
The first part of art. 3(a) deals with actual delivery, the second with constructive delivery. If neither the addressee's place of business, nor habitual residence, nor mailing address can be found after making a reasonable enquiry, receipt of a written communication is deemed if that communication is sent to the addressee's last known place of business, habitual residence, or mailing address by registered letter or any other means which provides a record of the attempt to deliver it.

Article 4

Waiver of right to object

A party who knows that any provision of this Law from which the parties may derogate or any requirement under the arbitration agreement has not been complied with and yet proceeds with the arbitration without stating his objections to such non-compliance without undue delay or, if a time-limit is provided therefor, within such period of time, shall be deemed to have waived his right to object.

GENERAL NOTE

Conditions for Operation of the Waiver Principle
　　Readers will recognise that the concept of waiver corresponds to the principle of personal bar. The operation of art. 4, however, is subject to a number of express conditions.
　　Firstly, the party must have known of the non compliance. Secondly, the objector must make his objection within the time limit provided by the Model Law or the arbitration agreement. Where neither the Model Law nor the arbitration agreement impose a time limit, then the objection must be stated without undue delay if the right to object is not to be deemed to be waived.
　　Another requirement for the application of art. 4 is that the party who has failed to state an objection should proceed with the arbitration.

Article 5

Extent of court intervention

　　In matters governed by his Law, no court shall intervene except where so provided in this Law.

GENERAL NOTE
　　Despite its brevity, this is one of the most important articles in the Model Law and one which is liable to occasion considerable uncertainty in practice.

Article 6

Court for certain functions of arbitration assistance, supervision and enforcement

　　The functions referred to in articles 11(3), 11(4), 13(3), 14, 16(3), 34(2), 35 and 36 shall be performed by:
　　(a)　the Court of Session; or
　　(b)　where it has jurisdiction, the sheriff court.

GENERAL NOTE
　　Art. 6 is fairly straightforward. Various articles refer to "the court" performing various functions, and it is necessary for that court to be designated.
　　It can be seen that the competent court in Scotland is to be either the Court of Session or the Sheriff Court where it has jurisdiction.

CHAPTER II

ARBITRATION AGREEMENT

Article 7

Definition and form of arbitration agreement

　　(1) "Arbitration agreement" is an agreement by the parties to submit to arbitration all or certain disputes which have arisen or which may arise between them in respect of a defined legal relationship, whether contractual or not. An arbitration agreement may be in the form of an arbitration clause in a contract or in the form of a separate agreement.
　　(2) The arbitration agreement shall be in writing. An agreement is in writing if it is contained in a document signed by the parties or in an exchange of letters, telex, telegrams or other means of telecommunication which provide a record of the agreement, or in an exchange of statements of claim and defence in which the existence of an agreement is alleged by one party and not denied by another. The reference in a contract to a document containing an arbitration clause

constitutes an arbitration agreement provided that the contract is in writing and the reference is such as to make that clause part of the contract.

GENERAL NOTE

Para. (1)
Definition of Arbitration Agreement
Art. 7(1) encompasses within the definition any agreement to refer existing or future disputes to arbitration.
It is clear from the terms of art. 7(1) that a legal dispute is contemplated and it is expressly stated that this dispute need not be contractual.

Para. (2)
Form of the Arbitration Agreement
Para. (2) is concerned with the form of the arbitration agreement.

Agreement in Writing
The Model Law contemplates first and foremost that the arbitration agreement shall be in writing (although this is later subject to considerable qualification).

Incorporation of Arbitration Clause
What is the position where the arbitration agreement is to be found in some document other than those embodying the contract between the parties? The last sentence of art. 7(2) represents the Model Law's solution of this problem. Thus we have the position that the requirements of form are satisfied where an arbitration clause is simply referred to, provided that the contract is in writing and the reference makes the clause part of the contract.

What is Writing?
Clearly probative writing is not required. There may be a document signed by both of the parties or an exchange of letters, telexes, telegrams or other means of telecommunication which provide a record of the agreement.

Deemed Writing—Exchange of Statements of Claim and Defence
The requirement that the agreement be in writing is deemed to be met if the parties have exchanged statements of claim and defence (see note to art. 23) in which the existence of an agreement is alleged by one party and not denied by the other.

Article 8

Arbitration agreement and substantive claim before court

(1) A court before which an action is brought in a matter which is the subject of an arbitration agreement shall, if a party so requests at any time before the pleadings in the action are finalised, refer the parties to arbitration unless it finds that the agreement is null and void, inoperative or incapable of being performed.
(2) Where an action referred to in paragraph (1) of this article has been brought, arbitral proceedings may nevertheless be commenced or continued, and an award may be made, while the issue is pending before the court.

GENERAL NOTE

Para. (1)
What is the effect of an arbitration agreement upon a party's right to raise the matter before the courts? Most readers will be familiar with the statement of Lord Dunedin in *Sanderson* v. *Armour & Co.* 1922 S.C. (H.L.) 117 at 126,
"If the parties have contracted to arbitrate, to arbitration they must go".
The plea that the matter is subject to an arbitration agreement must be raised by one of the parties, and it is not open to the court to raise the point of its own motion. Moreover, art. 8(1) stipulates a time limit by which the plea must be raised if it is to be entertained by the court.
Art. 8(1) further provides that even if the existence of the arbitration agreement is timeously raised, the court shall not refer the matter to arbitration if it feels that the agreement is "null and void inoperative or incapable of being performed".
It can be appreciated then that the issue of the validity of the agreement must be raised by the party who has raised the action. The court will not enquire into its validity of its own motion.

Para. (2)
This provision allows arbitral proceedings to be commenced or continued even to the extent of making an award where an action is brought before the court.

Article 9

Arbitration agreement and interim measures by court

(1) It is not incompatible with an arbitration agreement for a party to request, before or during arbitral proceedings, from a court an interim measure of protection and for a court to grant such measure.

(2) In paragraph (1) of this article "interim measure of protection" includes, but is not limited to, the following:

(a) arrestment or inhibition to ensure that any award which may be made in the arbitral proceedings is not rendered ineffectual by the dissipation of assets by another party;

(b) interim interdict or other interim order.

(3) Where:

(a) a party applies to a court for an interim interdict or other interim order; and

(b) an arbitral tribunal has already ruled on the matter,

the court shall treat the ruling or any finding of fact made in the course of the ruling as conclusive for the purposes of the application.

GENERAL NOTE
This Article is relatively straightforward. Art. 9(1) serves to emphasise that a party is not barred from arbitrating by seeking interim measures of protection from a court, whether before or during arbitral proceedings. Nor is a court barred from granting such measures of protection because of the existence of an arbitration agreement.

CHAPTER III

COMPOSITION OF ARBITRATION TRIBUNAL

Article 10

Number of arbitrators

(1) The parties are free to determine the number of arbitrators.

(2) Failing such determination, there shall be a single arbitrator.

GENERAL NOTE

Para. (1)
This is a familiar position for Scots lawyers.

Para. (2)
This is a straightforward provision.

Article 11

Appointment of arbitrators

(1) No person shall be precluded by reason of his nationality from acting as an arbitrator, unless otherwise agreed by the parties.

(2) The parties are free to agree on a procedure of appointing the arbitrator or arbitrators, subject to the provisions of paragraphs (4) and (5) of this article.

(3) Failing such agreement,

(a) in an arbitration with three arbitrators, each party shall appoint one arbitrator, and the two arbitrators thus appointed shall appoint the third arbitrator; if a party fails to appoint the arbitrator within thirty days of receipt of a request to do so from the other party, of if the two arbitrators fail to agree on the third arbitrator within thirty days of their appointment, the appointment shall be made, upon request of a party, by the court specified in article 6;

(b) in an arbitration with a single arbitrator, if the parties are unable to agree on the arbitrator, he shall be appointed, upon request of a party, by the court specified in article 6.

(4) Where, under an appointment procedure agreed upon by the parties:

(a) a party fails to act as required under such procedure, or

(b) the parties, or two arbitrators, are unable to reach an agreement expected of them under such procedure, or

(c) a third party, including an institution, fails to perform any function entrusted to it under such procedure,

any party may request the court specified in article 6 to take the necessary measure, unless the agreement on the appointment procedure provides other means for securing the appointment.

(5) A decision on a matter entrusted by paragraph (3) or (4) of this article to the court specified in article 6 shall be subject to no appeal. The court, in appointing an arbitrator, shall have due regard to any qualifications required of the arbitrator by the agreement of the parties and to such considerations as are likely to secure the appointment of an independent and impartial arbitrator and, in the case of a sole or third arbitrator, shall take into account as well the advisability of appointing an arbitrator of a nationality other than those of the parties.

GENERAL NOTE

Para. (1)
Introduction
This paragraph is really directed towards those jurisdictions which insist that the arbitrator is a different nationality from the parties. Scots law has never taken up such a position.

The remainder of art. 11 stipulates that prima facie the parties will agree on procedures for appointing arbitrators, but provides certain procedures which will operate in the absence of agreement, allowing the court to take such steps as will secure the appointment where procedures break down. This article should be read in conjunction with arts. 14 and 15. Together the three articles deal exhaustively with the issue of appointment, including the consequences of any failure in appointment.

Para. (2)
Agreement of the Parties
The Model Law looks initially for the parties to agree upon an appointment procedure, the seeming qualification of paras. (4) and (5) relating only to the consequences of appointment procedures breaking down.

Appointment in the Case of Failure to Agree
Art. 11(3) lays down procedures for the appointment of an arbitrator when the parties have failed to agree upon a procedure for appointment—in the case of a three arbitrator tribunal under art. 11(3)(c), and in the case of a single arbitrator under art. 11(3)(b).

Appointment by Court where Agreed Procedure Breaks Down
Art. 11(4) allows for any party to petition the court where the appointment procedure agreed upon by the parties breaks down, *unless that procedure "provides other means for securing the appointment".*

Para. (5)
Criteria to be Followed by Court in Making Appointment
Para. (5) indicates the criteria by which the court should be guided in appointing an arbiter under paras. (3) or (4).

Article 12

Grounds for challenge

(1) When a person is approached in connection with his possible appointment as an arbitrator, he shall disclose any circumstances likely to give rise to justifiable doubts as to his impartiality or independence. An arbitrator, from the time of his appointment and throughout the arbitral proceedings, shall without delay disclose any such circumstances to the parties unless they have already been informed by them by him.

(2) An arbitrator may be challenged only if circumstances exist that give rise to justifiable doubts as to his impartiality or independence, or if he does not possess qualifications agreed to by the parties. A party may challenge an arbitrator appointed by him, or in whose appointment he has participated, only for reasons of which he becomes aware after the appointment has been made.

GENERAL NOTE

Para. (1)
Arbitrator's Duty of Disclosure
Art. 12(1) imposes a duty upon an arbitrator to disclose circumstances which are likely to give

40–124

rise to justifiable doubts as to his impartiality and independence. This duty is imposed at two stages. The first is when he is approached in connection with his possible appointment. The provision demands disclosure at a second stage specifically to the parties—at the time of his appointment and throughout the arbitral proceedings—unless the parties have already been informed of the circumstances.

Para. (2)
Grounds of Challenge
The meaning of "circumstances that give rise to justifiable doubts as to his impartiality or independence" is somewhat dubious. The other ground for challenge is that the arbitrator lacks qualifications agreed to by the parties.

Finally, the last sentence recites that a party may challenge an arbitrator appointed by him or in whose appointment he participated, only for reasons of which he becomes aware after the appointment is made. In other words if a party participates in an arbitrator's appointment knowing full well that circumstances exist which make the arbitrator liable to challenge, he is not thereafter allowed to rely on these circumstances to challenge the arbitrator.

Article 13

Challenge procedure

(1) The parties are free to agree on a procedure for challenging an arbitrator, subject to the provisions of paragraph (3) of this article.

(2) Failing such agreement, a party who intends to challenge an arbitrator shall, within fifteen days after becoming aware of the constitution of the arbitral tribunal or after becoming aware of any circumstances referred to in article 12(2), send a written statement of the reasons for the challenge to the arbitral tribunal. Unless the challenged arbitrator withdraws from his office or the other party agrees to the challenge, the arbitral tribunal shall decide on the challenge.

(3) If a challenge under any procedure agreed upon by the parties or under the procedure of paragraph (2) of this article is not successful, the challenging party may, within thirty days after having received notice of the decision rejecting the challenge, request the court specified in article 6 to decide on the challenge, which decision shall be subject to no appeal. While such a request is pending, the arbitral tribunal, including the challenged arbitrator, may continue the arbitral proceedings and make an award.

GENERAL NOTE
Having specified the grounds of challenge under art. 12, art. 13 considers the issue of a procedure for making such a challenge.

Para. (1)
Agreed Challenge Procedures
The article starts out from the initial premise that the parties are free to agree upon their own challenge procedure. The freedom of the parties is, however, subject to important limitations imposed by para. (3).

Para. (2)
Challenge Procedure Where No Agreement can be Reached
Should the parties fail to agree on a challenge procedure, one is provided for them. It will be noted that the challenge must be directed to the arbitral tribunal. Three possibilities are then canvassed. The arbitrator withdraws from office. The other party accepts the challenge, in which case the arbitrator is effectively removed from office. Thirdly, neither of these things happen, in which case the arbitral tribunal itself decides upon the challenge. Obviously then, the challenged arbitrator will participate in the decision on the challenge.

Of course, the challenged arbitrator may be the sole arbitrator. At first sight there would appear to be obvious dangers in permitting the arbitral tribunal itself to rule on the challenge, but these are seen to be illusory in light of the safeguards provided in para. (3).

A time limit is provided for making a challenge—15 days from the date of becoming aware of the tribunal's constitution or of a ground of challenge.

Para. (3)
Appeal Against Tribunal's Decisions
Whether the parties have agreed upon a provision or that prescribed by para. (2) above is followed, the party making the challenge is guaranteed a right of appeal to the court should his challenge prove unsuccessful. Any appeal must be made within 30 days of receiving notice of the rejection of the challenge. The decision of the court is not subject to appeal. The arbitral tribunal can in the meantime continue the proceedings and even make an award.

Article 14

Failure or impossibility to act

(1) If an arbitrator becomes de jure or de facto unable to perform his functions or for other reasons fails to act without undue delay, his mandate terminates if he withdraws from his office or if the parties agree on the termination. Otherwise, if a controversy remains concerning any of these grounds, any party may request the court specified in article 6 to decide on the termination of the mandate, which decision shall be subject to no appeal.

(2) If, under this article or article 13(2), an arbitrator withdraws from his office or a party agrees to the termination of the mandate of an arbitrator, this does not imply acceptance of the validity of any ground referred to in this article or article 12(2).

GENERAL NOTE

Para. (1)
Impossibility to Act
The idea of an arbitrator being *de jure* or *de facto* unable to perform his functions is straightforward.

Failing to Act Without Undue Delay
The most difficult issue is what is meant by the arbitrator who fails to act without undue delay.

Possible Outcomes
Once it is suggested that an arbitrator has failed to act without undue delay, or is *de jure* or *de facto* unable to act, then three outcomes are possible: (i) the arbitrator withdraws and his mandate terminates; (ii) the parties agree that his mandate terminates; (iii) he does not withdraw and the parties do not agree that the mandate terminates.

In the last situation either party may ask the court to decide whether the mandate should terminate, which decision is not open to appeal.

Para. (2)
This provision is designed to facilitate such withdrawal or consent in order to prevent lengthy controversies.

Article 15

Appointment of substitute arbitrator

Where the mandate of an arbitrator terminates under article 13 or 14 or because of his withdrawal from office for any other reason or because of the revocation of his mandate by agreement of the parties or in any other case of termination of his mandate, a substitute arbitrator shall be appointed according to the rules that were applicable to the appointment of the arbitrator being replaced.

GENERAL NOTE

Revocation of Mandate by Agreement/Resignation of Arbitrator
It is clear that it is open to the parties to revoke the arbitrator's mandate by agreement.
Also, it is open to an arbitrator to resign at any time and for whatever reason.

Obligation to Appoint Substitute Arbitrator
The seeming effect of art. 15 is that in *all* cases where the mandate of an arbitrator terminates, a substitute arbitrator must be appointed according to the rules applicable to the appointment of the arbitrator to be replaced. Of course the parties cannot be obliged to continue with arbitration against their wishes.

CHAPTER IV

JURISDICTION OF ARBITRAL TRIBUNAL

Article 16

Competence of arbitral tribunal to rule on its jurisdiction

(1) The arbitral tribunal may rule on its own jurisdiction, including any objections with

respect to the existence or validity of the arbitration agreement. For that purpose, an arbitration clause which forms part of a contract shall be treated as an agreement independent of the other terms of the contract. A decision by the arbitral tribunal that the contract is null and void shall not entail ipso jure the invalidity of the arbitration clause.

(2) A plea that the arbitral does not have jurisdiction shall be raised not later than the submission of the statement of defence. A party is not precluded from raising such a plea by the fact that he has appointed, or participated in the appointment of, an arbitrator. A plea that the arbitral tribunal is exceeding the scope of its authority shall be raised as soon as the matter alleged to be beyond the scope of its authority is raised during the arbitral proceedings. The arbitral tribunal may, in either case, admit a later plea if it considers the delay justified.

(3) The arbitral tribunal may rule on a plea referred to in paragraph (2) of this article either as a preliminary question or in an award on the merits. If the arbitral tribunal rules on such a plea as a preliminary question, any party may, within thirty days after having received notice of that ruling, request the court specified in article 6 to decide the matter, which decision shall be subject to no appeal. While such a request is pending, the arbitral tribunal may continue the arbitral proceedings and make an award.

GENERAL NOTE

This is perhaps one of the most significant and controversial provisions in the Model Law.

Para. (1)
Competence-Competence

This establishes the celebrated principle of Competence-Competence, the ability of the arbitral tribunal to rule on its own jurisdiction, and to permit the operation of that principle acknowledges the severability of the arbitration agreement from the contract. This is a mandatory provision. It is clear from the terms of para. (1) that the arbitral tribunal need not rule upon jurisdictional questions merely in response to objections raised by the parties, but may do so "on its own motion".

It will be noted that the tribunal may consider objections as to the "existence" of the arbitration agreement.

Para. (2)
The Stage at Which Jurisdictional Pleas Must be Raised

The main point of art. 16 is to ensure that jurisdictional arguments are not used as a means of delaying the proceedings. This is achieved in two main ways, firstly by allowing the tribunal itself to pronounce upon jurisdictional matters—see para. (1) above, and secondly by placing a time limit on the making of a complaint that the tribunal does not have jurisdiction. Thus para. (2) provides that a plea that the tribunal has no jurisdiction must be raised no later than the submission of the statement of defence. The paragraph, having dealt with initial lack of jurisdiction, then goes on to deal with a lack of jurisdiction arising during the proceedings, *i.e.* where the tribunal exceeds the scope of its authority. In this case a plea must be raised "as soon as the matter alleged to be beyond the scope of its authority is raised during the arbitral proceedings".

Para. (3)
Appeals to the Court Against Jurisdictional Rulings

Para. (3) seeks to reconcile the need for court control with the desire to avoid appeals to the court being used as a means of obstructing the progress of the arbitration. Thus the tribunal is empowered to rule on a plea under para. (2) either as a preliminary question or in the award.

The tribunal's ruling on a plea as a preliminary question is subject to immediate appeal. That appeal must be made within a rather tight time limit. The court's decision is subject to no further appeal and the tribunal has a discretion to continue the proceedings while the outcome of the appeal is awaited.

Article 17

Power of arbitral tribunal to order interim measures

(1) Unless otherwise agreed by the parties, the arbitral tribunal may, at the request of a party, order any party to take such interim measures of protection as the arbitral tribunal may consider necessary in respect of the subject-matter of the dispute. The arbitral tribunal may require any party to provide appropriate security in connection with such measure.

(2) An order under paragraph (1) of this article shall take the form of an award and articles 31, 35 and 36 shall apply accordingly.

GENERAL NOTE

Para. (1)

This article gives the arbitral tribunal an implied power to order a party to take interim measures of protection. The parties are expressly empowered to contract out of the implication of such a power. The arbitral tribunal may not make such an order on its own initiative, but must wait for a party to request an order.

When a tribunal does order such a measure it may of its own volition require a party to provide appropriate security in connection therewith.

Para. (2)
Tribunal Order to Take Form of Award

Such an order is effectively treated as an interim award.

CHAPTER V

CONDUCT OF ARBITRAL PROCEEDINGS

Article 18

Equal treatment of parties

The parties shall be treated with equality and each party shall be given a full opportunity of presenting his case.

GENERAL NOTE

This article is the shortest article in the Model Law, but one of the most significant. The principle of equality and the right to be heard should be observed not only by the arbitral tribunal but also by the parties when laying down any rules of procedure.

Article 19

Determination of rules of procedure

(1) Subject to the provisions of this Law, the parties are free to agree on the procedure to be followed by the arbitral tribunal in conducting the proceedings.

(2) Failing such agreement, the arbitral tribunal may, subject to the provisions of this Law, conduct the arbitration in such manner as it considers appropriate. The power conferred upon the arbitral tribunal includes the power to determine the admissibility, relevance, materiality and weight of any evidence.

GENERAL NOTE

Para. (1)
Parties' Control of Arbitral Procedure

The parties may devise their own set of procedural rules, or, as is more likely, adopt a particular set of arbitration rules which may indeed allow them to "take full advantage of the services of permanent arbitral institutions".

Para. (2)
Control of Procedure by Arbitral Tribunal

Where the parties do not reach agreement in any procedural matter, then the arbitral tribunal may adopt whichever procedure seems appropriate, subject of course to the mandatory provisions of the Model Law.

Evidence and the Arbitral Tribunal

The second sentence of para. (2) makes it clear that the arbitral tribunal's discretion covers the determination of the "admissibility, relevance, materiality and weight of any evidence". The tribunal's power is subject to the contrary agreement of the parties.

Article 20

Place of arbitration

(1) The parties are free to agree on the place of arbitration. Failing such agreement, the place

of arbitration shall be determined by the arbitral tribunal having regard to the circumstances of the case, including the convenience of the parties.

(2) Notwithstanding the provisions of paragraph (1) of this article, the arbitral tribunal may, unless otherwise agreed by the parties, meet at any place it considers appropriate for consultation among its members, for hearing witnesses, experts or the parties, or for inspection of goods, other property or documents.

GENERAL NOTE

Para. (1)
The parties may agree on the place of arbitration, failing which agreement the arbitral tribunal will determine that place.

Nevertheless in doing so it must "have regard to the circumstances of the case including the convenience of the parties."

Para. (2)
Location of Actual Meetings of Arbitral Trust
Para. (2) gives the arbitral tribunal discretion, subject to the contrary agreement of the parties, to meet wherever it considers appropriate. The holding of such meetings will have no effect on the place of arbitration in its technical sense.

Article 21

Commencement of arbitral proceedings

Unless otherwise agreed by the parties, the arbitral proceedings in respect of a particular dispute commence on the date on which a request for that dispute to be referred to arbitration is received by the respondent.

GENERAL NOTE
Subject to the contrary agreement of the parties, arbitral proceedings commence on the date when the respondent receives a request for the dispute to be referred to arbitration. However, the main purpose served by art. 21 is to indicate "the decisive moment for the cessation of the running of the limitation period".

Article 22

Language

(1) The parties are free to agree on the language or languages to be used in the arbitral proceedings. Failing such agreement, the arbitral tribunal shall determine the language or languages to be used in the proceedings. This agreement or determination, unless otherwise specified therein, shall apply to any written statement by a party, any hearing and any award, decision or other communication by the arbitral tribunal.

(2) The arbitral tribunal may order that any documentary evidence shall be accompanied by a translation into the language or languages agreed upon by the parties or determined by the arbitral tribunal.

GENERAL NOTE

Para. (1)
Determination of Language(s) of Proceedings
Art. 22 permits the parties, or failing whom the arbitral tribunal, to decide upon the language(s) to be used in the proceedings.

Para. (2)
Discretion as to Translation of Documents
This paragraph gives the tribunal a discretion whether or not to order translation of documents into the applicable language(s).

Article 23

Statements of claim and defence

(1) Within the period of time agreed by the parties or determined by the arbitral tribunal, the

claimant shall state the facts supporting his claim, the points at issue and the relief or remedy sought, and the respondent shall state his defence in respect of these particulars, unless the parties have otherwise agreed as to the required elements of such statements. The parties may submit with their statements all documents they consider to be relevant or may add a reference to the documents or other evidence they will submit.

(2) Unless otherwise agreed by the parties, either party may amend or supplement his claim or defence during the course of the arbitral proceedings, unless the arbitral tribunal considers it inappropriate to allow such amendment having regard to the delay in making it.

GENERAL NOTE

Para. (1)
Form of the Statements
Essentially all that is required is a statement from each party. Prima facie, the claimant should state the facts supporting his claim, the points at issue and the relief or remedy sought, and the respondent should state his defence in respect of these particulars—but the parties may agree otherwise.

Para. (2)
Supplementary Claims and Defences
It may be noted to begin with that this provision is subject to the contrary agreement of the parties.
Apart from this, parties have freedom to amend/supplement their claims/defences as they see fit, subject to the arbitral tribunal's discretion described in the last paragraph of the provision.
The tribunal has a discretion to disallow attempted amendments where it considers that this would be inappropriate, with delay being the sole criterion governing the exercise of this discretion.

Article 24

Hearings and written proceedings

(1) Subject to any contrary agreement by the parties, the arbitral tribunal shall decide whether to hold oral hearings for the presentation of evidence of for oral argument, or whether the proceedings shall be conducted on the basis of documents and other materials. However, unless the parties have agreed that no hearings shall be held, the arbitral tribunal shall hold such hearings at an appropriate stage of the proceedings, if so requested by a party.

(2) The parties shall be given sufficient advance notice of any hearing and of any meeting of the arbitral tribunal for the purposes of inspection of goods, other property or documents.

(3) All statements, documents or other information supplied to the arbitral tribunal by one party shall be communicated to the other party. Also any expert report or evidentiary document on which the arbitral tribunal may rely in making its decision shall be communicated to the parties.

GENERAL NOTE

Para. (1)
Whether Hearings Must or May be Held
This provision establishes the following propositions: firstly, if the parties agree that oral hearings must occur, then the tribunal must hold such hearings; secondly, if the parties agree that there should be no oral hearings, the tribunal is not entitled to arrange such hearings; thirdly, if the parties have not reached agreement on the matter one way or another, the tribunal has a discretion whether to hold hearings or not—*but* in this case it still must hold hearings at an appropriate stage of the proceedings if a party so requests.

Form and Scope of Hearings
Generally, subject to the agreement of the parties, the arbitral tribunal under art. 24(1) is free to decide on the mode of the proceedings.

Para. (2)
Advance Notice of Hearings, etc.
This provision directs that the parties shall be given "sufficient" notice of any hearing or meeting for the purpose of inspecting documents, etc.

Para. (3)
This provision is inspired by art. 15(3) of the UNCITRAL Arbitration Rules.

Article 25

Default of a party

Unless otherwise agreed by the parties, if, without showing sufficient cause,

(a) the claimant fails to communicate his statement of claim in accordance with article 23(1), the arbitral tribunal shall terminate the proceedings;

(b) the respondent fails to communicate his statement of defence in accordance with article 23(1), the arbitral tribunal shall continue the proceedings without treating such failure in itself as an admission of the claimant's allegations;

(c) any party fails to appear at a hearing or to produce documentary evidence, the arbitral tribunal may continue the proceedings and make the award on the evidence before it.

GENERAL NOTE

Introduction—Sufficient Cause for Default

Thus art. 25 deals with various aspects of a party's failure to participate, whether fully or partially, in the arbitral proceedings. The provisions of the article are subject to the contrary agreement of the parties. Nor will the provisions of the article apply if a party can show sufficient cause for his default. It is up to the arbitral tribunal to decide whether or not "sufficient cause" has been shown.

Subpara. (a)
Consequences of Failure to Communicate Statement of Claim

Subject to the qualification mentioned above, where a claimant fails to communicate his statement of claim within the period of time agreed by the parties or determined by the arbitral tribunal (see art. 23(1)), the tribunal shall terminate the proceedings.

Subpara. (b)

Subject to the qualifications considered in the introduction, if the respondent fails to communicate his statement of defence within the period of time agreed by the parties or determined by the arbitral tribunal, then the tribunal will continue the proceedings, without treating such a failure in itself as an admission of the claimant's allegation.

Subpara. (c)
Consequences of Failure to Appear at Hearing/Produce Evidence

Where any party fails to appear at a hearing or to produce documentary evidence, the tribunal may continue the proceedings and make the award on the evidence before it.

Article 26

Expert appointed by arbitral tribunal

(1) Unless otherwise agreed by the parties, the arbitral tribunal:

(a) may appoint one or more experts to report to it on specific issues to be determined by the arbitral tribunal;

(b) may require a party to give the expert any relevant information or to provide access to any relevant documents, goods or other property for his inspection.

(2) Unless otherwise agreed by the parties, if a party so requests or if the arbitral tribunal considers it necessary, the expert shall, after delivery of his written or oral report, participate in a hearing where the parties have the opportunity to put questions to him and to present expert witnesses in order to testify on the points at issue.

GENERAL NOTE

Para. (1)(a)
Power to Appoint Expert/Rôle of Expert

This provision gives the arbitral tribunal a discretion to appoint an expert or experts to report to it on any issue(s) it may determine. The provision is subject to the contrary agreement of the parties.

Para. (1)(b)
Duty of a Party to Cooperate with Expert

Again subject to the contrary agreement of the parties, the arbitral tribunal is empowered to require a party to give the expert any relevant information or to produce or provide access to any relevant documents, goods or other property for his inspection.

Para. (2)
Expert Appearing at Hearing
   Obviously, this provision is once again subject to the contrary agreement of the parties.

Article 27

Court assistance in taking evidence

The arbitral tribunal or a party with the approval of the arbitral tribunal may request from the Court of Session or the sheriff court assistance in taking evidence and recovering documents. The court may execute the request within its competence and according to its rules on taking evidence and recovery of documents.

GENERAL NOTE
   This is a mandatory provision.

CHAPTER VI

MAKING OF AWARD AND TERMINATION OF PROCEEDINGS

Article 28

Rules applicable to substance of dispute

(1) The arbitral tribunal shall decide the dispute in accordance with such rules of law as are chosen by the parties as applicable to the substance of the dispute. Any designation of the law or legal system of a given State shall be construed, unless otherwise expressed, as directly referring to the substantive law of that State and not to its conflict of laws rules.

(2) Failing any designation by the parties, the arbitral tribunal shall apply the law determined by the conflict of laws rules which it considers applicable.

(3) The arbitral tribunal shall decide ex aequo et bono or as amiable compositeur only if the parties have expressly authorised it to do so.

(4) In all cases, the arbitral tribunal shall decide in accordance with the terms of the contract and shall take into account the usages of the trade applicable to the transaction.

GENERAL NOTE

Para. (1)
Choice of Applicable "Rules of Law" by the Parties
   The arbitral tribunal shall decide the dispute according to the "rules of law" chosen by the parties. The parties may "choose" such rules by invoking the rules of an arbitral institution. However, it is not open to the parties under art. 2(i) to allow a third party to make such a determination for them. Either they must choose the applicable law, or the arbitral tribunal must do so.

Para. (2)
Determination of Applicable Law by Arbitral Tribunal
   If the parties fail to choose the rules of law which will govern the substance of the dispute, then it falls to the tribunal to apply the law determined by the conflict of law rules which it considers applicable.
   The only guidelines which assist the tribunal in determining the "appropriate" conflict of law rules are those provided by para. (4) (see below).

Para. (3)
Decision ex Aequo et Bono or as Amiable Compositeur
   Such a decision must be expressly authorised by the parties. The two terms are practically interchangeable.
   Their natural meaning of amiable composition is that decisions are reached on the basis of fairness or justice rather than principles of law.

Para. (4)
Taking into Account the Terms of the Contract/Applicable Usages of Trade
   This provision underpins paras. (2) and (3) in the sense that the tribunal's choice of conflict of law rules or approach to amiable composition shall be informed by the terms of the contract and any applicable usages of trade.

Article 29

Decision making by panel of arbitrators

In arbitral proceedings with more than one arbitrator, any decision of the arbitral tribunal shall be made, unless otherwise agreed by the parties, by a majority of all its members. However, questions of procedure may be decided by a presiding arbitrator, if so authorised by the parties or all members of the arbitral tribunal.

GENERAL NOTE

Introduction
Majority Rule
This article insists on majority rule, where unanimity is not possible, unless the parties agree otherwise. This principle applies to all decisions of the arbitral tribunal whether substantive (*i.e.* as to the award itself) or procedural, although in this latter case the second sentence of the provision admits of a different possibility.

Procedural Questions and the Presiding Arbitrator
The second sentence of art. 29 allows procedural questions to be decided by a presiding arbitrator if so authorised by the parties, or all members of the arbitral tribunal.
What is a presiding arbitrator? No indication is given as to the meaning of this term in the Model Law. However, it is quite common for an arbitral tribunal to have a chairman, or third arbitrator, or presiding arbitrator who takes primary responsibility for conducting the arbitration. Nonetheless, it is important to recognise that there may not in fact be a presiding arbitrator, and that the Model Law does not require one.

Article 30

Settlement

(1) If, during arbitral proceedings, the parties settle the dispute, the arbitral tribunal shall terminate the proceedings and, if so requested by the parties and not objected to by the arbitral tribunal, record the settlement in the form of an arbitral award on agreed terms.

(2) An award on agreed terms shall be made in accordance with the provisions of article 31 and shall state that it is an award. Such an award has the same status and effect as any other award on the merits of the case.

GENERAL NOTE

Para. (1)
A Settlement in the Form of an Award
This provision begins by directing the arbitral tribunal to terminate the proceedings where a dispute is settled. One must presume in any case that settlement would automatically terminate the mandate of the tribunal and bring the proceedings to an end. However, the parties may wish that the terms of their settlement take the form of an award, perhaps to dispose of the dispute formally once and for all, perhaps better to aid enforcement. Thus para. (1) permits the parties to request that the arbitral tribunal record the settlement in the form of an arbitral award on agreed terms.

Objection by Arbitral Tribunal
Of course, it is by no means guaranteed that the arbitral tribunal will automatically comply with such a request, since it is permitted to object to recording the settlement in the form of an award. It will be noted that the provision does not suggest criteria by reference to which the arbitral tribunal might so object.

Para. (2)
This provision stipulates that such an award shall comply with the formalities required by art. 31 and must state it is an award. In all respects it is exactly like any other award.

Article 31

Form and contents of award

(1) The award shall be made in writing and shall be signed by the arbitrator or arbitrators. In

arbitral proceedings with more than one arbitrator, the signatures of the majority of all members of the arbitral tribunal shall suffice, provided that the reason for any omitted signature is stated.

(2) The award shall state the reasons upon which it is based, unless the parties have agreed that no reasons are to be given or the award is on agreed terms under article 30.

(3) The award shall state its date and the place of arbitration as determined in accordance with article 20(1). The award shall be deemed to have been made at that place.

(4) After the award is made, a copy signed by the arbitrators in accordance with paragraph (1) of this article shall be delivered to each party.

GENERAL NOTE

Para. (1)
Award to be in Writing and Signed by the Arbitrators
This is a mandatory provision. Where there are a number of arbitrators it is enough that a majority sign, as long as the reason for the omitted signature is stated. Any reason will suffice.

Para. (2)
The Giving of Reasons
This paragraph insists that the award shall state the reasons on which it is based unless (obviously) it is an award on agreed terms, or the parties agree that no reason should be given.

Para. (3)
Award to State its Date and the Place of Arbitration
This is a mandatory provision—the award must state both its date and the place of arbitration as determined in accordance with art. 20(1).

The second sentence of the provision creates an irrebuttable presumption that the award is in fact made at the place so stated. Yet, just as the arbitral tribunal may sit elsewhere than the place of arbitration determined under art. 20(1), so too the award may in fact be "made" other than at the stated place.

It is noteworthy that, although the award must state its date, the date thus stated is not subject to the same presumption as the place of the award.

Para. (4)
Copy of Award to be Delivered to Each Party
Once the award has been made a copy signed by the arbitrator(s), or at least by a majority of the arbitrators, must be delivered to each party. This provision is mandatory.

Article 32

Termination of proceedings

(1) The arbitral proceedings are terminated by the final award or by an order of the arbitral tribunal in accordance with paragraph (2) of this article.

(2) The arbitral tribunal shall issue an order for the termination of the arbitral proceedings when:
  (a) the claimant withdraws his claim, unless the respondent objects thereto and the arbitral tribunal recognises a legitimate interest on his part in obtaining a final settlement of the dispute;
  (b) the parties agree on the termination of the proceedings;
  (c) the arbitral tribunal finds that the continuation of the proceedings has for any other reason become unnecessary or impossible.

(3) The mandate of the arbitral tribunal terminates with the termination of the arbitral proceedings, subject to the provisions of articles 33 and 34(4).

GENERAL NOTE

Para. (1)
Termination by Final Award
The proceedings are to be terminated by the final award or by the order of the arbitral tribunal. The term "award" is nowhere defined in the Model Law. Nor is the term "final award". Yet it is obvious that the Model Law contemplates that provisional and part awards may be made. Indeed it is implicit in the use of the term "final award".

Para. (2)
Termination by Order of Arbitral Tribunal
Para. (2) considers the various situations in which the proceedings will be terminated by order of the arbitral tribunal rather than a final award.

Subpara. (a)
Withdrawal of Claim
It is unremarkable that the tribunal should ordinarily be obliged to issue an order terminating proceedings when the claimant withdraws his claim. The interesting feature of this subparagraph is the view "that the withdrawal of a claim should not *ipso facto* terminate arbitral proceedings". The tribunal is given this discretion to continue the proceedings where the respondent objects to termination and it recognises his "legitimate interest . . . in obtaining a final settlement of the dispute". The aforesaid discretion appears to be entirely subjective.

Subpara. (b)
Agreements on Termination
The tribunal must order the termination of the proceedings where the parties agree on their termination.

Subpara. (c)
The Continuation of the Proceedings has Become Unnecessary or Impossible
This provision asks the tribunal to determine whether the continuation of the proceedings has become unnecessary or impossible, and if the answer is in the affirmative, to issue an order. The Model Law is entirely unforthcoming as to what "unnecessary" or "impossible" means in this context.

Para. (3)
Termination of the Proceedings Terminates the Tribunal's Mandate
The mandate of the arbitral tribunal terminates with the termination of the proceedings. There are two exceptions to this. Firstly, even after the award has been made, one of the parties may under art. 33 request the arbitral tribunal to correct computational, clerical or other errors of a similar nature in the award, or to interpret the award, or to make an additional award (see notes on art. 33). Secondly, after the award has been given, a court under art. 34(4) may, in setting aside proceedings, give the arbitral tribunal the opportunity to resume the arbitral proceedings or take such other action as in the tribunal's opinion will eliminate the grounds for setting aside.

Article 33

Correction and interpretation of award and making of additional award

(1) Within thirty days of receipt of the award, unless another period of time has been agreed upon by the parties:
   (a) a party, with notice to the other party, may request the arbitral tribunal to correct in the award any errors in computation, any clerical or typographical errors or any errors of similar nature;
   (b) if so agreed by the parties, a party, with notice to the other party, may request the arbitral tribunal to give an interpretation of a specific point or part of the award.
If the arbitral tribunal considers the request to be justified, it shall make the correction or give the interpretation within thirty days of receipt of the request. The interpretation shall form part of the award.

(2) The arbitral tribunal may correct any error of the type referred to in paragraph (1)(a) of this article on its own initiative within thirty days of the date of the award.

(3) Unless otherwise agreed by the parties, a party, with notice to the other party, may, within thirty days of receipt of the award, request the arbitral tribunal to make an additional award as to claims presented in the arbitral proceedings but omitted from the award. If the arbitral tribunal considers the request to be justified, it shall make the additional award.

(4) The arbitral tribunal may extend, if necessary, the period of time within which it shall make a correction or interpretation under paragraph (1) of this article.

(5) The provisions of article 31 shall apply to a correction or interpretation of the award or to an additional award.

GENERAL NOTE

Time Limits
The article specifies that 30 days from the receipt of the award is the period for requesting (i) a correction in the award of any computational, clerical or typographical error, or any error of similar nature; (ii) an interpretation of a specific point or part of the award; (iii) an additional award in terms of para. (3).
The arbitral tribunal is also allowed 30 days from the receipt of the request to make a correction or give an interpretation (and 30 days from the date of the award to make a correction on its own initiative).

Although precise time limits are specified the parties may vary by agreement the period within which they must request a correction, interpretation or additional award, while the tribunal under para. (4) may extend, if necessary, the period within which it shall make such a condition, or interpretation.

It does not appear to be open to the tribunal to extend the period for making such a request. The arbitral tribunal may extend the period of time within which it must itself act "if necessary".

Notice to the Other Party

The other consideration which underpins this article generally is the requirement that any party requesting a correction/interpretation/additional award notify the other party.

Para. (1)
Requesting the Arbitral Tribunal to Correct Errors

It was agreed that this was a mandatory provision, save that the parties could stipulate a different period for making the request.

The tribunal must make the correction if it considers the request to be justified. Obviously, therefore, it is up to the tribunal to decide whether the correction should be made.

Subpara. (b)
Interpretation of Specific Point by Arbitral Tribunal

This arbitral tribunal is empowered to interpret an award only "if so agreed by the parties". Moreover, "it was agreed that a request for interpretation of the award should be limited to specific points in order to avoid possible abuses and delays".

Once again the arbitral tribunal need only give an interpretation if it considers the request to be justified, thus conferring an absolute discretion.

The interpretation forms part of the award.

Para. (2)
Tribunal Correcting Error on Own Initiative

Without waiting for a party to approach it the tribunal may correct an error on its own initiative within 30 days of the award. It relinquishes this power once the 30 days has elapsed.

Para. (3)
Request for Additional Award

This provision allows a party to request that the tribunal make an additional award covering "claims presented in the arbitral proceedings but omitted from the award". What is envisaged is the situation where a "final" award is issued which does not deal with all the matters submitted to the tribunal, rather than a "part" award. Para. (3) is not mandatory, applying only if the parties have not agreed to the contrary.

Para. (5)
Form of Correction/Interpretation/Additional Award

Any correction, interpretation or additional award must comply with the formalities specified in art. 31 (writing, the giving of reasons, statement of date and place, delivery of signed copy to each party).

CHAPTER VII

RECOURSE AGAINST AWARD

Article 34

Application for setting aside as exclusive recourse against arbitral award

(1) Recourse to a court against an arbitral award may be made only by an application for setting aside in accordance with paragraphs (2) and (3) of this article.

(2) An arbitral award may be set aside by the court specified in article 6 only if:

(a) the party making the application furnishes proof that:

(i) a party to the arbitration agreement referred to in article 7 was under some incapacity, or the said agreement is not valid under the law to which the parties have subjected it or, failing any indication thereon, under the law of Scotland; or

(ii) the party making the application was not given proper notice of the appointment of an arbitrator or of the arbitral proceedings or was otherwise unable to present his case; or

(iii) the award deals with a dispute not contemplated by or not falling within the terms of the submission to arbitration, or contains decisions on matters beyond the scope of the submission to arbitration, provided that, if the decision on matters submitted to arbitration can be separated from those not so submitted, only that part of the award which contains decisions on matters not submitted to arbitration may be set aside; or

(iv) the composition of the arbitral tribunal or the arbitral procedure was not in accordance with the agreement of the parties, unless such agreement was in conflict with a provision of this Law from which the parties cannot derogate, or, failing such agreement, was not in accordance with this Law; or

(v) the award was procured by fraud, bribery or corruption; or

(b) the court finds that:

(i) the subject-matter of the dispute is not capable of settlement by arbitration under the law of Scotland; or

(ii) the award is in conflict with public policy.

(3) An application for setting aside may not be made after three months have elapsed from the date on which the party making that application had received the award or, if a request had been made under article 33, from the date on which that request had been disposed of by the arbitral tribunal. This paragraph does not apply to an application for setting aside on the ground mentioned in paragraph (2)(a)(v) of this article.

(4) The court, when asked to set aside an award, may, where appropriate and so requested by a party, suspend the setting aside proceedings for a period of time determined by it in order to give the arbitral tribunal an opportunity to resume the arbitral proceedings or to take such other action as in the arbitral tribunal's opinion will eliminate the grounds for setting aside.

GENERAL NOTE

Para. (1)
Only Recourse Against an Award is an Action for Setting Aside
The only means of challenging an award under the Model Law will be a setting aside action in the Court of Session, or (where it has jurisdiction) the Sheriff Court. No special procedure will apply and the decision of either court will be subject to appeal in the normal way.

Para. (2)
Grounds for Setting an Award Aside

Incapacity of Party/Invalidity of Arbitration Agreement
This provision sets up two quite separate grounds; that a party to the arbitration agreement was under some incapacity or that the arbitration agreement itself is not valid under the law to which the parties have subjected it, or, failing any indication thereof, under the law of Scotland.

Party Unable to Present Case/Not Given Proper Notice of Proceedings/Arbitrator's Appointment
A party may have the award set aside if he can prove that he was not given proper notice of the appointment of an arbitrator or of the arbitral proceedings, or that he was otherwise unable to present his case.

Award Exceeds Tribunal's Jurisdiction
The award may be set aside if it covers matters beyond the scope of the jurisdiction of the arbitral tribunal. The present provision stipulates however that only that part of the award which suffers from an excess of jurisdiction may be set aside, if this part can be separated from the rest of the award.

Procedure/Composition of Tribunal not in Accordance with Agreement of Parties/Model Law
The effect of this provision is that the award may be set aside where the composition of the arbitral tribunal or the arbitral procedure was not in accordance with a mandatory provision of the Model Law, or with the agreement of the parties which does not contradict such a mandatory provision, or failing such agreement, with a provision of the Model Law.

Award Procured by Fraud, Bribery or Corruption
The three month time limit for setting aside an award established by para. (3) does not apply in this instance.
It may be noted that fraud, etc. may be that of the arbitrators, parties or witnesses.

Subject of Arbitration not Arbitrable under Law of Scotland
The award will be set aside if its subject matter is not arbitrable under the law of Scotland. It

may be noted that in relation to this provision and the public policy ground covered by para. 2(b)(ii) the court is envisaged as taking a more active rôle. Thus if an award is to be set aside under para. 2(a), the party seeking to have it set aside must furnish proof in relation to one of the grounds specified thereunder, while an award can be set aside under the present provision if the court finds that its subject matter is not arbitrable under the law of Scotland. Yet the court still may not act unless a party has sought to have the award set aside.

Award Conflicts with Public Policy
A court may set aside an award if it finds the award to be in conflict with public policy.

Para. (3)
Time Limit for Application to Set Award Aside
An award becomes immune from challenge if an application for setting aside has not been made within three months of the date when the party seeking to make the challenge received the award. There are two exceptions to this rule. If a party has requested under art. 33 a correction or interpretation of the award or an additional award, the three month period does not begin to run until the arbitral tribunal has disposed of this request. Secondly, if the ground on which it is sought to have the award set aside is that mentioned in para. 2(a)(v), an application may be made at any time.

Para. (4)
Suspension of Setting Aside Proceedings for Remedial Measures
The power only arises in the context of setting aside proceedings and therefore as an alternative to setting aside. Secondly, the court can only intervene when so requested by a party. Thirdly, the purpose of its intervention must be to give the arbitral tribunal an opportunity to resume the proceedings or take such other action as will eliminate the grounds for setting aside.
It may be noted that para. (4) only allows the court to suspend the setting aside proceedings to give the tribunal an *opportunity* to take such action as in the *tribunal's opinion* will eliminate the grounds for setting aside. Obviously the court may not indicate to the tribunal what action it must take and order it to take it. If the arbitral tribunal declines to take advantage of the opportunity and does not take the appropriate measures, the court must proceed to set the award aside. Finally, the court may only intervene "where appropriate". The exercise of this power will only be "appropriate" when there is "a possibility of curing the defect in arbitral proceedings".

CHAPTER VIII

RECOGNITION AND ENFORCEMENT OF AWARDS

Article 35

Recognition and enforcement

(1) An arbitral award, irrespective of the country in which it was made, shall be recognised as binding and, upon application in writing to the competent court, shall be enforced subject to the provisions of this article and of article 36.
(2) The party relying on an award or applying for its enforcement shall supply the duly authenticated original award or a duly certified copy thereof, and the original arbitration agreement referred to in article 7 or a duly certified copy thereof. If the award or agreement is not made in English, the party shall supply a duly certified translation thereof into English.

GENERAL NOTE

Conditions for Recognition and Enforcement
If a party wishes the award to be recognised or enforced, he must supply two things: the fully authenticated original award or a duly certified copy thereof, and the original arbitration agreement or a duly certified copy thereof.
If either the award or the arbitration agreement is in a language other than English the party seeking recognition or enforcement shall supply a duly certified English translation thereof.

Article 36

Grounds for refusing recognition or enforcement

(1) Recognition or enforcement of an arbitral award, irrespective of the country in which it was made, may be refused only:

(a) at the request of the party against whom it is invoked, if that party furnishes to the competent court where recognition or enforcement is sought proof that:

(i) a party to the arbitration agreement referred to in article 7 was under some incapacity; or the said agreement is not valid under the law to which the parties have subjected it or, failing any indication thereon, under the law of the country where the award was made; or

(ii) the party against whom the award is invoked was not given proper notice of the appointment of an arbitrator or of the arbitral proceedings or was otherwise unable to present his case; or

(iii) the award deals with a dispute not contemplated by or not falling within the terms of the submission to arbitration, or it contains decisions on matters beyond the scope of the submission to arbitration, provided that, if the decision on matters submitted to arbitration can be separated from those not so submitted, that part of the award which contains decisions on matters submitted to arbitration may be recognised and enforced; or

(iv) the composition of the arbitral tribunal or the arbitral procedure was not in accordance with the agreement of the parties or, failing such agreement, was not in accordance with the law of the country where the arbitration took place; or

(v) the award has not yet become binding on the parties or has been set aside or suspended by a court of the country in which, or under the law of which, that award was made, or

(b) if the court finds that:

(i) the subject-matter of the dispute is not capable of settlement by arbitration under the law of Scotland; or

(ii) the recognition or enforcement of the award would be contrary to public policy.

(2) If an application for setting aside or suspension of an award has been made to a court referred to in paragraph (1)(a)(v) of this article, the court where recognition or enforcement is sought may, if it considers it proper, adjourn its decision and also, on the application of the party claiming recognition or enforcement of the award, order the other party to provide appropriate security.

GENERAL NOTE

Introduction
Art. 36 lays down the grounds upon which recognition or enforcement may be refused. The article provides an exclusive list of grounds.
Moreover, the grounds are mirrored in the grounds for setting aside an award under art. 34.

Para. (1)(a)
The burden of proof of the grounds on which recognition or enforcement can be denied lies upon the party against whom recognition or enforcement is sought.

The Grounds for Refusing Recognition or Enforcement
Since the grounds are largely the same as those upon which the award may be set aside, there is little point in reproducing at this stage the discussion which may already be found in art. 34. Therefore, discussion of individual grounds will tend to concentrate on pointing out differences, if any, between individual subparas. and their counterparts under art. 34(2)(a).

Para. (1)(a)(iv)
Procedure/Composition of Tribunal not in Accordance with Agreement of Parties or Law of Forum State
This provision differs significantly from the terms of art. 34(2)(a)(iv). This article gives absolute priority to the agreement of the parties irrespective of whether such agreement is in conflict with a "mandatory" provision of the applicable procedural law.

Para. (1)(a)(v)
Award Not Yet Binding/Has Been Set Aside
This provision establishes two separate grounds: (1) that the award has not yet become binding on the parties; (2) that the award has been set aside or suspended by a court of the country in which or under the law of which that award was made.

Para. (2)
This provision confers discretion on the court to adjourn its decision on recognition and enforcement, if the party resisting enforcement has sought to have the award set aside or suspended by a court of the country in which or under the law of which the award was made.

The court also has a discretion in such circumstances, on the application of the party seeking recognition or enforcement, to order the party seeking to have the award set aside to provide appropriate security.

Section 74   SCHEDULE 8

AMENDMENT OF ENACTMENTS

PART I

AMENDMENTS TO THE LICENSING (SCOTLAND) ACT 1976

1. The Licensing (Scotland) Act 1976 shall be amended as follows.
2. In subsection (2) of section 5 (restriction on power of licensing board to delegate functions) at the end there shall be added the following paragraph—
    "(1) making a decision on an application for the grant of a children's certificate under section 49 of the Law Reform (Miscellaneous Provisions) (Scotland) Act 1990."
3. In subsection (6) of that section after the words "(a) to (i)" there shall be added the words "and (l)"
4. In subsection (3) of section 6 (voting by chairman) the words from "Provided that" to the end of the subsection shall cease to have effect.

GENERAL NOTE
The amendment means that the chairman now has a second or casting vote in relation to all applications, and the proviso that he did not have a casting vote in applications for the grant or provisional grant of new licences is no longer of effect. For a discussion of some of the difficulties which arise in respect of this second or casting vote, see Allan and Chapman, *The Licensing (Scotland) Act 1976* (2nd ed.), note to s.6, p. 39.

5. In section 16 (persons who may object to licence applications)—
    (a) in subsection (1), at the end there shall be added—
        "(e) the fire authority for the area in which the premises are situated;
        (f) a local authority for the area in which the premises are situated.";
    (b) in subsection (3), after "made," there shall be inserted the words "or, in the case of the agent of an applicant, shall be his place of business,"; and
    (c) in subsection (5), for the word "hear" there shall be substituted the words ", whether or not the objector appears, consider."

GENERAL NOTE

Subpara. (a)
This amendment extends the right to the fire authority and the local authority, for the area in which the premises are situated, to make objections to a licensing application. *Kelvinside Community Council* v. *City of Glasgow District Licensing Board*, 1990 S.L.T. 725 raised, but did not decide the issue as to whether a neighbouring community council, which did not qualify as a council "for the area in which the premises were situated", could qualify as an objector under one of the other heads; *e.g.* under s.16(1)(a) as persons owning or occupying property situated in the neighbourhood.
Boards were required to consult with the fire authority under s.24 of the 1976 Act. This procedure meant that applicants were disadvantaged in not being able to answer properly the observations made by the fire authority at a board meeting, which amounted to an objection to the grant of the licence. Following the case of *Centralbite* v. *Kincardine and Deeside District Licensing Board*, 1990 S.L.T. 231, such observations by the fire authority, which could be said to amount to an objection, might have been liable to challenge as incompetent objections.
A "local authority" is defined by s.235(1) of the Local Government (Scotland) Act 1973 to mean "a regional, islands or district council". Where the local authority objector is also the district or island council providing the licensing board under s.1 of the 1976 Act, care will have to be taken to ensure that the rules of natural justice are not broken, so that the board members are not represented on the same committee that recommends that an objection be made, or are not involved in the decision to make an objection to the board meeting.

Subpara. (b)
This makes provision for the service of objections on an agent, in conformity with the provisions of the new s.139(6) added by para. 18 (*infra*).

Subpara. (c)

The use of the word "hear" in the subsection was interpreted to mean that personal appearance by the objector or his agent was necessary before the objection would be entertained, but this amendment means that objections can be considered by the board in the absence of the objector.

6. In section 17 (grounds for refusal of an application), for paragraph (d) of subsection (1) there shall be substituted the following paragraph—

"(d) that, having regard to—
>   (i) the number of licensed premises in the locality at the time the application is considered; and
>   (ii) the number of premises in respect of which the provisional grant of a new licence is in force,
> the board is satisfied that the grant of the application would result in the over provision of licensed premises in the locality,".

GENERAL NOTE

This paragraph amends s.17(1)(d) quite radically. The old section had been construed to mean that it was the over-provision of specific facilities of the kind to be provided which had to be considered: see *Augustus Barnett* v. *Bute & Cowal District Licensing Board*, 1989 S.L.T. 572 and note to s.17 in Allan and Chapman, *The Licensing (Scotland) Act 1976* (2nd ed.), p. 51. The amendment has the effect of providing that it is the number of licensed premises as a whole, including premises in respect of which there is a provisional grant, which have to be considered, when determining whether or not the grant will result in over-provision.

7. In section 18 (giving of reasons for decisions of a licensing board)—
>   (a) in subsection (1), after "shall" there shall be inserted the words ", within 21 days of being required to do so under subsection (2) below," and the words "when required to do so under subsection (2) below" shall cease to have effect; and
>   (b) in subsection (4), at the beginning there shall be inserted the words "The period of 21 days referred to in subsection (1) above and."

GENERAL NOTE

This amendment provides a time-limit of 21 days within which a licensing board is required to give its written decision, when required so to do. "Within" requires the written decision to be provided by the 21st day. Difficulties had arisen where the clerks of some boards were dilatory in giving out the board's written reasons for a decision. The amendment to subs. (4) provides that in calculating the 21 days, Sundays, Christmas Day, New Year's Day, Good Friday, a bank holiday, or a public holiday, or a day appointed for public thanksgiving or mourning, are not to be included.

8. In section 21 (issue of licences)—
>   (a) in subsection (1), at the end there shall be added the words "and shall do so within 28 days of the grant of the licence";
>   (b) in subsection (2), for the words "when lawfully required" there shall be substituted the words "on application"; and
>   (c) after subsection (2) there shall be added the following subsection—
> "(3) The period of 28 days referred to in subsection (1) above shall not include a day which is a Sunday, Christmas Day, New Year's Day, Good Friday, a bank holiday, or a public holiday, or a day appointed for public thanksgiving or mourning."

GENERAL NOTE

This amendment introduces a time-limit of 28 days within which the clerk shall make out and deliver a licence, and is designed to deal with cases where a Clerk had been dilatory in giving out a licence. The words "lawfully required" which had given rise to some difficulty, are now replaced with the requirement "on application" to give out a duplicate. See note 7 (*supra*) regarding "within 28 days". The new subs. (3) excludes Sunday, etc. from the calculation of days; see note 7 (*supra*).

9. In section 33 (occasional licence for premises other than licensed premises)—
>   (a) in subsections (1) and (2) for the words "on such day" in each place where they occur there shall be substituted the words "for such period of not more than 14 days";
>   (b) in subsection (9) there shall be added at the end the words "but the board shall not cause to be published the address of the applicant if the applicant provides the name and address of an agent through whom he may have intimated to him any objections."

10. In subsection (1) of section 34 of that Act (occasional permission to sell alcoholic liquor) for the words "on such day" there shall be substituted the words "for such period of not more than 14 days."

GENERAL NOTE

These amendments overcome the difficulty caused by the restriction of an occasional licence and permission to "on such day" in the singular. Events which lasted two or more days required a separate occasional licence or permission for each day. The amendment allows for intimation of objections to be made to an agent in conformity with the new s.139(6) added by para. 18 (*infra*).

11.—(1) Section 39 (appeals against the decisions of licensing boards) shall be amended as follows.
(2) After subsection (2) there shall be inserted the following subsection—
"(2A) A licensing board may be a party to any appeal under this section."
(3) In subsection (5) for the words "grounded on paragraph (b) of subsection (4) above" there shall be substituted the words "under this section."

GENERAL NOTE

Subpara. (2)
This amendment clarifies the contradictory decisions in *Hutcheon* v. *Hamilton District Licensing Board*, 1978 S.L.T. (Sh.Ct.) 44, which held that a licensing board could not be party to an appeal, and *Joe Coral (Racing)* v. *Hamilton District Council*, 1981 S.L.T. (Notes) 106, which held that a board could be a party to an appeal. This section confirms that the board may be a party to an appeal under s.39, which has become the common practice.

Subpara. (3)
This important amendment allows the sheriff to hear evidence in an appeal on any of the grounds in subs. (4) and not just ground (4)(b) as was the former law; see Note 5 to s.39 of Allan and Chapman, *The Licensing (Scotland) Act 1976* (2nd ed.), p. 75. The difficulties which arose when the hearing of evidence was restricted to ground (4)(b) (incorrect material fact) was highlighted in *Tennant Caledonian Breweries* v. *City of Aberdeen District Licensing Board*, 1987 S.L.T. (Sh.Ct.) 2, where it was held that the appellants could not lead evidence of actings by a member of the board, which were said to amount to a breach of natural justice, being ground of appeal (c).

12. In section 64—
(a) in subsection (1), after the words "an entertainment licence" there shall be inserted the words ", a refreshment licence"; and
(b) after subsection (8) there shall be inserted the following subsection—
"(9) Where a licensing board has refused an application under subsection (1) above for the grant of an occasional or regular extension of permitted hours in respect of any premises, the board shall not, within one year of its refusal, entertain a subsequent application for such an extension in respect of the same premises unless the board, at the time of refusing the first-mentioned application, makes a direction to the contrary."

GENERAL NOTE

Subpara. (a)
This amendment allows the holder of a refreshment licence to apply for an extension.

Subpara. (b)
This amendment to s.64 introduces to applications for occasional and regular extensions a similar prohibition to that which applies under s.14 of the 1976 Act to applications for a new licence which have been refused to the effect that a further application cannot be made for two years without a direction made at the time of refusal that such an application could be made. The amendment provides that where an applicant for an occasional or regular extension is refused, a further application cannot be made within one year of the refusal unless the board at the time of the refusal makes a contrary direction. Where a refusal is intimated at a board meeting, it is important that the party or agent appearing makes an immediate application for such a direction, because *the direction must be given at the time of the refusal*; see note to s.14 in Allan and Chapman, *The Licensing (Scotland) Act 1976* (2nd ed.), p. 47.

13. In each of subsections (1) and (2) of section 69 (prohibition on children being in certain licensed premises) at the beginning there shall be inserted the words "Subject to section 49 of the Law Reform (Miscellaneous Provisions) (Scotland) Act 1990."

14. In section 70 (children in premises in respect of which a refreshment licence is held) for the number "21" there shall be substituted the number "18."

GENERAL NOTE

This amendment reduced the age from 21 to 18 years for an adult accompanying a child and reflects the age of majority introduced by the Age of Majority (Scotland) Act 1969.

15. In section 97 (restrictions on supply of alcoholic liquor on off-sale premises)—
(a) in subsection (1) for the words "supplies to any person, gratuitously or otherwise," there shall be substituted the words "sells to any person"; and
(b) in subsection (2) the words "or supply" shall be omitted.

GENERAL NOTE

This paragraph amends the law in relation to off-sales premises, so that it is now only an offence to sell alcoholic liquor. The gratuitous supply of liquor is no longer an offence.

16. In paragraph (j) of section 108 (grounds of objection to renewal of registration by club) after the word "is" there shall be inserted the words "or, in the case of an application for the renewal of a certificate of registration, has been, at any time during the currency of the certificate of registration in respect of which the application for renewal is made,".

GENERAL NOTE

The amendment corrects a possible problem in relation to objections to the renewal of a club's registration in that subs. (j) could have been interpreted to mean that only present disorderly conduct could be taken into account. The amendment allows past conduct to be considered when an application for renewal of the registration is made.

17. In subsection (1) of section 109 (cancellation of certificate of registration of club) after the word "being" there shall be inserted the words "or has been, at any time during the currency of the certificate of registration,".

GENERAL NOTE

See note 16 (*supra*). The amendment allows past conduct of the club to be considered, when an application for cancellation of a certificate is made.

18. In section 139 (interpretation) after subsection (4) there shall be inserted the following subsections—
"(5) Any requirement under this Act to cause to be published the address of—
(a) an applicant in respect of any competent application made to a licensing board;
(b) an employee or agent of an applicant who is not an individual natural person; or
(c) a person who is to be the holder of a licence under Part III of this Act,
may be satisfied by causing to be published the address of his agent and the clerk of a licensing board shall cause to be published the address of the agent rather than the address of any person mentioned in paragraphs (a) to (c) above if so requested by that person.
(6) Any requirement in this Act to intimate anything to an applicant may be satisfied by so intimating to his agent."

GENERAL NOTE

This sensible amendment allows the name and address of the agent to be used in publication of applications or for the service or intimation of anything under the Act. It is sensible because the agent is probably the person who needs timeous intimation of objections or other notices and it allows for confidentiality of the applicant's address. Concern had been expressed that applicants who perhaps had banned undesirable elements from their public-house were at risk by having to reveal their addresses.

PART II

MISCELLANEOUS

The Probate and Legacy Duties Act 1808 (c. 149)

19. In section 38 of the Probate and Legacy Duties Act 1808 (executors to exhibit inventories of estate)—
(a) for the words "oath or solemn affirmation" in both places where they occur there shall be substituted "declaration"; and

(b) the words from "(which oath" to "administer)" shall cease to have effect.

The Confirmation of Executors (Scotland) Act 1823 (c. 98)

20.—(1) In section 3 of the Confirmation of Executors (Scotland) Act 1823 (which requires applications for confirmation to relate to the whole known moveable estate), for the word "oath" in both places where it occurs there shall be substituted "declaration."

(2) In section 4 of that Act (confirmation by executor's creditor), for the word "oath" there shall be substituted "declaration."

The Judicial Factors Act 1849 (c. 51)

21.—(1) In section 5 (factor to lodge monies in one of the banks of Scotland) of the Judicial Factors Act 1849—
   (a) in subsection (1), for the words "banks in Scotland established by Act of Parliament or royal charter" there shall be substituted the words—
   "following institutions, that is to say—
   (a) an institution authorised under the Banking Act 1987;
   (b) the National Savings Bank; or
   (c) a building society incorporated (or deemed to be incorporated) under the Building Societies Act 1986,";
   and
   (b) at the end of that section there shall be inserted the following subsection—
   "(4) In lodging money under subsection (1) above the judicial factor shall not require to have regard to any provision of the Trustee Investments Act 1961 which would, apart from the provisions of this subsection, require him to seek advice before depositing money in any of the institutions mentioned in that subsection.".

(2) In section 33 (power of accountant to require information) of that Act, for the word "bank"—
   (a) in the first place where it occurs, there shall be substituted the words "institution such as is mentioned in paragraphs (a) to (c) of section 5(1) of this Act"; and
   (b) in the second and third places where it occurs, there shall be inserted the word "institution."

(3) In section 34 (discharge of factors, tutors and curators) of that Act, at the beginning there shall be inserted the words "Subject to section 34A of this Act,".

(4) In section 37 (accumulation of principal and interest on accounts and deposits) of that Act—
   (a) for the words "bank in Scotland" there shall be substituted the words "institution such as is mentioned in paragraphs (a) to (c) of section 5(1) of this Act"; and
   (b) for the words "any bank" there shall be substituted the words "any such institution."

The Confirmation of Executors (Scotland) Act 1858 (c. 56)

22.—(1) In section 2 of the Confirmation of Executors (Scotland) Act 1858 (petition for confirmation to be subscribed by petitioner or his agent), at the end there shall be added "or by an executry practitioner or a recognised financial institution providing executry services within the meaning of section 23 of the Law Reform (Miscellaneous Provisions) (Scotland) Act 1990."

(2) In Schedules D and E to that Act (forms of confirmation), for the word "oath" there shall be substituted "declaration."

The Promissory Oaths Act 1868 (c. 72)

23. In the second part of the Schedule to the Promissory Oaths Act 1868 (officers required to take oath of allegiance and judicial oath), after the words "Judges of the Court of Session in Scotland" there shall be inserted the words ", temporary judges of the Court of Session and High Court of Justiciary appointed under section 35(3) of the Law Reform (Miscellaneous Provisions) (Scotland) Act 1990,".

The Intestates Widows and Children (Scotland) Act 1875 (c. 41)

24.—(1) In section 3 of the Intestates Widows and Children (Scotland) Act 1875 (commissary clerk to prepare inventory etc for widow or children where deceased's estate small)—
   (a) for the word "oath" in the first place where it occurs there shall be substituted "declaration"; and
   (b) for the words "shall take the oath of the applicant thereto" there shall be substituted "on the inventory and declaration being signed by the applicant."

(2) In Schedule A to that Act (form of inventory etc)—

(a) for the word "oath" in both places where it occurs there shall be substituted "declaration";

(b) for the words from "in presence of" to "depones" there shall be substituted "*[name and address of applicant]* (hereinafter referred to "the applicant") hereby declares";

(c) for the words "deponent" wherever it occurs and "deponent's" there shall be substituted respectively "applicant" and "applicant's"; and

(d) the words from "All which" to the end shall cease to have effect.

(3) In Schedule B to that Act (form of confirmation)—

(a) for the word "oath" in both places where it occurs there shall be substituted "declaration"; and

(b) for the word "deponed" there shall be substituted "declared."

The Small Testate Estates (Scotland) Act 1876 (c. 24)

25.—(1) In section 3 of the Small Testate Estates (Scotland) Act 1876 (simplified procedure for confirmation to small estates)—

(a) for the word "oath" there shall be substituted "declaration"; and

(b) for the words "being duly sworn to" there shall be substituted "and declaration being duly signed."

(2) In Schedule A to that Act (form of inventory etc)—

(a) for the word "oath" in both places where it occurs there shall be substituted "declaration";

(b) for the words from "In presence of" to "depones" there shall be substituted "*[name and address of applicant]* (hereinafter referred to "the applicant") hereby declares";

(c) for the word "deponent" wherever it occurs there shall be substituted "applicant"; and

(d) the words from "All which" to the end shall cease to have effect.

(3) In Schedule B to that Act (form of confirmation), for the word "oath" there shall be substituted "declaration."

The Sheriff Courts (Scotland) Act 1971 (c. 58)

26.—(1) For subsection (1) of section 33 (Sheriff Court Rules Council) of the Sheriff Courts (Scotland) Act 1971 there shall be substituted the following subsection—

"(1) There shall be established a body (to be known as the Sheriff Court Rules Council, and hereafter in this section and section 34 called "the Council") which shall have the functions conferred on it by section 34, and which shall consist of—

(a) two sheriffs principal, three sheriffs, one advocate, five solicitors and two whole-time sheriff clerks, all appointed by the Lord President of the Court of Session, after consultation with such persons as appear to him to be appropriate;

(b) two persons appointed by the Lord President after consultation with the Secretary of State, being persons appearing to the Lord President to have—

(i) a knowledge of the working procedures and practices of the civil courts;

(ii) a knowledge of consumer affairs; and

(iii) an awareness of the interests of litigants in the civil courts; and

(c) one person appointed by the Secretary of State, being a person appearing to the Secretary of State to be qualified for such appointment."

(2) In subsection (3) of that section, for the words "consultation with such persons as may appear to him appropriate" there shall be substituted the words "such consultation as is mentioned in paragraph (a) or, as the case may be, (b) of subsection (1) above."

The Criminal Procedure (Scotland) Act 1975 (c. 21)

27.—(1) The Criminal Procedure (Scotland) Act 1975 shall be amended as follows.

(2) After section 282 there shall be inserted the following sections—

"Right of audience of solicitor before the High Court

282A. Without prejudice to section 250 of this Act, any solicitor who has, by virtue of section 25A (rights of audience) of the Solicitors (Scotland) Act 1980 a right of audience in relation to the High Court of Justiciary shall have the same right of audience in that court as is enjoyed by an advocate.

Further provision as to rights of audience

282B. Any person who has complied with the terms of a scheme approved under section 26 of the Law Reform (Miscellaneous Provisions) (Scotland) Act 1990 (consideration of applications made under section 25) shall have such rights of audience before the High Court of Justiciary as may be specified in an Act of Adjournal made under subsection (7)(b) of that section.".

(3) In subsection (1)(b) of section 407 (imprisonment of non-payment of fine), at the end there shall be inserted "either with immediate effect or to take effect in the event of the person failing to pay the fine or any part or instalment of it by such further time as the court may order."

GENERAL NOTE

Subpara. (3)

Under s.407(1)(a) of the Criminal Procedure (Scotland) Act 1975, a court has power, when imposing a fine, also to impose imprisonment on default: by s.407(1)(b) the court has power to impose imprisonment when a person fails to pay a fine or any part or instalment of a fine. However, in *Stevenson* v. *McGlennan*, 1990 S.L.T. 842 and *Craig* v. *Smith*, 1990 S.C.C.R., it was held that in exercising its power under s.407(1)(b), the court had to impose imprisonment to take effect immediately. The effect of para. 27(3) is to amend s.407(1)(b) to enable the court to impose imprisonment either with immediate effect or to have effect if the offender failed to pay the fine or any part or instalment of it by such further time as the court may order. This provision came into force on November 1, 1990.

The Community Service by Offenders (Scotland) Act 1978 (c. 49)

28. In section 4 of the Community Service by Offenders (Scotland) Act 1978 (which, amongst other things, gives the court powers to deal with failure to comply with community service orders) there shall be added at the end the following subsection—
"(3) The evidence of one witness shall, for the purposes of subsection (2) above, be sufficient evidence.".

The Solicitors (Scotland) Act 1980 (c. 46)

29.—(1) The Solicitors (Scotland) Act 1980 shall be amended as follows.
(2) In section 9 (removal of name from roll on request)—
(a) after the words "his name" there shall be inserted the words ", or any annotation made against his name under section 25A(3),"; and
(b) after the words "that solicitor" there shall be inserted the words "or, as the case may be, the annotation against his name,".
(3) In section 10 (restoration of name to roll on request), in subsection (1A)—
(a) after the words "whose name" there shall be inserted the words ", or any annotation against whose name,"; and
(b) after the words "that solicitor" there shall be inserted the words "or, as the case may be, the annotation,".
(4) In section 20 (duty of Council to supply lists)—
(a) in subsection (1), after paragraph (a) there shall be inserted the following paragraph—
"(ab) to the Principal Clerk of Session"; and
(b) subsection (2) there shall be substituted the following subsection—
"(2) The Council shall send a list of all solicitors who have rights of audience in—
(a) the Court of Session, to—
(i) the Principal Clerk of Session;
(ii) the Principal Clerk of the Judicial Office of the House of Lords; and
(iii) the Registrar to the Judicial Committee of the Privy Council;
and
(b) the High Court of Justiciary, to the Principal Clerk of Justiciary,
as soon as practicable after December 1, in each year; and where, by virtue of an order under section 53(2)(ba), 53A(2)(ba) or 55(1)(ba), a solicitor's right of audience in any of those courts is suspended or revoked, the Council shall forthwith inform the persons mentioned in this subsection of that fact.".
(5) In section 26 of the 1980 Act (offence for solicitors to act as agents for unqualified persons)—
(a) in subsection (1)(c), at the beginning there shall be inserted "subject to subsection (4),";
(b) in subsection (1)(d), at the beginning there shall be inserted "subject to subsection (4),";
(c) in subsection (2), at the end there shall be inserted "or employed by a law centre,"; and
(d) after subsection (3) there shall be inserted—
"(4) Subsection (1)(c) and (d) shall not apply in relation to—
(a) writs relating to heritable or moveable property drawn or prepared upon the account of or for the profit of independent qualified conveyancers providing conveyancing services within the meaning of section 23 (interpretation of sections 16 to 22) of the Law Reform (Miscellaneous Provisions) (Scotland) Act 1990; or
(b) papers to found or oppose an application for a grant of confirmation in favour of executors drawn or prepared upon the account of or for the profit of an executry

practitioner or recognised financial institution providing executry services within the meaning of the said section 23."

(6) In section 32 (which makes it an offence for unqualified persons to prepare writs and papers relating to certain matters)—

(a) in subsection (2)(a), after the words "fee, gain or reward" there shall be inserted the words "(other than by way of remuneration paid under a contract of employment)"; and

(b) after subsection (2) there shall be inserted the following subsections—

"(2A) Subsection (1)(a) shall not apply to a qualified conveyancer providing conveyancing services within the meaning of section 23 of the Law Reform (Miscellaneous Provisions) (Scotland) Act 1990.

(2B) Subsection (1)(b) shall not apply to a person who is, by virtue of an act of sederunt made under section 32 (power of Court of Session to regulate procedure) of the Sheriff Courts (Scotland) Act 1971, permitted to represent a party to a summary cause.

(2C) Subsection (1)(c) shall not apply to an executry practitioner or a recognised financial institution providing executry services within the meaning of section 23 of the Law Reform (Miscellaneous Provisions) (Scotland) Act 1990.".

(7) At the end of section 33 (unqualified person not entitled to fees etc.) there shall be inserted the words "or in relation to writs framed or drawn by a person who is by virtue of an act of sederunt made under section 32 of the Sheriff Courts (Scotland) Act 1971, permitted to represent a party to a summary cause."

(8) In section 42A (powers of Council where inadequate professional services alleged), at the end of subsection (2) there shall be inserted the following paragraph—

"(d) to direct the solicitor to pay to the client by way of compensation such sum, not exceeding £1,000, as the Council may specify."

(9) In section 51(3) (complaints to Scottish Solicitors Discipline Tribunal)—

(a) after paragraph (b) there shall be inserted—

"(ba) the Dean of the Faculty of Advocates;"; and

(b) for paragraph (f) there shall be substituted—

"(f) the Scottish legal services ombudsman.".

(10) In section 53 (powers of Tribunal)—

(a) after subsection (2)(b) there shall be inserted the following paragraph—

"(ba) order that any right of audience held by the solicitor by virtue of section 25A be suspended or revoked";

(b) in subsection (2)(c), for the words "£4,000" there shall be substituted the words "£10,000";

(c) after subsection (3A) there shall be inserted the following subsection—

"(3B) The power conferred by subsection (2)(ba) may be exercised by the Tribunal either independently of, or in conjunction with, any other power conferred by that subsection."; and

(d) in subsection (6), after the words "as a solicitor" there shall be inserted the words "or that any right of audience held by the solicitor by virtue of section 25A be suspended or revoked."

(11) In section 53A (inadequate professional services: powers of Tribunal),

(a) after subsection (2)(b) there shall be inserted the following paragraph—

"(ba) to order that any right of audience held by the solicitor by virtue of section 25A be suspended or revoked;";

and

(b) after subsection (2)(c) there shall be inserted the following paragraph—

"(d) to direct the solicitor to pay to the client by way of compensation such sum, not exceeding £1,000, as the Tribunal may specify."

(12) In section 55 (powers of court)—

(a) after subsection (1)(b) there shall be inserted the following paragraphs—

"(ba) suspend the solicitor from exercising any right of audience held by him by virtue section 25A of such period as the court may determine; or

(bb) revoke any right of audience so acquired by him; or"; and

(b) after subsection (3) there shall be inserted the following subsection—

"(3A) A solicitor whose rights of audience under section 25A have been revoked in pursuance of an order made by the court under subsection (1) may apply to the court for an order restoring those rights, and the court may make such order.".

(13) After section 56 there shall be inserted the following section—

"Further provision as to compensation awards

56A.—(1) The taking of any steps under section 42A(2) or 53A(2) shall not be founded upon in any proceedings for the purpose of showing that the solicitor in respect of whom the steps were taken was negligent.

(2) A direction under section 42A(2)(d) or 53A(2)(d) to a solicitor to pay compensation to a client shall not prejudice any right of that client to take proceedings against that solicitor for damages in respect of any loss which he alleges he has suffered as a result of that solicitor's negligence, and any sum directed to be paid to that client under either of those provisions may be taken into account in the computation of any award of damages made to him in any such proceedings.

(3) The Secretary of State may by order made by statutory instrument amend subsection (2)(d) of sections 42A and 53A by substituting for the sum for the time being specified in those provisions such other sum as he considers appropriate.

(4) Before making any such order the Secretary of State shall consult the Council.

(5) An order made under this section shall be subject to annulment in pursuance of a resolution of either House of Parliament."

(14) In section 63 (penalties and time limit for prosecution of offences)—

(a) in subsection (1)—
    (i) for the words "level 3" there shall be substituted the words "level 4"; and
    (ii) the words from "and to imprisonment" to the end shall cease to have effect; and

(b) after subsection (2) there shall be inserted the following subsections—

"(3) Where an offence under this Act is committed by a body corporate and is proved to have been committed with the consent or connivance of or to be attributable to any neglect on the part of—

(a) any director, secretary of other similar officer of the body corporate; or

(b) any person who was purporting to act in any such capacity,

he (as well as the body corporate) shall be guilty of the offence and shall be liable to be proceeded against the punished accordingly.

(4) Where an offence under this Act is committed by a partnership or by an unincorporated associated (other than a partnership) and is proved to have been committed with the consent or connivance of a partner in the partnership or, as the case may be, a person concerned in the management or control of the association, he (as well as the partnership or association) shall be guilty of the offence and shall be liable to be proceeded against and punished accordingly.".

(15) In subsection (1) of section 65 (interpretation)—

(a) after the definition of "the court" there shall be inserted—

" "the Director" means the Director General of Fair Trading;

"foreign lawyer" means a person who is not a solicitor or an advocate but who is a member, and entitled to practise as such, of a legal profession regulated within a jurisdiction outwith Scotland;";

(b) after the definition of "judge" there shall be inserted—

" "law centre" means a body—

(a) established for the purpose of providing legal services to the public generally as well as to individual members of the public; and

(b) which does not distribute any profits made either to its members or otherwise, but reinvests any such profits for the purposes of the law centre;";

(c) after the definition of "Lord President" there shall be inserted—

" "multi-disciplinary practice" means a body corporate or a partnership—

    (a) having as one of its directors or, as the case may be, partners, a solicitor or an incorporated practice; and

    (b) which offers services, including professional services such as are provided by individual solicitors, to the public; and

    (c) where that solicitor or incorporated practice carried out, or supervises the carrying out of, any such professional services as may lawfully be carried out only by a solicitor;

"multi-national practice" means—

    (a) a partnership whose members are solicitors or incorporated practices and registered foreign lawyers; or

    (b) a body corporate whose members include registered foreign lawyers, and membership of which is restricted to solicitors, incorporated practices, registered foreign lawyers and other multi-national practices;";

(d) after the definition of "property" there shall be inserted—

" "registered foreign lawyer" means a foreign lawyer who is registered under section 60A";

(e) after the definition of "the Society" there shall be inserted—

" "Scottish legal services ombudsman" means the ombudsman appointed under section 34 of the Law Reform (Miscellaneous Provisions) (Scotland) Act 1990"; and

(f) in the definition of "unqualified person," after the word "person" there shall be inserted ", other than a multi-disciplinary practice,".

(16) In Schedule 1 (The Law Society of Scotland), after paragraph 11 there shall be inserted—

"Exemption from liability for damages

11A. Neither the Society nor any of its officers or servants shall be liable in damages for anything done or omitted in the discharge or purported discharge of its functions unless the act or omission is shown to have been in bad faith."

(17) In Schedule 4 (constitution, procedure and powers of Tribunal)—

(a) in paragraph 1—

    (i) in sub-paragraph (a), at the end there shall be inserted the words "appointed by the Lord President";

    (ii) in sub-paragraph (b), for the word "4" there shall be substituted the word "8";

    (iii) at the end of sub-paragraph (b) there shall be inserted the words "appointed by the Lord President after consultation with the Secretary of State"; and

    (iv) the words "appointed by the Lord President," where they appear at the end of that paragraph, shall cease to have effect;

(b) in paragraph 2—

    (i) after the words "Lord President" there shall be inserted the words "after consultation with the Secretary of State"; and

    (ii) for the words "so re-appointed" there shall be substituted the words "re-appointed by the Lord President";

(c) in paragraph 3, after the words "as the case may be," there shall be inserted the words "after consultation with the Secretary of State,";

(d) in paragraph 14, for the words from "may be published" to the end there shall be substituted the words "shall, subject to paragraph 14A, be published in full";

(e) after paragraph 14 there shall be inserted the following paragraph—

"14A. In carrying out their duty under paragraph 14, the Tribunal may refrain from publishing any names, places or other facts the publication of which would, in their opinion, damage, or be likely to damage, the interests of persons other than—

    (a) the solicitor against whom the complaint was made; or

    (b) his partners; or

    (c) his or their families,

but where they so refrain they shall publish their reasons for so doing.";

(f) in paragraph 17—

    (i) the words from "also" to "before the order" shall cease to have effect;

    (ii) after the words "and shall" there shall be inserted the words ", without prejudice to paragraph 14,"; and

    (iii) the words from "and in such other manner" to the end shall cease to have effect; and

(g) after paragraph 18 there shall be inserted the following paragraph—

"18A. Without prejudice to paragraph 18, the Council shall ensure that a copy of every decision published under paragraph 14 is open for inspection at the office of the Society during office hours by any person without payment of any fee.".

GENERAL NOTE

The most significant amendments made to the 1980 Act are the ones authorised by paras. 29(8) and 29(11)(b), which grant a power to both the Council of the Law Society and the Scottish Solicitors' Discipline Tribunal to award compensation of up to £1,000 to a client who has received inadequate professional services. These amendments were also added at Report Stage in the House of Commons and constitute changes in the law for which consumer bodies have pressed over a number of years.

The Criminal Justice (Scotland) Act 1980 (c. 62)

30.—(1) For section 76 of the Criminal Justice (Scotland) Act 1980 (presumption as to the contents of containers) there shall be substituted the following section—

"Presumption as to contents of container

76. Section 127 of the Licensing (Scotland) Act 1976 shall apply for the purposes of any trial in connection with an alleged contravention of any provision of this Part of this Act as it applies for the purposes of any trial in connection with an alleged contravention of any provision of that Act."

(2) Nothing in this paragraph shall apply to the prosecution of any person for an offence committed before the commencement of this paragraph.

The Matrimonial Homes (Family Protection) (Scotland) Act 1981 (c. 59)

31.—(1) In section 6(3)(e) of the Matrimonial Homes (Family Protection) (Scotland) Act 1981 (occupancy rights after dealing with third parties)—

(a) the words ", at or before the time of the dealing," shall cease to have effect; and

(b) in sub-paragraph (i)—

    (i) after the word "not" there shall be inserted "or were not at the time of the dealing"; and

    (ii) after the word "has" there shall be inserted "or had."

(2) In section 8 of that Act (interests of heritable creditors)—

(a) in subsection (2), the words "before the granting of the loan" shall cease to have effect; and

(b) in subsection (2A)—

    (i) the words "at or before the granting of the security" shall cease to have effect;

    (ii) after the word "not" in paragraph (a) there shall be inserted "or were not at the time of the granting of the security"; and

    (iii) after the word "has" in paragraph (a) there shall be inserted "or had."

GENERAL NOTE

Under the Matrimonial Homes (Family Protection) (Scotland) Act 1981, ss.6 and 8, affidavits that the property was not subject to a non-entitled spouse's statutory right of occupation had to be produced to the seller or heritable creditor at or before the time of the dealing or at or before the granting of the security. These amendments enable affidavits to be effective if produced after the dealing or after the security has been granted.

The Representation of the People Act 1983 (c. 2)

32. Section 42(3)(b) of the Representation of the People Act 1983 (nomination paper in local election to contain statement of acceptance of office) shall cease to have effect.

The Companies Act 1985 (c. 6)

33.—(1) The Companies Act 1985 shall be amended as follows.

(2) In section 38(1) (appointment of attorney to execute deeds abroad), the words "under the law of England and Wales" shall cease to have effect.

(3) In section 39(3) (official seal for use abroad), the words "or, in the case of a company registered in Scotland, subscribed in accordance with section 36B," shall cease to have effect.

(4) In section 186 (share certificate to be evidence of title), the words "(or, in the case of a company registered in Scotland, subscribed in accordance with section 36B)" shall cease to have effect.

(5) In section 188(2) (issue and effect of share warrant to bearer), the words "(or, in the case of a company registered in Scotland, subscribed in accordance with section 36B)" shall cease to have effect.

(6) Subsection (2) of section 462 (power of company to create floating charges under Scots law) shall cease to have effect.

The Family Law (Scotland) Act 1985 (c. 37)

34. In section 8(1) of the Family Law (Scotland) Act 1985 (orders for financial provision on divorce etc.)—

(a) in paragraph (a), the words "or the transfer of property" shall cease to have effect; and

(b) at the end of paragraph (a) there shall be inserted the following paragraph—

"(aa) an order for the transfer of property to him by the other party to the marriage.";

GENERAL NOTE

This amendment to s.8(1) of the Family Law (Scotland) Act 1985 makes it clear that a court has power to make an order for both a capital sum payment and a property transfer in a claim for financial provision on divorce. Hitherto, there had been doubt whether this was competent: see *Walker* v. *Walker*, 1990 S.L.T. 229 and *Little* v. *Little*, 1990 S.L.T. 230. The Inner House, however, took the view that such an order was competent: *Walker* v. *Walker* 1990 G.W.D. 34–1958. This amendment puts the matter beyond doubt.

The Insolvency Act 1986 (c. 45)

35. Section 53(3) of the Insolvency Act 1986 (execution of instrument appointing receiver) shall cease to have effect.

The Legal Aid (Scotland) Act 1986 (c. 47)

36.—(1) In subsection (3) of section 4 (Scottish Legal Aid Fund) of the Legal Aid (Scotland) Act 1986—

(a) paragraph (a) shall cease to have effect; and

(b) in paragraph (c), after the word "property" there shall be inserted "(including money)."

(2) In subsection (1) of section 6 (definitions) of that Act, for the words "if and so far as may be necessary," in both places where they occur, there shall be substituted the words "where appropriate."

(3) In subsection (2) of section 13 (meaning of "civil legal aid") of that Act, for the words "(so far as is necessary)" there shall be substituted the words ", where appropriate,".

(4) In subsection (3) of section 14 (availability of civil legal aid) of that Act, at the beginning there shall be inserted the words "Subject to subsections (4) to (6) below,".

(5) After the said subsection (3) there shall be inserted the following subsections—

"(4) Where—

(a) the Board has refused an application for civil legal aid by a person who has applied for such aid for the purpose of raising an action against the Board; and

(b) the applicant has applied to the Board for a review of his application,

the Board shall, unless they decide to grant the application forthwith, refer the application, together with all relevant precognitions, statements and other papers, including any observations they wish to make on the application, to the sheriff for Lothian and Borders at Edinburgh.

(5) Subject to section 15 of this Act, and to subsection (2) above, where the sheriff decides—

(a) that the applicant has a *probabilis causa litigandi*; and

(b) that it is reasonable in the particular circumstances of the case that he should receive legal aid,

he shall so inform the Board, and the Board shall make civil legal aid available to the applicant.

(6) A decision made by the sheriff under subsection (5) above shall be final."

(6) After subsection (2) of section 17 (contributions and payments out of property received) of that Act, there shall be inserted the following subsections—

"(2A) Except in so far as regulations made under this section otherwise provide, any sum of money recovered under an award of or an agreement as to expenses in favour of any party in any proceedings in respect of which he is or has been in receipt of civil legal aid shall be paid to the Board.

(2B) Except in so far as regulations made under this section otherwise provide, where, in any proceedings, there is a net liability of the Fund on the account of any party, the amount of that liability shall be paid to the Board by that party, in priority to any other debts, out of any property (wherever situate) which is recovered or preserved for him—

(a) in the proceedings; or

(b) under any settlement to avoid them or to bring them to an end.".

(7) Subsections (3) to (5) of that section shall cease to have effect.

(8) In subsection (6) of that section, for the words "subsection (5)" there shall be substituted the words "subsection (2A) or (2B)."

(9) In subsection (8) of that section, for the words from "subsection" to the end there shall be substituted the words "subsection (1) above and in section 33 of this Act to "fees and outlays" include references to sums which would have been payable to that solicitor if he had been so employed."

(10) In subsection (4) of section 21 (scope and nature of criminal legal aid) of that Act, for the words "(so far as is necessary)" there shall be substituted the words ", where appropriate,".

(11) In subsection (8) of section 29 (legal aid in certain proceedings relating to children) of that Act, for the words "(so far as is necessary)" there shall be substituted the words ", where appropriate,".

(12) In subsection (4) of section 30 (legal aid in contempt proceedings) of that Act, for the words "(so far as is necessary)" there shall be substituted the words ", where appropriate,".

(13) In subsection (1) of section 31 (solicitors and counsel) of that Act, for the words "his counsel" there shall be substituted the words "or a solicitor holding rights of audience by virtue of section 25A (rights of audience) of the Solicitors (Scotland) Act 1980, his counsel or such a solicitor."

(14) In subsection (9)(b) of the said section 31, at the beginning there shall be inserted "Subject to subsection (11) below,".

(15) At the end of the said section 31 there shall be inserted the following subsection—

"(11) Nothing in subsection (9)(b) above shall enable the Secretary of State to make regulations authorising the granting of legal aid only to solicitors holding rights of audience under section 25A (rights of audience) of the Solicitors (Scotland) Act 1980."

(16) In subsection (3) of section 33 (fees and outlays of counsel and solicitors) of that Act—

(a) in paragraph (c) the words "and taxation" and "or taxation"; and

(b) in paragraph (d) the word ", taxation,"

shall cease to have effect.

The Criminal Justice (Scotland) Act 1987 (c. 41)

37. In section 6(1) of the Criminal Justice (Scotland) Act 1987 (definition of implicative gifts), for the words "mentioned in section 5(2) of this Act" there shall be substituted "on which, in respect of a person suspected of, or charged with, an offence to which section 1 of this Act relates, the warrant to arrest and commit was granted, or a restrain order was made (whichever first occurs)."

The Court of Session Act 1988 (c. 36)

38. For section 48 (limited right of audience of solicitor before the court) of the Court of Session Act 1988 there shall be substituted the following sections—

"Right of audience of solicitor before the court
48.—(1) Any solicitor who has, by virtue of section 25A (rights of audience) of the Solicitors (Scotland) Act 1980 a right of audience in relation to the Court of Session shall have the same right of audience in that court as is enjoyed by an advocate.
(2) Any solicitor shall have a right of audience—
(a) before the vacation judge; and
(b) in such other circumstances as may be prescribed.

Further provision as to rights of audience
48A. Any person who has complied with the terms of a scheme approved under section 26 of the Law Reform (Miscellaneous Provisions) (Scotland) Act 1990 (consideration of applications made under section 25) shall have such rights of audience before the court as may be specified in an act of sederunt made under subsection (7)(a) of that section.".

The Antarctic Minerals Act 1989 (c. 21)

39. In subsection (2) of section 7 of the Antarctic Minerals Act 1989 (which relates to the Secretary of State's power to give directions), for the words "section 91 of the Court of Session Act 1868" there shall be substituted the words "section 45 of the Court of Session Act 1988."

Section 74   SCHEDULE 9

REPEALS

Chapter	Short title	Extent of repeal
1808 c. 149.	The Probate and Legacy Duties Act 1808.	In section 38, the words from "(which oath" to "administer)".
1858 c. 56.	The Confirmation of Executors (Scotland) Act 1858.	Section 11.
1875 c. 41.	The Intestates Widows and Children (Scotland) Act 1875.	In section 6, the words from the beginning to "affirmations.". In Schedule A, the words from "All which" to the end.
1876 c. 24.	The Small Testate Estates (Scotland) Act 1876.	Section 6. In Schedule A, the words from "All which" to the end.
1900 c. 55.	The Executors (Scotland) Act 1900.	Section 8.
1907 c. 51.	The Sheriff Courts (Scotland) Act 1907.	In section 40, the words from "agents" to "1967)".
1975 c. 24.	The House of Commons Disqualification Act 1975.	In Schedule 1, the words "lay observer appointed under section 49 of the Solicitors (Scotland) Act 1980".

Chapter	Short title	Extent of repeal
1976 c. 66.	The Licensing (Scotland) Act 1976.	In section 6, the words from "Provided that" to the end of the subsection. In section 18, in subsection (1), the words from "when" to the end. Section 55. Section 61. In section 97(2), the words "or supply". Sections 131 and 132. In section 133(4), the words "and (6)". In Schedule 4, in paragraph 1, the words from "as" to "Act", paragraphs 12, 13 and 14, in paragraph 15, the words "or 12 above", paragraphs 16, 17 and 19 to 22.
1977 c. 50.	The Unfair Contract Terms Act 1977.	In section 15(1), the words "applies only to contracts,". In section 25, subsections (3)(d) and (4).
1980 c. 46.	The Solicitors (Scotland) Act 1980.	In section 20(1), the word "and". Section 27. Section 29. Section 31(3). Section 49. In section 63(1), the words "and to imprisonment for a period not exceeding one month". In section 65(1), the definition of "lay observer". In Schedule 4, in paragraph 1, the words "appointed by the Lord President" following sub-paragraph (b), and in paragraph 17, the words from "also" to "before the order" and the words from "and in such other manner" to the end. Schedule 5.
1981 c. 59.	The Matrimonial Homes (Family Protection) (Scotland) Act 1981.	In section 6(3)(e), the words ", at or before the time of the dealing,". In section 8, in subsection (2), the words "before the granting of the loan", and in subsection (2A), the words "at or before the granting of the security".
1983 c. 2.	The Representation of the People Act 1983.	Section 42(3)(b).
1983 c. 12.	The Divorce Jurisdiction, Court Fees and Legal Aid (Scotland) Act 1983.	In Schedule 1, paragraph 7.
1985 c. 6.	The Companies Act 1985.	In section 39(1), the words "under the law of England and Wales". In section 39(3), the words "or, in the case of a company registered in Scotland, subscribed in accordance with section 36B,". In section 186, the words "(or, in the case of a company registered in Scotland, subscribed in accordance with section 36B)". In section 188(2), the words "(or, in the case of a company registered in Scotland, subscribed in accordance with section 36B)". Section 462(2).
1985 c. 37.	The Family Law (Scotland) Act 1985.	In section 8(1)(a), the words "or the transfer of property".
1985 c. 73.	The Law Reform (Miscellaneous Provisions) (Scotland) Act 1985.	In Part I of Schedule 1, paragraphs 4 and 5.

Chapter	Short title	Extent of repeal
1986 c. 45.	The Insolvency Act 1986.	Section 53(3).
1986 c. 47.	The Legal Aid (Scotland) Act 1986.	In section 4(3), paragraph (a) and, in paragraph (b), the words "a court". In section 13(2), the words "(so far as is necessary)". Section 17(3) to (5). In section 33(3), in paragraph (c), the words "and taxation" and "or taxation", and, in paragraph (d), the word ", taxation".
1988 c. 34.	The Legal Aid Act 1988.	In paragraph 3 of Schedule 4, sub-paragraphs (b) and (c).
1988 c. 36.	The Court of Session Act 1988.	Section 5(g).
1989 c. 40.	The Companies Act 1989.	Section 130(3). In Schedule 17, paragraphs 1(2), 2(4), 8 and 10.

INDEX

References are to section numbers (but see the rubric under "solicitors, rights of audience")